"With *First Great Sorrow*, author Donna Chaffee has produced an inspiring tribute to a man for whom she worked and campaigned—Robert F. Kennedy. Her book is filled with fascinating, inside details of RFK's career and how he inspired those who knew him. An intimate portrait about a time when anything seemed possible. Oh, what might have been." ~ Ray E. Boomhower, author of *Robert F. Kennedy and the 1968 Indiana Primary*

* * *

"Through fresh eyes, Donna reminds us why Bobby Kennedy was just the right man for his times and remains an inspiration for ours." ~ Larry Tye, New York Times bestselling author of *Bobby Kennedy: The Making of a Liberal Icon*

* * *

"This is a lovely memoir by Donna Chaffee, who, as a young woman still in college, accepted a job on the Senate staff of Robert F. Kennedy. She writes with deep respect and insight about the empathy and authenticity of her boss, with whom, truth be told, she was at least a little bit in love. This is not a tell-all book—far from it. It is a story told with accessibility and heart about a singular politician from the 1960s whose concern for people on the margins of American life made him, some of us believe, the greatest Kennedy of them all." ~ Frye Gaillard, author of *A Hard Rain: America in the 1960s*

First Great Sorrow

First Great Sorrow

My Years with Robert F. Kennedy

Donna Chaffee

Library Tales Publishing

Published by Glass Compass Press, LLC
under the Library Tales Publishing imprint.

Library Tales Publishing is a trademark of
Morgan Entertainment Group, LLC, used under license.

Distributed by Empire City Press, LLC
www.librarytalespublishing.com
www.empirecitypress.com
www.glasscompasspress.com

* * *

ISBN
979-8-89441-084-5
979-8-89441-059-3

First Edition, 2026
Printed in the United States of America

For my son Ian who is my inspiration in all things,
and
for Dr. Eric T. Lee who—more than anyone else—encouraged me to
write this memoir

"She had no tears this morning. She had wept them all away last night, and now she felt that dry-eyed morning misery, which is worse than the first shock, because it has the future in it as well as the present. Every morning to come, as far as her imagination could stretch, she would have to get up and feel that the day would have no joy for her. For there is no despair so absolute as that which comes with the first moments of our first great sorrow, when we have not yet known what it is to have suffered and be healed, to have despaired and to have recovered hope. "

— George Eliot

Contents

Prologue   1
1. MY INTRODUCTION TO POLITICS   3
2. THE JFK YEARS   9
3. THE ASSASSINATION OF JFK   25
4. WASHINGTON, D.C.   36
5. WORKING FOR RFK   50
6. THE SPRING OF 1965   70
7. HYANNISPORT   81
8. THE BEACH BOYS   90
9. THE FALL OF 1965   99
10. THE SENATOR'S STAFF   112
11. THE NEW YEAR, 1966   134
12. GUNS VS. BUTTER   144
13. THE SENATOR AND I   152
14. LEAVING WASHINGTON   162
15. THE SUMMER OF 1966   174
16. THE PLEASURE OF HIS COMPANY   184
17. 1967 BEGINS   199
18. MY RETURN TO WASHINGTON   210
19. THE DECISION TO RUN   227
20. THE CAMPAIGN   238
   March   238
   April   242
   May   252
   June   253
21. THE ASSASSINATION   258
22. THE AFTERMATH   272
23. EPILOGUE   309

Prologue

What made us dream that he could comb gray hair?
~ W.B. Yeats

Television floodlights cast eerie shadows through the leaves, and candlelight flickered in the darkness. A near-full moon rode high in the sky. I climbed the hill to the gravesite behind a long line of mourners: serious young men in dark suits and ties; sad-eyed college girls in black.

I wore white.

"Always the rebel," he would have remarked with that cryptic half-smile of his. But it was the only dress I owned.

With each step, my nails dug deeper into the slender white candle in my hand, scarring its glossy surface. Hot wax dripped onto my fingers. But I kept on going. I told myself, *I will do this one last thing.*

On and on we walked, aimlessly it seemed at first, but converging finally on a patch of ground not far from where his brother's body was buried. The service was brief, and when it was done, his family and the President disappeared quickly, swallowed by the shadows, never looking back.

The rest of us advanced in silent procession, filing past the casket one last time. Each mourner would stand a respectful distance away with head bowed and then move on.

When my turn came, I broke ranks and inched in closer. Dropping to my knees on the dry grass, I gently placed my hand on the side of his coffin. I leaned in and whispered to him, "Goodbye, Senator. I love you. I will never forget you."

Then, in further defiance of norms, I bent down and kissed the now-flagless casket—just as his widow had done. He would have chuckled at my boldness. I remember the wood felt smooth but cold against the warm night air.

Kneeling beside him in the stillness, I closed my eyes. I felt broken inside and half out of my mind with grief. I longed to lie down on the stretch of grass next to him, to play dead and spend the night there. But instead, I simply got up and walked away.

It was over.

At twenty-one years old, my life should have been just beginning, yet I felt that it was ending. Years would pass before I could make some sense of what had brought me to this time and this place. But in that moment, on a Virginia hillside overlooking Washington, I knew that, no matter where the future took me, my life would never be the same again.

I would never feel as happy, as alive, or as young again.

Chapter 1

My Introduction to Politics

According to the ancient Chinese proverb, a journey
of a thousand miles must begin with a single step.
~ John F. Kennedy

My family was not like the Kennedys. My parents were both born in 1917—the same year as President Kennedy—so they did have that in common. But my father was dirt poor growing up during the Great Depression, and by the age of fifteen he would spend his summers chopping tobacco on a Wisconsin farm, while JFK sailed his boat *Victura* on Nantucket Sound.

By the end of the 1940s, my mother and father had moved to California, a place where everyone was from someplace else. They brought their Midwestern values of hard work and frugality with them, so by the time I came along, we were fairly well off—upper middle class, I guess you'd say. It was the era of drive-in movies, dry martinis, and thirty-year mortgages, and my parents embraced it all with a newfound spirit of optimism. My dad, who was gifted with a magnificent voice, worked as a radio and television announcer for the National Broadcasting Company in Hollywood, and my mother, whose interests were more scholarly, became an English teacher at Hollywood High School. So they made a good living, but we weren't wealthy by any measure—certainly not like the Kennedys.

We didn't engage in political discussions at our nightly dinner table like Joe Kennedy and his brood either, but I do remember my parents talking politics from time to time. My mother would recount how she cried when President Roosevelt died, saying that if it weren't for FDR, neither one of them would have been able to attend college. Their parents simply couldn't afford it.

My paternal grandfather was a Norwegian immigrant and a tenant farmer—he never did own his own farm. He would move around from farm to farm seeking work, and as a result, my dad was shuffled from one school to another, something that seemed to leave lifelong scars.

My maternal grandfather, who, I was told, once had a few bucks to his name, apparently lost everything in the 1929 stock market crash and mostly worked odd jobs throughout my mother's childhood. But the only political heritage I had was through him—"Crazy Louie." My dad used to call him that because when he first started dating my mother in high school, her father would sometimes yell at him and chase him down the street.

I never met "Crazy Louie"—he died when my mother was still in college. I don't even know what he looked like, except that he was "bald as a billiard ball." My mother didn't own a single photo of him, which always struck me as a bit strange. But, based upon what she told me about him, I suspect he may have been bipolar, in addition to being something of an eccentric genius. He would experience tremendous highs and lows, which my mother found deeply frightening, particularly when he became violent. As far as I know, he never actually hit her or any other member of his family, but there were times when he would suddenly slam doors, throw things around, or tear down the Christmas tree in a fit of rage.

But "Crazy Louie" did more than just scare the hell out of my mother. He was also a friend and occasional adviser to Robert La Follette, Jr., and his brother Phil, who were members of a politically prominent Wisconsin family. Their father, known as "Fighting Bob," had been both a Congressman and a Senator and also served as Governor of Wisconsin from 1901 to 1906. He ran for President in 1924 as the standard-bearer of his own "Progressive Party" and has been described as "the most celebrated political figure in Wisconsin history." "Young Bob," as Robert La Follette, Jr. was known, also served as a U.S. Senator for twenty-five years, and his brother Phil was twice Governor of Wisconsin.

So, I guess that politics was in my blood from the start, but I didn't come to realize it until 1960 at the age of thirteen, when, by chance, I saw our future President in person for the first time. It was a moment in my young life that I would never forget.

On January 2, 1960, John F. Kennedy formally announced that he would seek the Democratic nomination for President. To be honest, at the time I didn't have a clue who Kennedy was. My parents were big supporters of Adlai Stevenson, even though he'd lost two previous bids for the Presidency and had declared in December of 1956 that he wouldn't run again. But in 1959, "Draft Stevenson" clubs began to pop up in several states, driven mostly by members of the Democratic Party's liberal wing. And even though Kennedy was well ahead in the delegate count and Stevenson wasn't officially running, it became clear that Adlai would accept the nomination if the convention came to him.

It was against this backdrop that, on Wednesday, July 13, 1960, the Democratic Party convened to choose a nominee. As luck would have it, the convention was being held that year in my hometown of Los Angeles. At the urging of my parents, my older sister, who was a senior in high school, and a friend of hers decided to drive down to the convention center and picket on behalf of Stevenson. Never wanting to miss out on an adventure, I asked to tag along, and they reluctantly agreed.

When we got to the Sports Arena, a huge crowd of more than 3,000 demonstrators had already gathered. We were handed placards, and we joined the throng and began chanting, "We want Stevenson. We want Stevenson."

As the time approached for Senator Eugene McCarthy to nominate Stevenson, his supporters began to pack the galleries inside the hall. McCarthy delivered an emotional speech, and those of us marching listened to it on our transistor radios:

> Do not leave this prophet without honor in his own party. Do not reject this man. I submit to you a man who is not the favorite son of any one state. I submit to you the man who is the favorite son of fifty states... This favorite son I submit to you: Adlai E. Stevenson of Illinois.

Outside the hall, we responded to the speech with a loud outburst and more chants of "We want Stevenson! We want Stevenson!" It went on for nearly a half hour. Then Eleanor Roosevelt rose to second the nomination, and the demonstrations erupted anew, lasting another fifteen minutes. Finally, after a few favorite son nominations, the gavel came down and they began calling the roll.

Once the roll call began, many of the Stevenson supporters began to pour out of the convention center. Seeing them, I suggested to my sister that we ask if we could use their tickets. She was hesitant, but she knew that once I got an idea in my head, there would be no talking me down. And that night, I was determined to get inside the convention hall no matter what it took. So off I scurried, not bothering to wait for her approval.

Incredibly, I was able to convince the first man I approached to hand over his ticket*. Perhaps he took pity on me. I was going through a particularly awkward phase in those days. People used to say that I resembled Hayley Mills—the child actress who had recently starred in the hit film *Pollyanna*. Like her, I was small and skinny for my age and looked younger than thirteen. Most of my girlfriends had already been through puberty, but I was slow to develop breasts, and there was still no hint of a "fur piece" (as my earthy Norwegian grandmother used to call it). Nevertheless, I insisted on wearing a bra that I didn't really need. To be honest, the contraption was more trouble than it was worth. I had to avoid getting too close to boys at school dances because I didn't fill up the padded cups, and if they pushed too hard against me, the bra would make an embarrassing popping noise. But, despite those physical shortcomings, I did have quite a mouth on me, and even though I could be shy, I was also pretty fearless, so it didn't bother me to approach a complete stranger to ask for his ticket. After quickly arranging with my sister to meet up later, I headed inside the convention center all by myself.

The fun was just beginning for me, but for Stevenson, the night was soon over. Kennedy won the nomination on the first ballot in something of a landslide, getting 806 votes to Johnson's 409 and Stevenson's 79.5. It wasn't a done deal, however, until they got to Wyoming, and a man in the delegation excitedly shouted, "Wyoming casts all fifteen votes for the next President of the United States— John Fitzgerald Kennedy."

Earlier in the day, Robert Kennedy, who was managing his brother's campaign, had told his people that there could be no second ballot—that they had to win it on the first ballot. And so they did.

As for me, coming into the convention hall that night was like entering another dimension—a world that, up until that moment, I didn't know existed. In my young life, I had never experienced anything like it. The feeling was electric and intoxicating.

---

* Many years later, I learned that the redistribution of gallery tickets to Stevenson supporters outside was actually part of the Stevenson campaign strategy.

Fortunately, my seat was in the front row of the spectators' gallery, and former First Lady Eleanor Roosevelt was sitting just a short distance away from me. I couldn't believe that I was so close to her—she was a true icon in my family. Being in her presence, I could feel the pull of history. I couldn't stop staring at her.

Once Stevenson lost, however, the former First Lady decided to call it a night. As she got up to leave, all of us in the gallery spontaneously rose to our feet and gave her a standing ovation.

Ticket to the DNC

But the most exciting part of the evening for me was yet to come. We soon learned that John F. Kennedy himself would be making a brief appearance at the convention—not to formally accept the nomination (that would be done two days later at the Los Angeles Memorial Coliseum), but to express his appreciation to the gathered delegates.

When he stepped to the podium, my heart raced. It was love at first sight. Even from way up in the gallery, I could tell how incredibly handsome he was. And that voice... it was magic.

A new chapter of my life was beginning.

Chapter 2

The JFK Years
1960 - 1963

All this will not be finished in the first one hundred
days. Nor will it be finished in the first one thousand days... But let us begin. ~ John F. Kennedy

On July 15, 1960, John F. Kennedy formally accepted the
Democratic Party's nomination for President of the
United States. In his acceptance speech, he spoke for the
first time about a "New Frontier." He declared that the old era was
ending and that old ways would no longer do, saying, "We stand
today on the edge of a New Frontier—the frontier of the 1960s—a
frontier of unknown opportunities and perils—a frontier of unful-
filled hopes and threats."

He told us that the New Frontier was here whether we sought it
or not and that beyond it were "the uncharted areas of science and
space, unsolved problems of peace and war, unconquered pockets of
ignorance and prejudice, unanswered questions of poverty and
surplus." He called on us to "be pioneers on that New Frontier." He

said, "My call is to the young in heart, regardless of age—to all who respond to the Scriptural call: Be strong and of good courage; be not afraid..."

My parents and I watched JFK's speech on television that night. We were hanging on his every word. My mother and father—who had once stubbornly supported a third Stevenson bid for the Presidency—were suddenly swept up by the Kennedy rhetoric. In comparison, Adlai Stevenson seemed something of a dinosaur—a holdover from the past. They were excited to hear this young man of their own generation talk about the future in a way that they hadn't heard before. As for me, I sat there captivated, ready to march off into that New Frontier armed only with my youthful idealism.

I was all in.

Beginning in the fall, the Kennedy campaign set up a storefront headquarters not far from my home. Back then, there was no Internet, and most of the electioneering—even for President—was done primarily at the grassroots level. So once the operation was in full swing, I went into the Kennedy for President headquarters to volunteer with a couple of friends from school. We were religious about our campaign work. Every afternoon, when classes finished at three o'clock, we would walk from the school bus stop to the headquarters and sit for hours at a time stuffing and addressing envelopes. We were probably the youngest people there, but the grunt work of volunteering didn't require advanced age, wisdom, or a degree from Harvard, so we were welcomed with open arms.

Frequently, the volunteers were also sent out to canvas neighborhoods, and that was where I think our youth and enthusiasm actually paid off. We were provided voter registration lists for a specific area and would knock on doors and ring doorbells. If someone answered the door, we would give them our most passionate pitch about why they should vote for Kennedy and hand them a campaign pamphlet to look at later.

The pamphlet outlined the Senator's experience in foreign policy as a member of the Senate Foreign Relations Committee as well as his position on military preparedness—"increased military strength was the soundest basis for a durable peace." It laid out his views and accomplishments in the area of a progressive labor policy—a higher minimum wage, increased unemployment compensation, and safer working conditions—plus his positions on civil rights and other issues.

JFK for President pamphlet

It was always a great thrill whenever people told us that they would indeed be voting for Kennedy. If nobody was at home, we would leave a tag on the door and a Kennedy campaign pamphlet in their mailbox. Most importantly, we would keep a careful record of whom we'd managed to talk to and whether they supported Kennedy or not. It was my first introduction to the nuts and bolts of politics, and I loved it. I began to feel that even young people like myself could have some influence on what was happening in the world.

In September, I started the ninth grade, and as a project for my social studies class, I began collecting and cataloguing every newspaper article I could find that dealt with the contest between Kennedy and Nixon. I soaked up every written word about the presidential campaign as eagerly as I'd once devoured Nancy Drew mysteries. Instead of spending my leisure hours at home reading how my favorite teenage sleuth solved *The Mystery at Lilac Inn*, I would pore over articles in the *Los Angeles Times* that spelled out how radio listeners had judged Nixon the victor of the first debate, while those watching on television thought Kennedy had won.

I couldn't wait until Election Day.

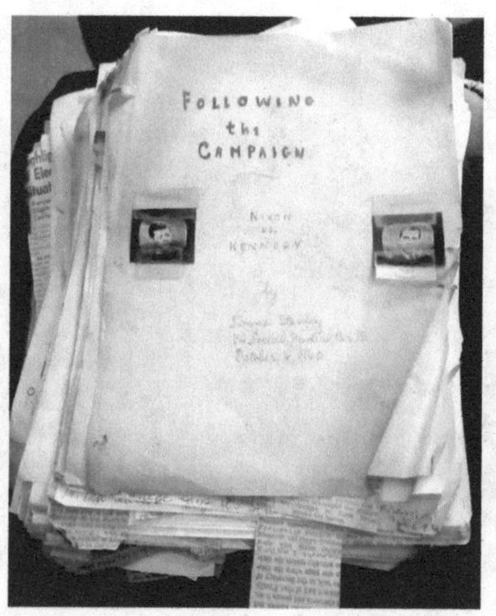

My Ninth-Grade Social Studies Project

On election night, I stayed up past midnight, glued to the television set, praying that Kennedy would be declared the winner. Finally, my parents insisted that I go to bed because the next day was a school day. When I woke up bleary-eyed in the morning, I was ecstatic to learn that my hero, John F. Kennedy, was going to be our next President.

The day before my fourteenth birthday, John Fitzgerald Kennedy was inaugurated as the thirty-fifth President of the United States. He was the youngest man ever elected to the office, but tragically, by my seventeenth birthday, he would be dead. Still, on that twentieth day of January in 1961, as we watched him raise his right hand to take the oath of office, we were hopeful. In subfreezing temperatures on the steps of the Capitol, he challenged "a new generation of Americans" to ask not what their country could do for them, but what they could do for their country. I heard his call and was ready to act.

But first, I had to get through high school.

The next one thousand days would mark a significant turning point both in the life of our country and in my young life personally. In the fall of 1961, I entered the tenth grade at Hollywood High School. The summer before, I grew seven inches in height, and my body began to change. That awkward, scrawny little girl who had attended the Democratic Convention the year before was finally starting to look more like a young woman. My interests had also grown—I began to paint and write—but I continued to closely follow what was going on at the Kennedy White House.

The President's first few months in office were by no means easy sailing for him. Right off the bat, he invited controversy by appointing his brother, Robert Kennedy, as Attorney General, despite pretty much universal opposition. Among others, *The New York Times* attacked the appointment, pointing to RFK's lack of experience and implying that he got the job solely as a result of nepotism*. According to historical accounts, JFK had actually intended to give his brother a different job in the administration. But his father, Joe, insisted that the President make Bobby AG instead, and Jack wasn't prepared to fight him on it.

Then, as T. S. Eliot had predicted, April was the cruelest month. The Soviets put a man into space on April 12, and less than a week later, on April 17, with Kennedy's operational approval, Cuban exiles launched a botched invasion of Cuba on its southwestern coast at a place called the Bay of Pigs. It was an unmitigated disaster.

The administration was eager to quickly change the narrative. The press was having a field day with stories about Kennedy's missteps, and he badly needed a win.

---

* Less than a year later, RFK would call out the hypocrisy of the attack when the publisher of *The New York Times*, Arthur Hays Sulzberger, retired and appointed his son-in-law to succeed him in the position. To this day, members of the Sulzberger family continue to run the *New York Times*.

On May 25, 1961, President Kennedy stood before a joint session of Congress and declared: "I believe that this nation should commit itself to achieving the goal, before this decade is out, of landing a man on the moon and returning him safely to earth." A year later, he would reaffirm this goal in his speech at Rice University, where he famously stated, "We choose to go to the moon in this decade and do the other things, not because they are easy, but because they are hard."

At the time, not all Americans thought that spending a lot of money to go to the moon was important or realistic. A poll following his speech to Congress in May 1961 found that a majority—58 percent—was opposed. But I was not one of them. I was excited. Yes—let's do what is hard. Let's try new things. Let's go to the moon. I would hazard a guess that most of my generation applauded Kennedy's space initiative. But there was something else that became even more important to me and to many other young people in the 1960s, and that was the civil rights struggle.

On May 4, 1961, the Congress of Racial Equality (CORE) organized the first "Freedom Ride" of young Black and white men and women from Washington, D.C., to New Orleans, Louisiana. As they traveled on buses through several Southern states, they were met with violence. At the time, I knew little about the civil rights movement. I had met few Black people, and I lived a rather insulated existence. I knew a lot of rich kids—kids whose parents were in show business, kids who lived in ranch-style homes in the Hollywood Hills, kids who were given sports cars wrapped with big red bows for their sixteenth birthdays—but, sadly, I didn't know any Black kids.

Still, I wasn't deaf, dumb, or blind (as we used to say back then). So, as the civil rights struggle gained momentum and there was increased television coverage of the violence in the South, I became more and more concerned about what was going on. In the spring of 1963, when I was a junior in high school, I joined the Student Nonviolent Coordinating Committee (SNCC) and became involved in fighting *de facto* segregation in the Los Angeles School District.

But I'm getting ahead of myself.

Throughout most of 1961 and 1962, I was primarily concerned with what was happening in my own little teenage bubble. In my first year at Hollywood High School, I had joined the drill team and was excited that we would be leading off the Hollywood Christmas Parade in November. I was active in several school organizations, was getting mostly A's in my classes, and I couldn't wait to get my copy of *Seventeen* magazine in the mail each month. I was planning to go to the next school dance with my girlfriends and worried about what I would wear. Would that cute boy in my English class—the shy one who kept to himself—be there? Would he ask me to dance? Then there was the weightiest question of all: how would I get to sleep the night before wearing those jumbo pink plastic hair curlers?

That was pretty much the extent of my teenage world.

Don't get me wrong. My family life wasn't like a *Father Knows Best* episode. My dad would sometimes linger too long having "one more for the road" at Nickodell's—a favorite watering hole down the street from NBC Studios—and my mother would threaten to leave him for the one hundredth time when he finally staggered in the door three hours later. By this time, both my brother and sister had already left home, so I was on my own to deal with all the drama.

In the summers, I would escape by ushering at the Greek Theatre in Los Angeles with a friend from school whose father was a violinist in the orchestra there. Harry Belafonte, Johnny Mathis, and Nat King Cole were regulars at the Greek, and as ushers, we were able to go backstage after their performances. They were probably the first Black men I ever met.

I'll never forget seeing Nat King Cole for the first time—talk about unforgettable. At six foot one, he seemed to tower over us. I remember that first night he was wearing a camel-hair overcoat (in summer, no less) draped regally over his shoulders like a cape, and a long cigarette holder was dangling from his mouth. He looked like a real movie star.

And then there was Harry Belafonte. My God, he was absolutely gorgeous and also very approachable. But he was more than just a handsome singer.

Since the 1950s, he had been close friends with Dr. Martin Luther King, Jr., and had become an activist in the civil rights movement. His wife, Julie, was also involved in the movement, cofounding the women's division of SNCC with actress Diahann Carroll, as well as helping to organize a women's march against the Vietnam War in 1968 with Coretta Scott King. We would frequently chat with both of them after his performances, and one night, I asked him to autograph a pencil sketch that I had drawn of him. He seemed genuinely touched.

My Pencil Drawing of Belafonte

Of course, for those who flocked to Southern California from somewhere else, Hollywood was a glamorous city—a place where stars were born, where small-town dreams of fame and fortune came true. But growing up in Hollywood and with my father working in television, it was difficult for me to appreciate what the city meant to people who didn't live there. As far as I was concerned, it was just home, and I became quite used to being around celebrities.

My dad actually worked with a number of stars—Cary Grant, Bette Davis, Vincent Price, Charles Boyer, and others—mostly in the 1940s, when he announced several old-time radio shows. Those were the days when they would have live audiences for the radio broadcasts. One of the shows that he announced was called *Mr. and Mrs. Blandings*, which Cary Grant starred in with his then-wife, Betsy Drake. My father told me that when he would introduce Grant, Cary would frequently come out wearing an old pair of jeans and tennis shoes with no socks, and the audience would usually seem surprised and a little disappointed. I guess they were used to the more elegant and urbane celluloid version of Grant that they'd seen on their local movie screens.

I was also told that when I was just a toddler, I would often share a playpen with Jeff Bridges. At the time, the Bridges lived down the street from us in the Mar Vista neighborhood of West Los Angeles. Back then, Lloyd Bridges was still doing B movies; his breakout role in *Sea Hunt* would come later. But at that time, my brother was in the same Cub Scout troop as Beau Bridges, and my mom used to go down to their house to exercise with his mother, Dorothy. I was about three years old, and Jeff was still a baby, but according to my mother, they would put us together in a playpen while the two of them worked out. Regretfully, I don't remember a thing about it.

Then, when I was a bit older and living on the other side of town near Universal City, my friends and I would frequently sneak into movie studios and wander around for hours. I remember how, back in 1955, when I was just eight years old, we climbed the fence at the old Republic Studios just off Ventura Boulevard in Studio City, where we spent a good half hour chatting with the actor John Payne (not to be confused with John Wayne). He was dressed in full cowboy garb and was filming a forgettable western called *Tennessee's Partner*, but he generously took the time to show us around the set, never asking who we were or what we were doing there. The film starred the future President, Ronald Reagan, as well, but we didn't see him that day.

One Halloween night—it must have been 1959 or 1960—I also managed to meet Rock Hudson in Newport Beach. My parents had a vacation home there in those days, and we had driven down for the weekend. Hudson had just moved from Malibu to Newport Beach in 1959, so a friend of mine and I decided to go trick-or-treating at his house on Lido Isle in Newport. We were actually rather astonished when he answered the door himself, dressed in a beautiful long silk kimono, apparently hosting a Halloween party. At that time, it was still not public knowledge that he was gay, but the house was filled with gorgeous young men—go figure. He didn't have any candy, so instead he gave us both a couple of dollars.

But things were different in Hollywood back then. Movie stars and other celebrities didn't hide out from the public so much. They didn't seem to require an entourage or bodyguards either—for the most part, they just acted like normal people. So I would frequently see them out and about by themselves—shopping at grocery stores or at filling stations getting gas.

In October 1962, however, everything in our world changed. The Kennedy administration—and indeed mankind—was facing an existential threat: the Cuban Missile Crisis. On October 22, 1962, President Kennedy gave a nationally televised address in which he announced that American surveillance had revealed that the Soviet Union was building offensive missile sites in Cuba. The President warned that the missiles in Cuba could be "none other than to provide a nuclear strike capability against the Western Hemisphere." In order to protect the United States from such a threat, he said that he would be imposing a "quarantine," or naval blockade, around Cuba.

In response to the President's address to the nation, my high school held an assembly to discuss what to do in the event of a nuclear strike. Duck and cover—were they kidding? All of us were old enough to understand that there was really nothing we could do if a nuclear missile hit Los Angeles. I remember peals of nervous laughter and dark humor coming from those of us in the audience. *Yeah, put your head between your legs and kiss your ass goodbye.* That was the general attitude. But underneath it all, we were genuinely scared. For the first time in most of our young lives, we were faced with the prospect of our own mortality. It was a heady realization and enough to get a kid thinking about more than just the next football game.

Fortunately, we survived those thirteen days of terror, and things went on much as before. But the world was changing, and young people were getting involved.

In the spring of 1963, I signed up to go door-to-door in South Central Los Angeles to talk to people in the community about *de facto* segregation in L.A. public schools, specifically as it related to Jordan and Lynwood high schools. The aim was to encourage the Black community to participate in a protest march from South Central's AME Church to the Board of Education, scheduled to take place in June of that year. Often, residents would invite us into their homes, and in their living rooms there would invariably be large framed photographs of the Reverend Martin Luther King, Jr., and President Kennedy hanging on the walls. It always touched me to see how the President was honored alongside Dr. King.

The person organizing this effort was a young Black man dressed in jeans and a faded denim work shirt. His name was Jimmy Garrett, and he was from the Student Nonviolent Coordinating Committee (SNCC). I'd never met anyone quite like him—someone who'd come out of an L.A. street gang to become an organizer in the civil rights movement.

I was in awe when he told me how, at the age of fifteen, he had participated in the sit-ins of 1960 and then gone on the Freedom Rides of 1961, actually getting arrested and spending time in solitary confinement. He was just a couple of years older than I was, but he seemed much older. I suspect it was because of everything he'd been through—things I could only imagine, given my privileged life. Jimmy was stone-cold serious and came from the real world—a world with which I was unfamiliar. He was also charismatic, passionate, and fully committed—someone whom I intuitively understood would never back down from the cause, even if it killed him.

Over the years, I would think about Jimmy from time to time and wonder whatever became of him. I had this awful feeling that his involvement in the cause would one day catch up with him. In fact, when I first heard that three civil rights workers had been murdered in Mississippi in 1964, I immediately imagined that he might be one of them. But fortunately, he wasn't.

After the community canvassing effort, I saw Jimmy just one more time, at a SNCC/CORE meeting that he invited me to attend in the early summer of 1963. I assumed that he was going to the March on Washington in August, but beyond that, I had no idea where he was headed.*

My activism that spring was inspired in part by what the Reverend Martin Luther King, Jr., was organizing down in the South. In April 1963, MLK and the Southern Christian Leadership Conference launched an anti-segregation campaign in Birmingham, Alabama, that included sit-ins, economic boycotts, and marches on City Hall. On April 12, King was arrested and put in solitary confinement. The demonstrations continued, but the city refused to budge. Beginning on May 2, 1963, school-aged children began to march. On May 3, the notorious "Bull" Connor ordered the police and fire department to use attack dogs and high-pressure water hoses against the protesters. Film showing peaceful demonstrators being brutally assaulted by the local authorities was all over the nightly

---

* *After my brief encounter with him in 1963, Jimmy Garrett went on to graduate from San Francisco State University (forming the first Black Student Union and Black Studies program there), earned a law degree, and ultimately received two PhDs, one from Harvard. He became a tenured associate professor at Howard University, where he taught political science, and later became Dean of Students at a community college in Oakland.*

news on television, and it caused Americans to finally sit up and pay attention.

Attorney General Robert Kennedy was one of those who took notice. Shortly after the Birmingham protests, he decided to sit down with some high-profile civil rights activists. He invited the novelist James Baldwin, together with Harry Belafonte, Lena Horne, and a dozen other cultural leaders, to meet with him at the Kennedy family apartment in New York City to discuss the state of race relations in the country. According to all accounts, it did not go well.

Throughout the nearly three-hour meeting, the mood was extremely tense and confrontational. The Black activists felt that RFK was being "naive" and did not understand the depth of the problem, while the Attorney General was shocked when some of the activists attacked him personally—despite all he had done to protect Freedom Riders and desegregate the University of Mississippi—and began talking about taking up arms and going into the streets. At one point during the meeting, Lena Horne told RFK, "Mr. Attorney General, you can take all those pious statements and stuff them up your ass."

After the meeting adjourned, Belafonte told Kennedy, "Of course you have done more for civil rights than anyone else," but it only managed to frustrate the Attorney General further. "Why didn't you say this to the others?" he asked. Belafonte responded that doing so would have lessened his own credibility and undermined his influence over the group. James Baldwin would later remark that Robert Kennedy was "insensitive and unresponsive" to the "torment" of Black people, and Harry Belafonte telephoned MLK the next day to tell him about the meeting, characterizing it as a "disaster." According to Belafonte, Dr. King replied, "Maybe it's just what Bobby needed to hear."

He was right. It became a turning point in Robert Kennedy's long-term attitude toward the civil rights struggle, even though, according to someone who knew RFK well, he "wasn't very forgiving about that meeting, ever." However, he was beginning to understand the depth of anger within the Black community. In fact, after the Watts riots in 1967, he would actually seek out militants to talk to because he wanted to hear what they were thinking.

And following his 1963 meeting with Baldwin and the others, he apparently shared his new understanding about the movement with his brother, the President. Less than a month later, President Kennedy delivered an address to the nation dealing with civil rights. In his speech, he spoke of it as a moral issue and proposed new civil rights legislation. (The bill would eventually be signed into law by President Lyndon Johnson following JFK's death.)

In his speech on June 11, President Kennedy said:

> "The heart of the question is whether all Americans are to be afforded equal rights and equal opportunities, whether we are going to treat our fellow Americans as we want to be treated.
>
> If an American, because his skin is dark, cannot eat lunch in a restaurant open to the public, if he cannot send his children to the best public school available, if he cannot vote for the public officials who represent him, if, in short, he cannot enjoy the full and free life which all of us want, then who among us would be content to have the color of his skin changed and stand in his place?
>
> Who among us would then be content with the counsels of patience and delay?"

That June was quite a consequential month for President Kennedy, filled with several other speeches and lots of traveling. It would prove to be consequential for me as well.

Just three days before his address to the nation on civil rights, JFK came to Los Angeles to speak at a breakfast meeting of the Women's Division of the California Democratic State Central Committee. It was being held at the Hollywood Palladium on Sunset Boulevard, not far from where my parents and I lived at the time. My mother and I decided to walk down to the Palladium to see if we could catch a glimpse of the President on his way to the breakfast. In checking out the location, we figured that his car would probably enter through the parking lot on a side street, so we positioned ourselves on the sidewalk next to the parking lot entrance. Surprisingly, we were the only ones there.

Our plan paid off. Suddenly, there the President was—in an open Lincoln convertible turning onto the street where we were standing. The car was going very slowly, and he passed right next to us—not more than a couple of feet away. We were waving and cheering, and he looked directly at me, smiling, and waved back. Needless to say, my mother and I were both over the moon.

The President also stopped at the NBC Hollywood Studios that day. Apparently, he was planning to sell the television rights for his book *Profiles in Courage* to NBC, so that must have been why he was there.

Just two days later, on June 10, the President gave a commencement address at American University. In his speech, he proposed a nuclear test ban treaty, which he would sign in October. It was a significant step forward toward preventing another nuclear missile crisis.

And then, two weeks after that, he traveled to Berlin, where on June 26 he gave his famous *Ich bin ein Berliner* speech to thousands of cheering Germans.

During the summer, the civil rights demonstrations of 1963 culminated with the March on Washington. On August 28, approximately a quarter of a million people gathered peacefully on the National Mall in Washington, D.C., to listen to speeches by civil rights leaders. Martin Luther King, Jr., addressed the crowd with his now-famous "I Have a Dream" speech. Sadly, despite my begging, my parents didn't allow me to go to Washington for the march.

On November 1, South Vietnamese President Diem was assassinated in a U.S.-supported coup. Robert Kennedy, among others, had opposed the coup. President Kennedy was shocked at the brutal killing of Diem and called it "abhorrent" in a recording made on November 4, 1963. At the time, I knew virtually nothing about Vietnam. But Americans would soon learn a great deal more about that tiny country in Southeast Asia.

Less than three weeks later, President John F. Kennedy traveled with the First Lady to Dallas, Texas.

Chapter 3

The Assassination of JFK

A man may die, nations may rise and fall, but an idea
lives on. Ideas have endurance without death. ~
John F. Kennedy

It was finally football season.

All was right in my world. After a hard-fought campaign, I was elected cheerleader in the spring of 1963. At last, I could wear that lusted-after red-and-white uniform and dance around beneath the grandstand while our brave boys knocked each other senseless out on the football field.

One of my best girlfriends had also been selected, and the two of us, with our cheerleader necklaces on full display, paraded up and down Balboa Island all summer as if we were members of some royal family. But then the summer was over, and out on the football field, it was showtime.

I was a senior in high school, and nothing could spoil the sense of joy and endless possibility that I felt as the days grew colder and football season heated up. Life was good.

Or so I thought.

In November 1963, I was a cheerleader at Hollywood High School.

On Friday morning, November 22, 1963, I was sitting in my current events class. It was a favorite of mine because we spent most of the time discussing what was going on in the world. We never knew what the topic of the day would be, since things kept changing—not always for the better. One day we might discuss foreign affairs: Why was the U.S. planning to suspend all arms shipments to South Africa at the end of 1963? The next day the topic might be civil rights: Would the mass boycott of Chicago schools have the desired effect of ending segregation there? We would have freewheeling conversations, and it was always exciting, given my interest in politics. Mr. Birnbaum was our teacher, and, like me, he was a big fan of President Kennedy, so he frequently steered the discussion in the direction of whatever the administration was doing.

There was nothing unusual about this particular day. As I recall, we were in the middle of one of our frequent pop quizzes when all at once we heard a disturbance in the hallway—people were speaking loudly, and there were voices coming from what sounded like a radio. Mr. Birnbaum excused himself and went outside the classroom to find out what was going on. A few minutes passed. We all just looked at each other blankly, wondering what was happening to cause such a commotion.

When our teacher returned, he took a deep breath and then announced solemnly, "The President has been shot." Mr. Birnbaum was no softie—he was also coach of the football team—but in those moments, he had a hard time keeping it together. His tough-guy exterior quickly dissolved, and his voice trembled with emotion. Hearing the news, at first it didn't sink in. Then suddenly, I felt as though someone had punched me in the gut. All the air went out of me, and I had trouble breathing. I was prepared to make whatever deals with God I needed to in order to save the President's life. *Please, God—let him live, and I promise I'll never talk back to my mother again.* But sadly, there were no deals to be had that morning.

As I look back, the rest is something of a blur to me. I don't remember exactly when I found out that President Kennedy had died, but I think it was before the bell rang for my next class.

I can't recall if I made it all the way through that class or not, but at some point I went to see the girls' vice principal and asked her if I could go home. Miss Standfast was her name; she adored the Kennedys and was in tears herself. I'm not sure she fully understood my question, but she said, "Okay," and I left.

I remember walking slowly up Highland Avenue from the school to Hollywood Boulevard, past the old Max Factor building just below the intersection. It was in that Art Deco building that Marilyn Monroe had become a blonde and Lucille Ball became a redhead.

Nothing seemed any different—everything appeared the same as always. There were people on the street going about their business, seemingly unaffected by the news. Maybe they simply hadn't heard about it yet, or were in some sort of shock. I would witness a similar lack of immediate reaction nearly thirty-five years later, when I happened to be in London the day Princess Diana died. It was as if, at first, people didn't really know what to do or how to react.

But at the corner, there was this tall bank building with a tower, and it had a flagpole atop the tower. It had been designed back in the late 1920s by the same architect who built the famous Chinese Theatre on Hollywood Boulevard—the one with all the handprints and footprints of Hollywood stars. I looked up and saw that the flag had been lowered to half-staff. That was when it finally hit me that this was real.

At the time, we lived not far from the school in a condo two blocks above Hollywood Boulevard on Whitley Avenue—just a ten-minute walk. I was in a daze and found my way home by rote. When I walked in the door, I could hear that the television was on in my parents' bedroom.

I entered the room, and there was my father sitting alone on the edge of the bed, his head in his hands. He was sobbing. It was the first time in my life I had ever seen him cry like that. He got up and, without saying a word, wrapped his arms around me.

For the next three days, like millions of others, I was glued to the television, even eating my meals on a TV tray in front of it. The awful images of that weekend are forever etched in my mind.

I watched in horror on Sunday when the accused assassin, Lee Harvey Oswald, was murdered live on national television. To this day, I can still hear the voice of NBC reporter Tom Pettit, who was the sole broadcaster on the scene, shouting to no one in particular, "He's been shot. He's been shot. Lee Oswald has been shot."

Mercilessly, they kept playing back the film. Over and over again, we watched Jack Ruby leap in front of Oswald, a pistol clutched tightly in his hand, and pull the trigger. Then Oswald, grimacing—his face contorted when the bullet hit him—slumped to the ground. And finally, the Dallas police, with their good-old-boy cowboy hats, grabbed Jack Ruby and hustled him away. After several minutes, word came down that Oswald was being transported by ambulance to Parkland Memorial Hospital, the same hospital where President Kennedy had died just two days before. For some reason, that outraged me. I didn't want Oswald to sully the place where the President had taken his last breath. For me, it was hallowed ground. Of course, it made no difference, really. But I wasn't thinking rationally at that point.

That same Sunday, the President's coffin was carried on a horse-drawn carriage to the Capitol, where he was to lie in state for eighteen hours. Hundreds of thousands of people had lined Pennsylvania Avenue to view the procession. In the Rotunda of the Capitol, Jacqueline Kennedy and her daughter Caroline were shown kneeling beside the President's casket. A pit formed in my stomach. It was gut-wrenching to watch them.

Monday, November 25, was declared a day of national mourning. It was also the day of JFK's state funeral. I watched as world leaders gathered at the White House—French President Charles de Gaulle in full military uniform towering above the rest. He had survived an assassination attempt on his own life just the year before. The President's widow, walking behind her husband's casket, together with Bobby and Ted Kennedy, led them on foot to St. Matthew's Cathedral. There, Cardinal Richard Cushing—the Archbishop of Boston and the man who, ten years before, had married Jack and Jackie—conducted the funeral Mass.

Afterwards, as they stood outside St. Matthew's, Jackie leaned down and whispered something to her young son. John-John, his shoulders squared, stepped forward and, as if from some ancient narrative, saluted his father's casket. I burst into tears. It was not the first or the last time I would cry during that long weekend.

Then the burial. Cardinal Cushing's gravelly monotone reciting the Lord's Prayer. The playing of the "Navy Hymn" as the American flag was folded into a crisp-edged triangle and presented to Mrs. Kennedy. Robert Kennedy—his face stone-like—standing frozen beside his beloved brother's grave. A twenty-one-gun salute reverberating in the distance. "Taps" playing—with a note touchingly off-key. The lighting of the eternal flame by Jackie, Bobby, and Ted in turn. Jackie's tear-stained face beneath that black veil. Finally, Bobby—ever devoted and protective of his brother—taking the widow's hand and leading her away from Jack's grave.

The scene was so heartbreaking that it was nearly unbearable for any of us to watch. I wanted to rewind the tape to the day before the Dallas trip. I wished that somehow we could turn back the clock—have President Kennedy decide not to go to Dallas after all. But there was no turning back. No magical thinking on my part could alter what had happened.

People would say that, with the assassination, we lost our innocence as a nation. I know that I lost mine the day that JFK was killed.

But, as much as it hurt, life went on. Years later, I would write this short poem:

> We are the children of the sixties,
> We watch our hair turn gray,
> And write our recollections of where
> we were that day.
> That day they shot the President,
> His bride wore pink, then black.
> We sat in silent vigil,
> As they brought his body back.
> We are the children of the sixties,
> We watch our own children play,
> Yet lost in deep reflection,
> We recall a darker day.

Following the funeral, I wrote a letter to Attorney General Robert Kennedy expressing my condolences. I did a charcoal drawing of President Kennedy and gave it to my parents. They framed it and hung it on the wall in their home. I tried to deal with my grief in productive ways. I decided that, in tribute to President Kennedy, I would devote my life to public service. Before the assassination, I had been trying to decide where I should go to college. With JFK's death, my mind was made up—I would attend university in Washington, D.C.

I was interested in a course of study that would prepare me for a job in the Foreign Service. Both Georgetown University and George Washington University had college programs geared to a career in the State Department. The downside of Georgetown was that, at that time, it was primarily a men's college, although it did admit women to its International Studies program. It was also a Jesuit school, and I wasn't Catholic. George Washington had a similar program of study, and it had the advantage of being in downtown Washington, just a few blocks from the White House and from "Foggy Bottom," where the State Department was located. It was also easier to get into. So GWU it would be.

Attorney General Robert Kennedy would not announce his candidacy for the Senate until the summer of 1964, so my decision to attend college in Washington was not influenced by that. Although Ted Kennedy was already a Senator, for some reason I never considered working for him. I guess it was because Robert Kennedy always seemed the natural successor to JFK and the one I expected to carry forward his brother's torch.

In March, I received a reply from Robert Kennedy to my letter of condolence. In it, he wrote, "I hope that the interest in politics and government which he kindled within you will continue to grow..."

Little did I know then that less than a year later, I would be working on his Senate staff.

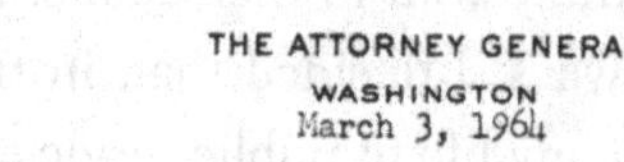

THE ATTORNEY GENERAL
WASHINGTON
March 3, 1964

Dear Miss Stanley:

Many thanks for your very thoughtful
letter. I was glad to hear from you and
to learn that you, although young in years,
were inspired and excited by my brother's
leadership. He had a special fondness
for young people and apparently this was
recognized and returned in large measure.

I hope that the interest in politics
and government which he kindled within
you will continue to grow and increase.

Sincerely,

Robert F. Kennedy

Miss Donna Stanley
1850 North Whitley Avenue
Hollywood 28, California

Attorney General RFK's letter to me

Shortly after I received the letter from RFK, President Kennedy's former press secretary, Pierre Salinger, declared his candidacy for the Democratic Senate nomination in California. The California primary was scheduled to take place on June 2. At first, there was some controversy over whether Salinger was even eligible to run in California, since he was registered to vote in Virginia. However, he had been born in San Francisco and had spent most of his life there, so he was eventually certified to run in the Democratic primary against California's state controller, Alan Cranston.

Once his campaign set up headquarters in the San Fernando Valley, I immediately went in to volunteer. At that point, I already knew the ropes, having worked in JFK's 1960 campaign. Basically, it was more of the same: envelope stuffing and neighborhood canvassing to win support and get out the vote. Salinger, with his trademark vest, his thick caterpillar eyebrows, and his ever-present cigar in hand, would often come into the headquarters—a cloud of smoke trailing behind him—to see how things were going. He was always friendly and approachable, so I managed to get a photo with him.

With Pierre Salinger during the 1964 California primary

It was a contentious campaign between Cranston and Salinger, but when all the votes were finally counted on June 2, "Plucky Pierre," as JFK used to call him, was declared the winner. That night, he made a victory speech at the headquarters, and I was there, standing right next to the candidate as he spoke to the press and the television cameras. In fact, the next day, the *Valley Times* ran a photo of Salinger and me in a front-page story.

With Salinger — Credit: George Brich/Valley Times

Valley Times newspaper—June 3, 1964

At the end of July 1964, when the incumbent in the California

Senate seat, retiring Democratic Senator Clair Engle, died, Governor Pat Brown appointed Pierre Salinger to the position. He would still have to run in November for a full 6-year term against the Republican candidate, former actor George Murphy. At that point, I was also headed to Washington, and I suppose I might have considered applying for a job in Salinger's office on Capitol Hill.

But on August 25, 1964, nine months after the death of his brother, Robert F. Kennedy announced that he would run for the Senate in New York State. His decision would change the direction of my life.

RFK for NY Senate flyer

Chapter 4

Washington, D.C.

Change is the law of life. And those who look only to
the past or the present are certain to miss the
future. ~ John F. Kennedy

In late August of 1964, my parents and I traveled by train to
Washington, D.C., where I was scheduled to begin the fall
semester at George Washington University. We went by train
primarily because my father was afraid to fly in those days (he
would later learn that if you downed a few martinis beforehand,
you could actually bring yourself to climb aboard a Boeing 707).
But going by train to Washington had an added advantage for me,
since I'd brought along a large trunk to accommodate all my
belongings.

To be honest, I wasn't much of a fan of railroad travel, but I was
used to it since, when I was growing up, we would take a train to the
Midwest every year to visit my grandparents on the farm. This was
well before Amtrak, so we always rode on the Santa Fe Super Chief

from Los Angeles to Chicago and then rented a vehicle to drive on to Wisconsin.

On those trips, my siblings and I used to enjoy sitting in the big dome car, from which we could get a good view of the passing landscape. Going through the Southwest, of course, it was mostly barren desert. Every now and then, we would pass by some forlorn little one-room adobe shack at the edge of the tracks and spot a Native woman hanging clothes on a line in the backyard.

One of the few stops along the route to Chicago was Albuquerque, New Mexico. The train would stay there for about twenty minutes, so there was enough time to go outside, stretch our legs, and look around. Walking up and down beside the train were Native American women dressed in bright tribal clothing, selling trinkets to the passengers. As a kid, I'd been fascinated by American Indians (as we used to call them then) and would read every book I could get my hands on about great chiefs like Sitting Bull and Cochise or fierce warriors like Geronimo and Crazy Horse. So seeing Native Americans reduced to hawking cheap souvenirs simply in order to survive was really quite depressing.

Robert Kennedy apparently felt the same way. In 1963, when he was Attorney General, he remarked in a speech to the National Council of American Indians (NCAI): "It is a tragic irony that the American Indian has for so long been denied a full share of freedom —full citizenship in the greatest free country in the world. And the irony is compounded when we realize how great the influence of Indian culture has been in shaping our national character."

Following his speech, RFK had been adopted into the tribes and given the name "Brave Heart," a name that I always thought suited him perfectly. It was clear that he had a special place in that heart for Native Americans and was deeply disturbed by their continued mistreatment in white America. His concern for their welfare would become even more apparent during his 1968 campaign for the presidency.

But back to my 1964 train trip. There was no direct service to

Washington, D.C., from Los Angeles, so we had to go through Chicago's Dearborn Station, where we could change trains for the East Coast. We were able to get on an overnight train from there connecting to Washington, and within twenty-four hours we arrived at Union Station in D.C. As we stepped off the train into the sweltering summer heat of the nation's capital, I was excited about what the future might hold for me. I never would have guessed that less than four years later, I would be arriving at that same station on a funeral train carrying the body of Senator Robert F. Kennedy.

George Washington University was not at all what I had expected. In the brochure they had sent me, there was an old colonial-style brick building pictured, situated in a park-like setting. Yes, that building did exist, but in those days it was the only one on campus with any sort of character. Most of the structures looked very much like the many government buildings that surrounded the campus and dotted the city—gray, boxy, and uninteresting. I suppose this was somewhat to be expected. After all, GWU was an urban school that, with both daytime and nighttime classes, reached out not only to graduating high school students but also to older civil servant types trying to further their college education.

For me, though, it was a big disappointment. I was looking for the full college experience, and in my mind's eye that included ivy-covered walls, lush greenery, and beautiful English Gothic–style buildings. As we toured the campus, I was immediately depressed. And the prospect that my parents would soon leave me there alone to fend for myself was somewhat terrifying.

George Washington University

My dormitory was a nondescript brick edifice, built in 1929, that was nine stories high. It was conveniently situated at the corner of 19th and F, just a couple of blocks down from Pennsylvania Avenue and the White House, so it was a perfect jumping-off point for exploring all that Washington had to offer. My room was located on one of the upper floors, with a window looking out over 19th Street.

My roommates and I got along well, but we were never particularly close, perhaps because I moved out after that first year and we didn't stay in touch. There were common bathrooms on each floor, and that's where I met some of the more interesting dorm rats who would become closer friends of mine. Nothing like spending hours together in front of the bathroom mirror under a cloud of Aqua Net hairspray to cement a close relationship.

One of those girls—I believe her name was Gail—was into politics as much as I was, and we would frequently hop the bus together down Pennsylvania Avenue to the Capitol to watch the Senate proceedings from the gallery. I remember that she had a bit of a crush on Senator Thurston Morton from Kentucky, who was a Republican, like she was, although not quite as middle-of-the-road. She enjoyed watching him from the gallery as he sashayed around the Senate floor like some modern-day Mark Antony making deals during the Second Triumvirate. She thought he had a "sexy way of walking." Frankly, I couldn't see it. Besides, he was rather ancient and a Republican to boot—not my kind of guy.

In fact, it was surprising that Gail and I got along at all. But the temper of the times was different back then—not as divisive as it is today. Democrats and Republicans could actually be friends, believe it or not—even have conversations about politics and discuss the issues without coming to blows. The only subject that became off-limits for the two of us was the Senate race in New York. Even though Gail was from Illinois, she was passionate about the New York contest, strongly supporting the incumbent Republican senator, Kenneth Keating. Naturally, I was all in for Robert Kennedy—the "carpetbagger," as she and other Republicans liked to derisively call him. After a few heated exchanges between us about the upcoming election in New York, we decided on a temporary truce, which worked well until the following January, when I actually started working for RFK up on the Hill. But more about that later.

During the fall of 1964, I would walk over to Arlington Cemetery to visit President Kennedy's grave at least a couple of times a week after classes. It was a bit of a hike from my dorm, but the exercise helped clear my head, and I felt I owed it to the President, who had been such an inspiration to me. I would generally go in the late afternoon so that I could reach his grave before the cemetery closed and to avoid most of the tourists. I later learned that Robert Kennedy would frequent the gravesite in the evenings too, but I never saw him there. This was before the memorial was built, so the grave was basically just a fenced-off grassy area with the eternal flame, surrounded by a military honor guard.

I would usually spend about twenty minutes there, waiting for the lights of the Lincoln Memorial to appear like magic in the distance. I would stand there in silence, remembering the President and reminding myself why I was in Washington. I went to the President's grave so often that one evening one of the soldiers asked me if I was a member of the Kennedy family. Sometimes I felt as though I was, but mostly my treks to Arlington were a way of dealing with my lingering grief.

It also provided me with some quiet time to meditate—not only about what was happening in my own little world but about the world at large. In fact, I specifically recall the day that Nikita Khrushchev was overthrown in the Soviet Union. It was in October 1964, and I was walking across the Memorial Bridge to Arlington, thinking about it and worrying about what might happen next. Would the new leader of the Soviet Union be more aggressive toward the United States? And what would President Kennedy have thought about what was going on in Russia? I don't believe I got any answers that day. But then, as they say, dead men don't talk. Of course, Khrushchev wasn't dead... but he might as well have been.

That fall, I also made a habit of sneaking into political events in Washington where I might encounter Robert Kennedy or other Democratic political figures, and my friend Gail frequently came along. Gail was a good wingman to have at my side—she was tall, probably five foot ten, and quite stunning in looks—so she served as a distraction to any red-blooded American male who might challenge us.

I was something of a veteran when it came to gate-crashing, after my childhood forays into studio back lots. In fact, just the year before, I'd even managed to sweet-talk my way into the Hollywood premiere of *Cleopatra*, where a school friend and I—still in our pleated skirts and cotton blouses with Peter Pan collars—stood next to mink-draped actresses and sipped expensive champagne out of plastic, gold-flecked glasses.

So I figured, why not try the same thing in Washington? The trick I had learned was to act as if I actually belonged at the event. Whenever one of the security men seemed as though he might be itching to confront me, all I had to do was look him directly in the eyes with complete disdain, stick my nose up in the air, and act like some entitled little snot who was there with someone really important. It worked every time. The truth was that most people could be convinced, with just the right look, that it was more important for them to stay *out of* trouble than to get me *into* trouble.

So, anyway, I managed to crash a few political gatherings that fall without credentials of any kind. It was really rather surprising—and alarming—since President Johnson was in attendance at a couple of the events. One would have thought that security by the Secret Service would have been paramount, given that President Kennedy had been assassinated just the year before. But sadly, that wasn't the case—I was never challenged, never even asked to show any sort of identification.

In late October 1964, former President Herbert Hoover died, and Gail and I managed to get into the Capitol Rotunda to view the ceremony that preceded his lying in state. Both President Johnson and former Vice President Nixon were there. As far as I could tell, RFK wasn't in attendance; at least, I never saw him (although I would later be surprised to learn that he admired President Hoover, having worked for him as a young lawyer on the Government Reorganization Commission, a.k.a. the Hoover Commission). This was the first of many times that I would see President Johnson in Washington. His daughter Lynda Bird was in one of my classes at GW, and I used to spot her Secret Service agents hanging around outside in the hall or inside the classroom, but I had never seen her father in person until that day. It was also the first and only time that I saw Richard Nixon —or "Tricky Dick," as my dad and others liked to call him.

Then, a little over a month later, on a gloomy and cold day in early December, there was a groundbreaking ceremony for the John F. Kennedy Center for the Performing Arts held along the banks of the Potomac. This time I went by myself. Not only was President Johnson there to perform the groundbreaking—with the same gold-plated shovel that had been used to break ground at the Lincoln and Jefferson Memorials—but both he and Robert Kennedy were scheduled to speak.

Incredibly, I simply walked into the outdoor event without an invitation and was able to sit down in the front row of the audience, just a few feet away from the podium where LBJ, RFK, and Supreme Court Justice Byron White were all seated. Most of the chairs in the front row were reserved, but I found one that didn't have a "Reserved" placard on it. That was another gate-crashing strategy of mine: I always sat in the front row if I could. Extreme boldness usually paid off because it wasn't expected of a gatecrasher. As it was, no one checked my ID or made sure I wasn't carrying a weapon. Fortunately, I wasn't. I was just a political junkie looking to participate in Washington life.

There were also a few Hollywood figures in attendance at the groundbreaking. They included Audrey Hepburn, her husband Mel Ferrer, Rex Harrison, and Lauren Bacall. Renowned Shakespearean actor Sir John Gielgud read from *Henry V* (an RFK favorite), and Jason Robards quoted extensively from a speech that the late President had made shortly before his death about art and the role of artists. Incredibly, Robards did it completely from memory because, as he told us all, he'd left his notes on the plane.

Robert Kennedy, who was seated next to President Johnson on the dais, had just been elected U.S. Senator from the state of New York the month before. I had been most looking forward to seeing him and hearing him speak.

As I watched RFK from the front row of the audience, he appeared very much absorbed in his own thoughts. There was a distinct aura of melancholy that seemed to envelop him. I would soon learn, when I went to work on his Senate staff, that this was often his demeanor, particularly during that first year. Even his smile was mixed with sadness. I sensed that his brother's death had changed him in some profound way. Yes, the death of a close family member changes us all. But for him, I don't know—it was somehow different. It's difficult to explain, but it was as if his entire being had been cut up into pieces and then put back together again—but rearranged differently than before.

Following his victory in the New York Senate race, he had remarked, "If my brother were alive, I wouldn't be here. I would rather have it that way." In seeing him that day at the groundbreaking ceremony, it seemed apparent that his feelings hadn't changed in that regard. There was no sense of jubilation about his winning the Senate seat in New York. Instead, when he rose to speak, he seemed distracted and almost reluctant to talk. I don't remember exactly what he said because I, too, was distracted—mostly by my own sadness over how lost he seemed.

But the breaking of ground for the center represented the fulfillment of one of President Kennedy's dreams. Early on in his administration, he had made the building of a national cultural arts center a top priority. To support the proposed center, he had declared the period November 26 through December 2, 1962, as "National Cultural Center Week." In a televised fundraiser on November 29, 1962, the President had said, "Art knows no national boundaries. Genius can speak in any tongue, and the entire world will hear it and listen... I am certain that after the dust of centuries has passed over our cities, we, too, will be remembered, not for our victories and defeats in battle or in politics but for our contribution to the human spirit."

Kennedy Center groundbreaking ceremony. Credit: AP

In the program for the groundbreaking event, historian Arthur Schlesinger, Jr., stated with equal eloquence, "President Kennedy, like the great Presidents of the early Republic, saw America not just as a state or a system but as a civilization... He therefore saw the arts, not as an interruption or distraction in the life of a nation, not as a luxury, but at the heart of a nation's purpose... In this same spirit, the American people today dedicate the John F. Kennedy Center for the Performing Arts."

GROUND-BREAKING CEREMONY
ON THE SITE OF
THE JOHN F. KENNEDY CENTER
for the Performing Arts

Wednesday, December 2, 1964 At Noon

PROGRAM

The National Anthem
Invocation
The Most Reverend Philip M. Hannan, D.D., V.G.
Auxiliary Bishop of Washington

Presiding
Roger L. Stevens

Readings from Shakespeare
Sir John Gielgud

Hymn "Eternal Father, Strong to Save"
The Sea Chanters

Readings from President John F. Kennedy
Jason Robards, Jr.

Remarks by Robert F. Kennedy

Address by the President of the United States

The ground-breaking ceremony will be performed
by the President of the United States

Swearing in of the Center's new Trustees

Music by the United States Navy Band and
the Sea Chanters
Lt. Comdr. Anthony A. Mitchell, USN, Leader

Program from Kennedy Center ceremony

Then, in January 1965, my gate-crashing skills were further put to the test when I set my sights on sneaking into the presidential inauguration of Lyndon B. Johnson. It was to be held on Wednesday, January 20—the day before my eighteenth birthday—outside at the East Portico of the Capitol building, with Chief Justice Earl Warren administering the oath of office.

My wingman, Gail, and I, along with a couple of other girls from the dorm, got to the Capitol early that morning in order to secure a good spot from which we could view all the goings-on. We decided that the best place to stand was right next to where people would be admitted into the VIP seating section, which was situated just beneath the podium where Johnson was to be sworn in.

As it got closer to noon, more and more of the VIPs began arriving. When I craned my head to see who was among those approaching, I noticed that Henry Cabot Lodge and his wife were standing right next to me, about to enter the roped-off VIP area. Lodge was a very recognizable figure then because he had been Nixon's running mate in 1960 and, more recently, had served as ambassador to South Vietnam. Since the passage of the Gulf of Tonkin Resolution by Congress in August 1964, and with more and more U.S. personnel being sent to Vietnam, the ambassador had been increasingly in the news over the last year—often wearing his trademark white suit.

Being ridiculously bold, I just reached up (he was very tall), put my arm through his, and walked right in with him. You should have seen the looks on the faces of my friends. Lodge himself seemed a bit startled at first but then just chuckled—like the trooper that he obviously was—and went along with it. The man responsible for checking the tickets gave me a look, but he didn't dare stop someone as important as Henry Cabot Lodge to ask who the hell I was.

Once we were inside the VIP area, I thanked the ambassador; he simply nodded in acknowledgment, and I proceeded down the aisle to find myself a seat. As I recall, the seats were not individually assigned, so I just searched for an empty one as close as possible to the podium and plopped myself down. Amazing how easy it was. Fortunately, the Secret Service didn't tackle me, and no one else came to arrest me. But again, it was something of an indictment of the security surrounding the leader of the free world.

Ambassador Henry Cabot Lodge with JFK; Credit: Robert Knudsen, White House Photographer

I also had the opportunity to attend the Inaugural Ball that evening. At the time, I had been briefly dating a guy who was on the congressional staff of newly elected Representative John Conyers, and he invited me to go to the ball with him. The only catch was that he wanted me to pay for my own ticket (I think it was just twenty-five or fifty dollars). I had only known the guy for a few weeks, and our relationship wasn't serious at that point. But I didn't have much money then, so I really couldn't afford to pay for my own ticket and buy a new dress to wear to the ball. So I declined the offer and, not happy with his demand that I pay for the ticket, I broke up with him.

Representative Conyers of Michigan went on to become the longest-serving member of Congress. However, his fifty-two-year career on Capitol Hill was cut short in 2017 by allegations of sexual harassment. It's ironic, because I remember when this fellow on his staff invited me late one night to see his new office and then tried to seduce me on the Congressman's sofa. Lord knows what else may have taken place on that sofa over the years. Fortunately, I managed to leave the Congressman's office in one piece that night.

Invitation to the Inaugural Ball

Chapter 5

Working for RFK

This world demands the qualities of youth; not a time
of life but a state of mind, a temper of the will, a
quality of the imagination, a predominance of
courage over timidity, of the appetite for adventure over the life of ease. ~ Robert F. Kennedy

From the moment that Robert Kennedy was elected to the Senate in November 1964, I was determined to get a job working in his Capitol Hill office. Even though I was just seventeen years old at the time—about to turn eighteen in January— I'd been around political campaigns long enough to see how rudderless they could sometimes be, and I imagined that it probably applied to a Senate office as well, particularly if they were just getting off the ground. One of the main things I had going for me—aside from my own determination—was the fact that the Senator had just been elected. Therefore, it was likely that whoever was in charge of his office hadn't yet had time to get fully staffed up, particularly when it came to lower-level positions. My gut feeling was that the place was bound to be pretty chaotic at first ... and I was right.

Beyond that, my strategy was three-pronged:

First and foremost, I had to arrange my school schedule for the upcoming semester so that I could work five days a week. Fortunately, George Washington University offered night classes, so I was able to set things up so that I would attend class only in the mornings and the late evenings. Most days of the week, then, I could get down to the Capitol by 1:00 in the afternoon at the latest—some days much earlier—and work until at least six at night.

Secondly, it was important that I start volunteering immediately before they filled all of their positions. I felt confident that if I was given sufficient time to show them what I had to contribute, they would eventually offer me a job. Actually, it was never really about the money for me. I was willing to work for nothing just to be around him. But the Kennedy name always attracted dozens of volunteers, and I wanted to become a real staffer, to get as close to him as possible.

Thirdly, I was willing to do any sort of work, no matter how menial it was. I was so idealistic, and RFK seemed to me to be the embodiment of those ideals. I didn't care what tasks I performed in his office—anything that might help him to do his job as Senator. That was what really mattered to me.

The trick was getting my foot in the door.

My plan worked. Robert Kennedy was sworn in as Senator from the State of New York on January 4, 1965. The following week, I walked into his office and volunteered my services. Within a month, the Senator hired me as a paid staffer.

It was obvious when I first started volunteering that my predictions about the office had been spot on. Almost everything was in complete disarray. There were so many boxes and pieces of mail stacked everywhere that you could barely navigate your way through the office.

The Senator himself had selected much of the professional staff immediately after the election, so that part of the operation was running relatively smoothly. There were the legislative assistants (Adam Walinsky, Peter Edelman, and Wendell Pigman), the office manager (Joe Dolan), the Senator's executive secretary (Angie Novello), the press secretary (Ed Guthman—he left in March and was replaced by Wes Barthelmes), and a few other professional staff members in the New York offices, such as Jerry Bruno in Syracuse, who were already in place. However, several of the lesser positions—primarily clerical and caseworker jobs—still needed to be filled, the majority of which would be assigned to mailroom operations.

In our first year, the Capitol Hill office would eventually consist of twenty-six full-time staff and twelve part-timers (including me), plus his driver, Jim Boyd, with an additional ten people in his two New York offices (New York City and Syracuse). Considering the Senator's high public profile and the fact that we were the only Senate office that answered out-of-state mail, it seemed like a relatively small staff, but by Senate standards it was actually quite large, and several of us had to be paid out of the Senator's own pocket because the Senate budget wasn't big enough. I received half my salary from the government and half from the Senator (or from the Joseph P. Kennedy Foundation). I heard that this arrangement cost RFK upwards of $100,000 per year because even some of his professional staff were paid this way, and they earned a great deal more than I did, of course.

When I showed up that first day, I was immediately directed to see Joe Dolan, who was the Senator's chief of staff and responsible for all hiring. Joe and the Senator had a long history together, going back to 1956, when Joe worked briefly as a legislative assistant for RFK's brother, Senator John Kennedy, then later became an advisor to his 1960 presidential campaign. He was subsequently appointed Deputy Attorney General in Robert Kennedy's Justice Department. Following RFK's election to the Senate, he chose Dolan to run his Senate office. Although Joe never received the same level of media attention as some of the others in RFK's inner circle, I think the Senator depended on him for political advice more than any other member of his staff. He likely would have become chief of staff in the White House if Robert Kennedy had been elected President.

Joe and I immediately hit it off, and I adored working for him. He had a quirky manner and a very relaxed approach to managing—it was all very free-form. He would sometimes burst into song without warning, but I never once heard him raise his voice in anger. He was much like the Senator that way—if he was disappointed in someone, he wouldn't yell; he would usually become silent or say something short and sweet like, "Well, do better next time," then turn his back and walk away. Whenever I would go see Joe in his office, he'd be slouching way down in his chair, often with his feet up on the desk, his shirt hanging out on one side. Behind his glasses, he had one eye that would wander around at will while his eyebrows hopped up and down in rhythm. I always had to force myself not to follow the errant eye or chuckle when I was talking to him face-to-face.

But, as he explained to me right off the bat, his first priority was to get a handle not only on the incredible backlog of mail that the Senator had already received but also to deal with each new day's flood of letters that were beginning to pile up. As we would soon learn, correspondence addressed to the office would regularly total about one thousand letters a day, and unless we quickly got on top of it, we might never be able to crawl out from under it all. In fact, the large volume of mail set a record for a freshman Senator, but it really wasn't one that we welcomed. Still, getting it under control was my first assignment. Working with Joe, I helped design a system for separating the mail by category and distributing it to the appropriate staff for action. There were eight basic categories:

1. **Casework**—Constituents would write in asking for the Senator's assistance in resolving problems they were having with various government agencies such as the

Veterans Administration, the Social Security Administration, Immigration, etc. These letters would go to our casework staff, which eventually consisted of about four or five full-time employees.

2. **Legislation**—The hot legislative issues would change from month to month, but they would generally be directed to Adam or Peter for a draft position response, depending on the specific issue. Wendell handled only water issues.

3. **Press**—This included requests for interviews with the Senator and other press inquiries.

4. **Joe Dolan**—Joe got all the political mail, postmaster appointments, and letters from job seekers.

5. **General mail**—This included requests for copies of bills, photos, general thank-you letters, etc.

6. **Receptionist**—The front office handled requests for flags to be flown over the Capitol, passes, D.C. information, etc.

7. **Angie's assistant**—She screened invitations for the Senator to speak.

8. **Angie Novello**—Angie handled the Senator's personal mail, VIP mail, VIP requests for autographed photos, appointments, etc.

It was all pretty straightforward, and my job was to read each of those one thousand letters and decide where it should go. The most important part of sorting the mail was quickly getting it to the right person to either reply individually or develop a proposed template response for multiple uses. The Senator was also interested in where his constituents stood on the important issues of the day, so I would keep tallies of the number of pro and con letters we received on major subjects like Vietnam. The legislative assistants would come up with draft responses on various issues for approval by the Senator, and other less important or less popular issues would usually get some sort of general response like "Thanks for your recent letter with your views on the issues."

Of course, one of the worst things that could happen if the mail was misdirected was sending one of the Senator's personal friends or a VIP a canned response. Let's say the President wrote, "Hey, Bobby—let's sit down together and hash out your objections to my proposed veteran benefits bill," and we sent the response: "Dear President Johnson: Thank you for your views. I always appreciate hearing from my constituents on issues of importance to New York." Well, you get the idea.

Thankfully, I believe I only screwed up once during the entire time that I worked for the Senator, when I sent one of RFK's close friends, who had written about a personal matter, a template response with an autopen signature rather than his standard scrawl of "Bob" for people he knew. Not bad, considering the nearly 400,000 letters that we received in a year; but the fact that I still remember it sixty years later says a lot about how much my mistake bothered me.

But the mail didn't just require sorting, distributing, and drafting position papers; it also required the physical process of opening, typing, and mailing out some one thousand signed responses per day. In fact, our entire crew of twelve part-time people was involved in the business of dealing with the mail. We probably had the most highly educated mailroom in the entire Senate—perhaps in all of Washington—since every one of the guys who ran not only the robo-signature machine but all the other machines involved in answering mail were attending law school, mostly at Georgetown and Howard. Then there was me. At age eighteen, I was the youngest paid member of the Senator's staff.

At one time or another, the mailroom workers included Robert Reich—former Secretary of Labor under President Bill Clinton—and Jules Kroll, renowned business entrepreneur and father to actor Nick Kroll. In a blog written in 2022, Reich described his intern job in RFK's mailroom as requiring "only half a brain." He recounted that he was in charge of our signature machine and that he had to make sure that the thousands of photos and letters he handled each day were lined up properly with the Senator's signature in the right place. He went on to say that he got so bored that at one point he began to compose mock letters to friends ("Congratulations, Mr. Dworkin, on possessing the largest nose in the entire Hudson Valley. Yours sincerely, Robert F. Kennedy."). He was actually thinking about quitting until one day he happened to run into RFK in the corridor, and the Senator remembered his name and exchanged a few pleasantries with him. That meeting, Reich recounted, was inspiration enough to keep him going for the rest of the summer, adding that "It doesn't take much to inspire; sometimes a smile and a hello, and remembering someone's name will do." I think we all felt that way, more or less—the personal interactions we had with the Senator were worth everything to us.

But during those first few months in 1965, even as we staffed up, we continued to struggle with the mail—in part because we were still crowded into temporary office space. It wasn't until March that we were able to move into permanent offices, which provided a bit more breathing room. The mailroom where I worked was three floors above the Senator's main office in the New Senate Office Building, and next door to us was where the caseworkers were housed.

Me in RFK's office with volunteers in temporary office space

Some of those who worked up on the third floor complained because they were separated from the Senator and from the other professional staff, who were located down on the first floor. It never really bothered me, though. For one thing, I would make a point of personally delivering mail downstairs to the Senator's main office a couple of times a day, so I had a lot of interaction with Angie and the other staff down there and would often run into the Senator as well. Secondly, RFK, who was sensitive to these things, made it a point to stop by and visit us up on the third floor from time to time.

In particular, he was always interested in coming by to shoot the breeze with Provi Paredes and me. Provi, who had been with the Kennedy family since the 1950s, worked directly with me on the mail. She would open the envelopes and then hand the letters over to me for reading and sorting. She also supervised the volunteers who sometimes assisted us. Even though she was more than twenty years my senior, from the start Provi and I became great pals. We would often get together outside of office hours, and we remained good friends for the rest of her life. At work, we were constantly laughing about one thing or another, so much so that the caseworker girls next door sometimes complained to us about the racket.

But Provi was someone who loved to have fun. I really admired her for her ability to always see the glass as half full rather than half empty. She had been through so much tragedy with the death of the President and taking care of Jacqueline Kennedy in her grief. But Provi still maintained her upbeat, positive attitude, no matter what was going on in her life. After the assassination, Jackie had wanted her to move to New York to continue as her personal assistant, like she'd been in the White House, but Provi had a young son at home and she didn't want to uproot him, so RFK arranged to have her work in his Senate office. Provi's son, Gustavo, was just six years younger than I—only twelve years old at that point. He had been practically raised with Caroline and John, Jr., spending Christmases with the

Kennedy family in Palm Beach and summers in Hyannis Port. He remained a close friend of JFK Jr. until the day John died.

But again, I digress. More about Provi and her relationship with the Kennedy family later.

As I said, RFK would sometimes stop by our office on the third floor to say hello and chat for a few minutes. I think, like me, he enjoyed being around Provi, and he knew that he could always have a few laughs with the two of us. Neither Provi nor I took ourselves too seriously, and I think he liked that about us. If Provi wasn't there when he came by, he'd invariably ask, "Where's your buddy?" We both knew who he meant. But anyway, he'd come by, feign interest in what we were working on (he really didn't care to hear specifics except to be assured that the mail was under control), shoot the breeze for a while, and then move on.

He was constantly on the move whenever I saw him, and even when he was in his office, he would rarely stay put behind his desk. He seemed very restless and would often roam the hallways. Sometimes he would have Brumus, his gigantic, smelly, slobbering Newfoundland dog, in tow. He seemed to get a kick out of shocking his fellow Senators by actually bringing Brumus into meetings. I don't think anyone at work was crazy about Brumus, except for the Senator, who probably loved him even more because of that. When RFK was Attorney General, he'd even been known to ask staff in his office to walk Brumus on their lunch hours. He told *The New York Times*, "Brumus gets lonely. I bring him down here to get pretty girls to take him for walks." Fortunately, he seemed to have abandoned that practice when he became Senator. Angie once asked RFK why he brought Brumus to work when he seemed to cause nothing but trouble, and he replied that he couldn't stand hearing the dog whine and cry when he left for work in the morning.

Occasionally, Ethel and some of the older children would also come by—she and the girls were always in their Sunday best and wearing gloves to boot—looking very 1950s even though this was 1965. And me? I was usually dressed California casual style, particularly in the warmer months—sleeveless top, short fringe skirt, bare legs, and sandals. There wasn't a dress code in the office, but I imagine some of the fresh-out-of-the-convent girls didn't approve of my choice in clothes. But did I care? Not really. As long as Joe and the Senator didn't have a problem with my attire, I was good.

I never had much contact with Ethel, but word from those who did was that she could be quite volatile and difficult—had quite a temper and would sometimes raise her voice with people who worked for her ... or even with the Senator. I think there was a lot of turnover out at the house, Hickory Hill, because of that. But again, this information was secondhand, so I couldn't swear to it—I never witnessed it personally.

The only one of the Senator's kids that I really interacted with in the office was his oldest son, Joe, who was about twelve years old then. He liked to come up to the mailroom and play around with the Senator's signature machine—forcing the robotic pen to sign his own name instead of his father's. He managed to break the machine on a couple of occasions, which set back the whole mail operation for a few days. If anyone had told me then that one day this bratty little boy would be elected to Congress himself and probably have his own signature machine, I wouldn't have believed it.

One of Joe Kennedy's signatures that managed to break the machine

Actually, some of the Senator's children did receive their own mail from other kids around the country. Robert Kennedy Jr., in particular, got quite a few letters, so we printed up a card with his signature to send in response. It was pretty well known that young Bobby loved to collect animals, and I guess that is what intrigued other children. Also, the story of how he had presented President Kennedy with "Shadrack," the dead salamander, had received a great deal of press attention at the time. Of course, he's been the subject of even more media scrutiny in recent years.

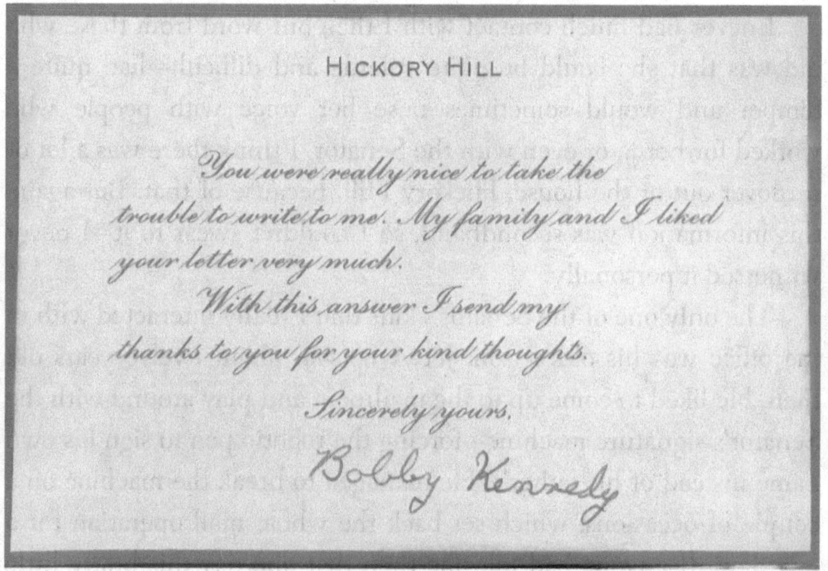

Robert Kennedy, Jr.'s response to letters

At any rate, in early February 1965, Joe Dolan called me into his office and offered me a paid position on staff. He said it was basically a done deal since I'd already been working there for a month and he knew what I was capable of doing. But he said that I would first have to go through the formality of meeting with the Senator in a sort of pre-employment interview. I didn't mind. In fact, being given the opportunity to talk to the Senator alone, one on one, was the most exciting thing that had happened to me thus far. Although he'd been up to the office where I was working a few times and had chatted with Provi and me, I'd never been alone with him before. The meeting with him was scheduled for later that afternoon.

It was an unusual interview. His office door was already open when I showed up at Angie's desk, and she said that he was waiting for me. I stuck my head around the corner, and he waved me in. As usual, his jacket was off, and he had on a black tie—in mourning for his brother—but it was loosened, and his shirtsleeves were rolled up, as was often his practice in the office. He was leaning back in his chair, reading some papers, which he promptly laid on the desk. I sat down, and he smiled, resting his hands in his lap. This is pretty much the way the conversation went:

"So, Donna, Joe tells me that you've managed to single-handedly get all of our mail in order."

I laughed and said, "Well, we're still working on it, Senator, but we've made a lot of progress."

"Good, good. So, you're from California, right? What are you doing working here?"

"Well, unfortunately, as you know, both of the Senators from California are now Republicans. I worked on Salinger's campaign last year, but ..."

"Yeah, too bad about Pierre ... You're from Los Angeles?"

I was going to tell him that I had been at the Sports Arena the night that President Kennedy was nominated, but I was afraid that mention of his slain brother might make him uncomfortable, so I didn't.

Instead, I said, "Yeah—born and raised there. That's where most of your hate mail comes from." I don't know why I brought that up—probably because I was nervous about not mentioning JFK.

"Really? I didn't know that. Do we get a lot of hate mail?" He didn't seem particularly concerned, just curious.

"Not too much ... but more than other offices, I think."

"That figures. So tell me, what do you like to read?"

"Other than your mail?"

He chuckled. "Yeah, I mean ... what books do you like to read?"

"Well, I'm currently reading *The Rise and Fall of the Third Reich*."

He looked surprised. "For school?"

"No. I started reading it on the way to Washington—just for

myself. My parents and I took a train here, so I figured it would keep me occupied for the whole trip. Plus, I'm something of a history buff. But it's over a thousand pages, so since I started school, I haven't been able to finish it."

"A train? Why did you take a train?"

"Well, my dad is afraid of flying, so ..."

"Oh, I see. Well, how do you like it here?"

"I love it, of course. Working for you is a dream come true."

"You and Provi are pals, right?"

"Yeah, she and I have a great time together. We really hit it off. I love her."

"We all love Provi. Here, this is for you." He reached across the desk and handed me a PT-109 pin. "Let me know if there's anything I can do for you."

I looked at him. "Thanks, Senator." He returned my gaze but was silent. I figured that the interview was over.

I took the pin and stood up. I smiled and headed for the door. I was quite pleased with how relaxed he was with me. I had been told that he was shy around strangers—I would see that for myself later—but on this day, he seemed very comfortable with me. And all the while that I was sitting there, I kept asking myself: How can anyone call this man ruthless? He was usually quite intense, but what was most noticeable to me was his complete absence of guile. He seemed nothing if not direct and authentic ... and his piercing blue eyes bore right through me.

Others on staff would talk about "the look"—a glare that the Senator gave when he was unhappy with someone. Adam would later describe it as his eyes going "dead flat cold"—that it was "enough to wither tree branches a hundred miles away." But I never experienced that. To me, I felt he could look directly into my soul with those eyes. I realize that sounds rather melodramatic, but it's true. I got the impression that whenever he met new people, he would immediately size them up—for better or worse—it was intuitive for him ... and if he didn't like you, it would probably be quite obvious. It was all about chemistry, you see, and we had really good chemistry. It was very natural between the two of us, perhaps in part because I didn't treat him like a celebrity and was able to relax around him, to be myself. So he, in turn, also seemed relaxed. Anyway, I was happy that I had apparently passed his test. And, of course, he had certainly passed mine.

PT-109 pin—gift from RFK

So the next thing I knew, I was over at the Capitol raising my right hand and swearing to support and defend the Constitution of the United States against all enemies.

The Senator always did his best to make everyone on staff feel that they were important to him, even if they didn't interact with him on a regular basis. Not long after my "interview" with him in February, he held the first of many after-work parties in his private Senate office. I think he did it for us—for the little people on his staff —to let us know that we were part of it all and mattered to him. The date of that first party was Friday, March 12, 1965—I happened to make a note of it. By this time, we were starting to get things in shape. The mail operation had moved into permanent offices, and even though there was still a backlog of unanswered correspondence, we'd managed to increase our outgoing mail to more than six hundred letters a day, which was quite a feat.

At 6:15 that evening, we all showed up promptly at the Senator's office. He stood framed in the doorway as we filed in. He welcomed each of us individually, shaking our hands, which seemed a little strange since I'm pretty sure that most of us had already met him. But anyway, once he'd greeted us all, he launched into a humorous story about how his dog Brumus had made a mess in Senator Byrd's office earlier that day. Apparently, RFK was there for a meeting with the senior Senator from Virginia, and he brought Brumus along with him. Well, Brumus decided to have a pee on the carpet in Byrd's inner office. The Senator (RFK, that is) seemed quite amused and pleased by what had happened, and we all got a big kick out of it.

After telling his story, he moved toward the back of the office and stood all by himself to the side of his desk, over near a window. His sleeves were rolled up, his tie undone, his arms folded, and his back a little hunched, as it always was. From time to time, one hand would go up to his face, drag across his chin, and rest there, fingers splayed. Then, a few minutes later, the hand would be folded back into his crossed arms. He had this strange way of standing sometimes with one knee bent and the toe of one shoe on top of the toe of the other—I wondered how he could keep his balance. That's pretty much where he remained, though, during most of the party—all alone in the corner of the room. He seemed to be lost in his own thoughts. Being around him, I often got the sense of his aloneness, his vulnerability, his fragility even. This particular evening, he seemed very shy and not really eager to engage in direct conversation with anyone. And, naturally, people were reluctant to go up to him and start talking. It felt too intrusive.

There were alcoholic drinks available for anyone at the party who wanted one. I don't remember exactly what I was drinking—I think maybe vodka with some sort of mixer in it. For some reason, I do remember what the Senator was drinking—bourbon and 7-Up. I think it's called a "7 and 7." I'm not sure how I knew what he was drinking—I must have overheard one of the men who was making the drinks ask him what he wanted, and he said, "7 and 7," a drink I've never heard anyone order since. I remember that, later, I asked someone what it was. At that point, I was not an experienced drinker. I would have the occasional beer at college parties (actually, I didn't really like beer), but I think this was the first time I'd ever had hard liquor. The drinking age in California was still twenty-one then, but in D.C., it was eighteen.

At the party, I was excited to check out his office. During my one-on-one interview, I hadn't had a chance to really look around.

The first thing I noticed was the oil painting of his older brother Joe on the wall. He was dressed in his World War II military flying gear—leather helmet and all—standing on an airfield. I knew that Joe had been killed on a secret flying mission during the war. It was a beautiful painting—rather large—and I was quite moved looking at it. I think it was just one of two—maybe three—oil paintings hanging in his office, at least that I recall. I remember that there was a large abstract painting behind his desk, although the Senator would change up the furniture arrangement from time to time.

Painting of RFK's brother Joe that hung in his Senate office;
credit: Robert Knudsen/White House Photo/JFK Library

On the wall near the door was a plaque that he'd had engraved with a quote from Theodore Roosevelt. It read, in part: "The credit belongs to the man ... who at the best knows in the end the triumph of high achievement, and who at the worst, if he fails, at least fails while daring greatly ..."

Then there was a table near the door, atop which were many framed photographs of President Kennedy and memorabilia from when he was in the White House. I spent a lot of time studying each photo. For some reason, it made me very sad to see all these things, and I think it showed on my face, because when I looked up and glanced his way, I saw that the Senator was watching me. I don't know—perhaps it was just projection on my part—but I felt such a strong bond with him in that moment. He had that look on his face like when he gave the speech about President Kennedy to the Democratic National Convention in 1964—that hurt, little-boy look. I wanted to go up and hug him and tell him how much I loved President Kennedy too, how I used to visit Arlington a couple of times a week, but I didn't. Months later, I did manage to talk to him about it briefly, but it didn't seem appropriate in that party setting.

He would have these office parties every month or every other month, and I think the staff really appreciated them. Also, it was nice for everyone to get together in one place from time to time. His style in the office was to deal one on one with people, and he was always available if you needed to talk to him about something. But he never really had large staff meetings—even with the professional staff. So it was rare that we would all be in the same room together at one time. Sometimes, a lot of us would be out at Hickory Hill in the summer months, but that was different because the Senator usually wouldn't be there. When he was up in Hyannis Port or New York, or when the family was off on a trip, he would always invite the staff to use the pool. Occasionally, he and Ethel would actually be in town on the weekends, and they would have us out to Hickory Hill for swimming and touch football.

Anyway, the next office party he held was in May, as I recall. As he got to know us all better, he became less shy, and we were able to spend more time talking directly with him. But one had to read his moods. His body language always told me a lot about how social he wanted to be, and despite my unorthodox manner, I tried to be respectful of his privacy and his space.

Even with people he knew, RFK could sometimes be quite with-drawn. In that regard, he was unlike his brother Ted, who always seemed very outgoing. I imagine he was different in that way from President Kennedy as well. I think it was not long after this first office party that we were all invited to another gathering at some hotel ball-room near the Capitol. I can't, for the life of me, remember what the occasion was. Perhaps someone was leaving the staff—maybe Ed Guthman; maybe it was for something else entirely. But anyway, what I do remember clearly is someone playing "When Irish Eyes Are Smiling" on the piano, and Senator Ted Kennedy standing next to the piano, singing at the top of his lungs—mostly off-key. He was very gregarious and often quite drunk back then—completely different from RFK in that sense. Two brothers hadn't served in the Senate together at the same time since 1803, but you couldn't find two men who were more unalike in so many ways.

Ted was also known as a big womanizer in those days. Perhaps his drinking had something to do with that too. But I know that the girls up on the Hill had a rule back then: Don't ever get into an elevator alone with Ted Kennedy. Ted wasn't the only one, of course; there were some other Senators for whom the rule also applied. Never RFK, however.

It's funny, though—whenever the Senator was with Ted, he became more outgoing himself. They would always be joking and teasing each other like a couple of college boys. I imagine that Presi-dent Kennedy brought out that side of him, too. I remember one time I ran into him and his brother, Ted, up at the Capitol—this was much later, maybe 1966. I waved at RFK as I was passing, and the Senator called me to come over. I gladly went up to them, and he asked, "What are you doing here, Donna?"

By this time, we knew each other quite well. I was something of a smart aleck, and he seemed to enjoy that about me. So I said, "I came over to pick up my check. Some of us have to work for a living, you know."

With this, Ted burst out laughing, and the Senator just smiled—

the smile of a man who didn't mind being spoken to that way. Then he asked me, gesturing to Ted, "Do you know who this is?"

I rolled my eyes and replied, "No, I don't have a clue."

Then he immediately added with a smirk, "This is the Senator from Massachusetts. He's a member of 'The Club.'" He said "The Club" in a derogatory sort of way.

I chuckled.

"Nice to meet you, Senator." (Even though I had met him before.)

Then I said, "Well, I better get going ... before they run out of money. See you boys later." I left them standing there like a couple of fraternity brothers waiting for the girls to show up for a beer bust.

It seemed that RFK was always teasing Ted about being a member of "The Senate Club." Reportedly, he would sometimes even walk up behind him when he was speaking on the floor of the Senate and whisper, "Is this how you become a member of the Club?" or something like that. Still, Ted would frequently give as good as he got—poking fun at his older brother about being the new kid on the block or about his inability to sit still.

But with RFK, the whole thing about the "Senate Club" wasn't just his way of teasing Ted. From day one, I think he was genuinely frustrated by the Byzantine ways in which things worked (or didn't work) in the Senate. He would often become restless at committee hearings with the other Senators who were asking stupid questions or droning on ad nauseam. He would get bored too, particularly if it wasn't an issue that he cared a lot about. So he would occasionally become a bit acerbic in his questioning, or he would just get up and leave in the middle of a hearing. Sometimes, I think other Senators got their feathers ruffled when he did that. Perhaps they even considered it rude. One of the unwritten rules of the Senate was that freshman Senators shouldn't assert themselves, but RFK often did, and so it was rough sailing for him from the get-go.

He also couldn't stand some of the hypocrisy going on there—Senators who would smile at you while they stabbed you in the back.

It wasn't that he didn't enjoy working as a Senator; he did like fighting for things that really mattered. But he was a man who wanted to get things accomplished, so he would become impatient with all the nonsense that frequently went on in Congress, and he would let people know it. Frankly, I admired that about him, but I don't think most of his Senate colleagues felt the same way.

Chapter 6

The Spring of 1965

It was a high counsel that I once heard given to a
young person: 'Always do what you are afraid to
do.' ~ Ralph Waldo Emerson

Less than two weeks after that first office party, the Senator
flew to Canada on March 23, 1965, to climb Mount
Kennedy. At nearly 14,000 feet, the mountain, which was
named for the late President, was located in the Yukon Territory and
was the highest unclimbed peak in the Saint Elias mountain range.
The National Geographic Society and the Boston Museum of
Science were planning to conduct a joint survey of the mountain so
that a detailed map of it could be drawn.

The Senator, who had never done any mountain climbing before,
was invited to join the climbing party, but he waited until the last
minute to make a final decision to go ahead with it. When he did, I
think most of us in the office were caught a bit off guard and worried
about his safety.

When asked by the press how he had prepared for the climb, the Senator famously quipped that he had practiced by running up and down the stairs at Hickory Hill, yelling, "Help!" It wasn't that far from the truth. With no climbing experience and a real fear of heights, he probably had second thoughts about his decision on the flight over to the Yukon. But he was never one to back down or shrink from a challenge just because it was dangerous or because he was afraid.

When he got to base camp, he was given a crash course in mountain climbing by a couple of veteran climbers who had been on the Mount Everest expedition in 1963. Jim Whittaker was one of them, and he led the three-man party up the final ridge. At that point, they unroped and let the Senator climb the last fifty yards alone so that he could be the first man to reach the top.

A local newspaper, *The Whitehorse Star*, shot a photo of the Senator in his climbing gear following the ascent, and it ran together with a news article about the climb. They sent a copy of the story to our office, and when I saw the photo, I had to have it. So I contacted the newspaper and asked them if I could get a print of it, which they kindly sent me. When the Senator came back to the office, I got him to sign it for me. I didn't find out until much later that he hated to see photos of himself in his climbing clothes.

He did make it clear after returning, though, that he didn't particularly enjoy the climb. But once he'd been asked to join them, I think he just couldn't bring himself to say "no" and have people think he was some sort of coward. Bravery was something that was always important to him—it didn't matter whether it involved fighting in a war, fighting organized crime, or climbing a mountain in the Yukon.

Jim Whittaker, who became a close friend of RFK's, later said about the Senator, "I think he could have climbed any mountain. I think he could have made Everest if he wanted to. I mean he could have done anything that he wanted to do. He had that determination and the willpower, you see; he could overcome physical problems and

other problems. I mean he had the determination and ... Well, he had
... I mean, God, he was beautiful."

Photo credit: Bob Erlam/Whitehorse Star

Much has been made over the years about why it was that Robert
Kennedy took so many risks, how sometimes he almost seemed to
court danger. I felt that after the President was shot, RFK became
quite fatalistic about his own life. Not just because he figured that
there was nothing he could do about it, although that might have
been part of it. But mostly, I think that he actually set out to tempt
fate. That was my impression about his need to take risks, anyway—to
climb Mount Kennedy or go white-water rafting, even why he would

wade into crowds, allow people to tear at his shirt sleeves, take his shoes and his cuff links, and leave his hands bloodied. It was almost as if he were challenging the gods—so you want to kill me? Go ahead and try. I will give you every chance, and if you don't succeed, then I'll know that you're not as powerful as you would have me believe.

He always put up a brave front, and I don't think that it was false bravado. It was something else. It came from somewhere down deep —a need to face up to the real dangers that threatened him, to take them head-on and to prevail. In the end, he lost that fight. But he never lost the will to fight.

A different kind of battle that RFK waged early on in his term as Senator was with the Johnson administration's foreign policy. In April 1965, he went to the White House to urge the President to halt the bombing in Vietnam. Johnson listened to him and later did agree to cease U.S. air strikes for six days in May as a concession to the Senator and other critics. But at the same time, the President asked Congress for another $700 million to support more troops in the region, so the temporary halt was rendered virtually meaningless.

A crisis had also been brewing closer to home that spring—in the Dominican Republic. Claiming that Communists were attempting to overthrow the government there, on April 27 President Johnson ordered American troops to invade the island nation. The Senator was furious. He felt that the unilateral military action by the United States made a mockery of the Organization of American States (OAS) and undermined the economic goals of the Alliance for Progress that his brother had proposed and championed.

On May 6, I watched from the Senate gallery as RFK rose in the chamber to speak about the administration's request for additional funds to support the Vietnam War effort. He also used the opportunity to raise his concerns about Johnson's invasion of the Dominican Republic, criticizing the administration for acting unilaterally without regard for other members of the OAS. As for Vietnam, he said that while he would vote in favor of the $700 million appropriation that Johnson wanted for our troops, he viewed it as a prelude to negotiations there, which he favored. He warned that escalation in Vietnam "might lead to nuclear warfare."

The press immediately jumped on the Senator's remarks and started pushing the narrative that there was a feud brewing between RFK and the President, with headlines like "Kennedy Blasts Johnson." The Senator's criticism of the administration's foreign policy was not aligned with public opinion either. According to polls at the time, 57 percent of Americans supported Johnson's handling of the Vietnam conflict, while an overwhelming 75 percent supported the invasion of the Dominican Republic.

On June 23, the Senator was scheduled to deliver his maiden speech on the floor of the U.S. Senate. The subject of the address was the proliferation of nuclear weapons—an issue that President Kennedy had been particularly concerned about during the last year of his life. The day of the speech, the Senator sent Adam Walinsky to the White House with a copy of it so that the President would not be caught off guard. Adam sat down with the Vice President to go over the final draft of the speech, and Humphrey seemed to be comfortable with it.

That afternoon, Angie called and asked me to deliver a copy of the speech to the Georgetown home of the Senator's friend, newspaper columnist Joseph Alsop. In those days, of course, there were no personal computers or fax machines, so other than reading the speech to Alsop over the telephone, the only way of getting it to him was by hand-delivering it. Angie told me that she would give me cab fare to get there and that I could go directly home afterward if I wanted. I was happy to run the errand for the Senator but was disappointed that I would not be able to get back to the Senate gallery in time to see him deliver his speech. In the months that followed, I would make a point of going over to the gallery as often as I could to watch him whenever he was scheduled to speak on the Senate floor.

In his remarks to the Senate, RFK called upon the U.S. government to extend the 1963 Nuclear Test Ban Treaty to underground testing and to develop a new treaty that would cover the nonproliferation of nuclear weapons. This, he said, was "the most vital issue now facing the nation and the world," and that without controls on nuclear weapons, we might face what could "well become the last crisis for all mankind."

For a freshman senator, this was an unusually heady speech to make so early in his term. It also had the potential to create a further rift in relations with the Johnson administration because it implied that they were not doing enough to stop the spread of nuclear weapons. But after Adam met with Humphrey, that did not seem to be a problem.

Following his speech, some seventeen senators rose to praise RFK's remarks, and most of the mail we received afterward was highly favorable. The Senator would often ask to see the letters sent to him on various issues, and he was particularly interested in the reaction to this speech, requesting to see the few negative pieces of mail that we received.

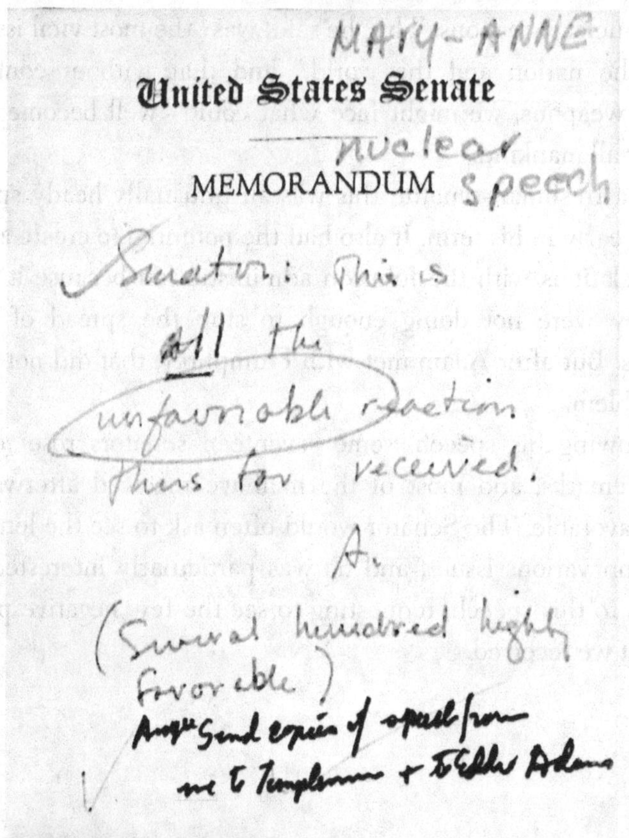

RFK handwritten note to Angie (bottom)

But despite the go-ahead signal that Vice President Humphrey had given Adam, we learned afterward that President Johnson was privately displeased with the speech. Reportedly, he resented the fact that RFK had quoted President Kennedy extensively and felt that some of the Senator's general statements about American attitudes toward war could be interpreted as an indictment of the administration's policy in Vietnam. In short, the President was not happy with the Senator from New York, but that was nothing new.

It was, of course, common knowledge among the staff that the Senator did not like Lyndon Johnson, and the President felt the same way about Robert Kennedy. Reportedly, RFK considered LBJ a bully and had once described him as "mean, bitter, vicious—an animal in many ways." Still, most of us on staff never heard him say a bad word about the President. But then, he never said a good word about him either. Actually, in the beginning, I never heard anyone in the office talk about Johnson at all in conversation—particularly not in the presence of the Senator. Rumor had it that RFK had to shut Adam down once when he'd said something negative about Johnson in front of him. But for the rest of us, it was like being in a family where the abusive father had gone off to buy cigarettes one day and never came back ... and then everyone pretended he didn't exist. The President's name was simply not part of our vocabulary. Over time, that would change, as Johnson's antagonism toward RFK mushroomed.

I think that the Senator did try very hard not to further fuel the media fixation about a rift between the two of them. For one thing, it was counterproductive in the sense that anything the Senator did that went against administration policy would be looked at through the lens of, "Oh, he's just doing that because he hates Johnson." But the press continued to push that narrative anyway, so I don't know that it made much difference. The half-truths were repeated over and over so often that they began to take on a life of their own.

But while the Senator clearly disliked Johnson, he had difficulty understanding why the President was so obsessed with him. He would raise the question with Dick Goodwin, who was still in the White House: "Why does he keep worrying about me? Hell, he's the President and I'm only a junior Senator." Over the months to come, Johnson's paranoia about RFK would only grow, and sadly, it began to influence the administration's policy decisions more and more. By the summer of 1966, Ambassador Chester Bowles would report that LBJ's obsession with Robert Kennedy had reached paranoiac proportions and only seemed to strengthen his resolve about winning the Vietnam War.

Years later, Doris Kearns Goodwin would quote President Johnson as saying that if he hadn't escalated the war, "there would be Robert Kennedy out in front leading the fight against me, telling everyone that I had betrayed John Kennedy's commitment to South Vietnam. That I had let a democracy fall into the hands of the communists. That I was a coward. An unmanly man. A man without a spine. Oh, I could see it coming, all right."

Given LBJ's feelings, it's not difficult to understand why RFK sometimes couldn't bear to be around the President if he didn't have to be. In fact, the night after the Senator's maiden speech, a Democratic Congressional Dinner was being held at the National Guard Armory in Washington. President Johnson was to be honored, and he was also the keynote speaker.

The Senator did his duty. As a loyal Democrat, he bought up several tables for the dinner—which must have cost him a pretty penny—and all of us on staff were able to attend the event for free. But unfortunately, the Senator had a "conflict" in his schedule, so he couldn't be there personally. Maybe he really did have to be somewhere else, but everyone, probably even LBJ, assumed that he just didn't want to attend. In any event, there was no love lost between the two men.

During the years that I spent working for Robert Kennedy, that was one thing that never changed.

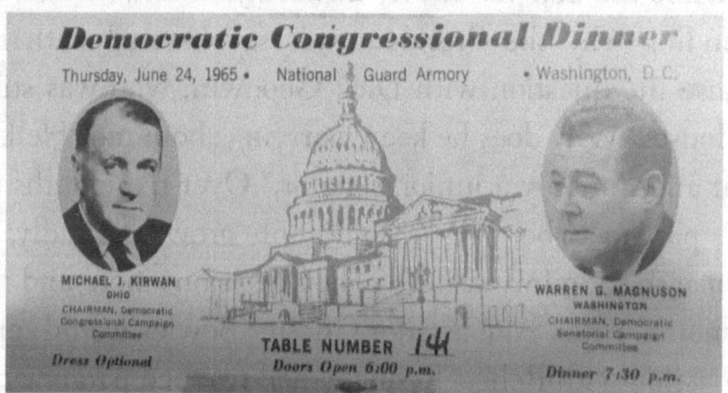

Ticket to Democratic Congressional Dinner

That Congressional Dinner was probably one of the few evenings out that I had in the first few months after I began working for the Senator. In fact, throughout the spring of 1965, I didn't have much of a social life at all. Most of my time was spent working in the Senator's office, attending classes, or studying. I managed to make the Dean's List at George Washington, so I was pleased with that, but I had little energy for anything else. I rarely went to parties or on dates. I was taking a full schedule of classes, and some of them were pretty difficult. In preparation for what I thought at the time would be a career in the State Department (perhaps assigned to the U.S. Embassy in Moscow), I was studying Russian, Russian history, and political science, in addition to a couple of other freshman-required courses.

The only guys I seemed to meet were working up on the Hill. I was always on the run from classes at GW to work, so I never had the opportunity to socialize with any of my classmates. Also, there were no co-ed dorms at the university in those days, so it was strictly girls in my residence hall.

There was one fellow, however, on whom I had developed a bit of a crush. I would often see him riding the same bus up to the Capitol. I would later learn that he was attending Georgetown University, so that was why he was already seated by the time I boarded the bus at the corner of Pennsylvania Avenue and 19th Street. One day, when the bus was fairly crowded, I finally screwed up the courage to sit down next to him and start a conversation.

He was tall and skinny, had very black hair and dreamy blue, blue eyes. His name was Gerry—Gerry McGowan. At the time, he was working in Senator Hart's office. Senator Phil Hart was a Democratic senator from Michigan, and I learned that Gerry was also from Michigan. I loved talking to him because he was super-smart and had a great sense of humor, sarcastic though it often was. He was also a bit moody—I never knew which Gerry I would find sitting there on any given day—but I was drawn to him, partly, I suppose, because he was something of an enigma to me and a challenge.

We became pretty good friends, but it never went beyond that. He never asked me out. I don't know why. Perhaps he was just shy or afraid of girls at that age, or maybe he simply wasn't as attracted to me as I was to him. Who knows? Maybe he just wasn't into the whole boyfriend business.

But anyway, I lost track of him after I left Washington. Then, in 2020, during the COVID pandemic, I decided to see if I could find out whatever became of Gerry. So I did a Google search ... and man, was I shocked.

It turned out that Gerry McGowan was a very close friend of another Georgetown student at the time—a guy by the name of Bill Clinton. (I never did run into Bill back then. If I had known him, my life might have gone in a completely different direction!) Anyway, Gerry—who went on to Georgetown Law School and then served as an Army First Lieutenant in the Vietnam War—eventually became a partner in a Washington law firm that specialized in telecommunications. Later, he also served on the board of Portugal Telecom.

Then, in 1997, his old friend, President Bill Clinton, appointed him as U.S. Ambassador to Portugal. Interestingly, Gerry and his late wife had seven children together (frankly, I would never have been up to that). Following his first wife's death, he married Susan Brophy, who was also working in the Clinton White House at the time. Apparently, President Clinton acted as something of a matchmaker, inviting both of them on a presidential trip to Ireland, which is how they met.

Well, it all just confirmed to me that there was, in fact, something very special about that skinny, blue-eyed boy who got away.

Chapter 7

Hyannisport

How many loved your moments of glad grace, And
loved your beauty with love false or true... ~
W.B. Yeats

I continued to work in Senator Kennedy's office over the
summer of 1965, only heading home to L.A. for a few weeks in
August. I was able to remain in the dorm during that period
even though I wasn't taking any classes. The place was pretty empty
during June, July, and August, so they rented out rooms to non-
students. When I was at the dorm, I met one of those "non-students"
—a woman who would become a good friend of mine. Judy was a few
years older than I. She was working as a secretary at a private
company near Dupont Circle and staying at the dorm until she could
find an apartment she could afford.

Anyway, July Fourth weekend was approaching, so Judy and I
were bouncing around ideas about what to do. Of course, there were
lots of festivities planned in Washington for the Fourth, but both of

us were eager to get out of town. The Senator and his family were going river rafting in Colorado that weekend with his newfound friend and fellow mountain climber, Jim Whittaker, so he had sent out a memo to all of the staff inviting us to use his pool at Hickory Hill. But Provi was in Hyannis Port with Jackie for most of the summer, so there was nobody from the office I really wanted to see at the Senator's place.

After considering various possibilities and rejecting them, I suddenly thought: Why not go up to Hyannis Port and visit Provi? Neither Judy nor I had ever been to Boston, and I figured that it might be fun to experience a new city. Judy was totally up for it, so we made reservations to fly from D.C. to Boston first thing Saturday morning. Since it was only an hour-and-a-half drive from Boston to Hyannis Port, we could rent a car and be up at the Cape by Saturday afternoon.

Everything went exactly as planned. We had pre-booked a room in Hyannis for Saturday night that wasn't far from the Kennedy property, so after dumping our bags there, we headed out. We had no trouble finding the compound, and when we got there, we parked a ways down the street and then walked up to talk to the security guard who was posted in a little kiosk outside Jackie's house. I told him that I was there to see Providencia Paredes and asked if he could call her on the telephone so that she could come out and talk to us. I explained that I was a friend of Provi's, that we worked together in RFK's office, but he just gave me a blank stare, as if he didn't understand what I was talking about. He acted as though he didn't know who Provi was either, which I knew was a lie, since anyone who ever worked for the Kennedys knew Provi.

Then, just as we were about to give up and walk away, who should emerge from Jackie's house at that moment but Gustavo, Provi's son. He spotted us immediately and came running over to the kiosk, very excited to see me. The first words out of his mouth were, "My mom's going to be so happy you're here, Donna. Come on inside." So off we went, following Gustavo into Jacqueline Kennedy's house. As I recall, the door led directly into the kitchen, and lo and behold, when we walked through it, there was Provi fussing over the stove.

She immediately started shrieking with delight. "Oh, Donna—I don't believe it!" Then, in her charming Dominican accent, she demanded, "What you doing here, Donna?" She ran over and hugged me. I introduced her to Judy and explained that we had decided, on a whim, to fly up to Boston for the weekend and that we had rented a room not too far from there.

"Sit down, sit down," she demanded. And so we did.

"What you want to drink, Donna? Did you eat yet?" In usual Provi fashion, she insisted on making sandwiches for us and served up a couple of daiquiris as well, even though it was just the afternoon. Provi was famous for her daiquiris, and they were as potent as they were delicious.

She sat down at the table with us, and we all started talking. She asked what was going on in the office, and I wanted to find out what she had been up to. As usual, we were having a rollicking good time— talking a mile a minute and laughing loudly.

Then, at some point, the kitchen door from the inside of the house opened, and in walked Jackie. Holy cow! As I've said before, growing up in Hollywood, it never really fazed me to see celebrities. But meeting Jacqueline Kennedy that day was something else entirely.

I have to tell you: she was more stunning than I ever could have imagined. She was dressed pretty simply—a yellow, short-sleeved cotton T-shirt and white pants. No jewelry that I noticed and very little makeup. But she was simply gorgeous, nonetheless. And so gracious.

Provi introduced us, telling her that I worked in RFK's office with her. She just said, "Very nice to meet you," or something along those lines. We made some small talk for a few moments; then she excused herself, picked up something from the counter, and went back inside.

After she was gone, Provi told us that Randolph Churchill—the son of Winston Churchill—was a guest at the house that weekend. I remembered that the Senator and Jackie had gone to dinner with Churchill back in May, when they both were in the UK for the Queen's dedication of Runnymede—an acre of Crown land given to the American people in honor of JFK. I later read that Jackie had dated Churchill briefly, but I don't know if that's true. They may have just been good friends, which is probably more likely, considering Churchill's declining health at the time.

But the whole thing was surreal. Here we were—a couple of complete strangers—sitting around her kitchen table being loud and raucous (I can't imagine that they hadn't heard us), and she was as hospitable as can be, treating us as though we were her guests or old friends. I was simply blown away. What a classy woman she was. It was such a thrill to meet her, but I wouldn't see her again in person for another twenty-eight years. The next time we would meet was at Gustavo's wedding to Elizabeth Alexander in 1993.

At any rate, after we finished our sandwiches and drinks, Provi offered to show us around the compound. The house itself, other than the kitchen area, was off-limits that weekend since Jackie was entertaining Churchill, so we went outside to take a look at the other homes and head down to the boat docks.

RFK's house was closest to where the President's home was situated; then, below it and nearest the water, was the Ambassador's house.

Postcard—Kennedy Compound—1965

Old Joe was still alive then, but not in great shape after his stroke. As we walked along below the elder Kennedy's home, the three of us continued gabbing and laughing quite loudly. Suddenly, we heard someone yelling from the house, "Provi, Provi!" We looked back, and in an upstairs window there was the Kennedy matriarch, Rose, leaning out. She yelled, "Stop making so much noise, Provi. The Ambassador is trying to sleep." Provi yelled back, "Sorry, Mrs. Kennedy!" The window slammed shut, and we all looked at each other and giggled. It seemed funny to us that Rose Kennedy would be screaming at the top of her lungs, chastising us for being too loud.

Anyway, we made our way down to the dock, and Provi said, "Come on, I want you to meet someone." Standing there was a young boy with a man. They were both in swim trunks, and the man was wrapping a towel around the boy. As we got closer, I realized that the child was John Kennedy Jr. He would have been about three and a half years old then. He was soaking wet, his little body shivering as the man tried to dry him off.

Provi said, "Jack, I want you to meet my girlfriend from the office, Donna, and her friend, Judy." It was Jack Walsh, JFK Jr.'s Secret Service agent. Provi had talked a lot about him when we were in the office. He was quite good-looking, and I knew Provi had a bit of a crush on him. We stood and chatted with him for a few minutes. I couldn't take my eyes off John, though. Here was that same little boy I had seen on TV saluting his father's casket less than two years before. He was so adorable, but I couldn't have guessed then how handsome and accomplished a man he would eventually become. The next time I would meet him was many years later at Hickory Hill following a twentieth-anniversary memorial service for his uncle Bobby.

After spending most of the afternoon with Provi, Judy and I headed back to our motel to clean up and change clothes. Provi had insisted on setting us up on "dates" with two of the Secret Service agents assigned to Mrs. Kennedy and her children. Apparently, they were able to get some time off in the evenings. We were supposed to meet them at a bar not far from the compound. We thought it might be fun, so we agreed.

It turned out that the Secret Service agents were quite a bit older than we were, and they really weren't our kind of guys. Both were beefy, linebacker types, as I recall. Even worse, the moment we sat down, they immediately started bad-mouthing Mrs. Kennedy. I don't know if they were just trying to impress us—hard to imagine that they thought we would be impressed by that—or if they really felt that way. But their criticisms of her were ridiculous and unfounded. They asserted that she cared more about herself than about her kids and that she was only interested in entertaining important friends rather than taking care of her own children. I asked for examples of what they meant, and all they could come up with was that she fed John and Caroline hot dogs and hamburgers while she ate expensive, fancy food. What? Angered, I immediately said, "What are you talking about? Hot dogs and hamburgers are what kids like to eat. Everybody feeds their kids that."

Anyway, their disloyalty and unprofessionalism really bothered me, so after finishing our drinks about ten minutes later, Judy and I got up and left them there. It did make me wonder, however, about the quality of the Secret Service agents assigned to Mrs. Kennedy. Judy and I were headed back to Boston the next day, so I didn't see

Provi again that weekend, but I told her about our conversation with them when she returned to the office. I have no idea whether she mentioned it to Mrs. Kennedy or not, but it was no surprise to me when Jackie later chose to marry Onassis. At least he could provide the level of protection she wanted for her children.

During the rest of the summer, Washington was relatively quiet. In the office, we started a college intern program, which in its first year included about twelve to fifteen college students. The Senator was eager to get it off the ground because we were still struggling with an overload of mail and too much work in the office with too few staff members. The only trouble was that we really had no place to put them, so they ended up being shuffled off to "seminars" and meetings with various federal officials around D.C. during their time with us. That way, they got a feel for how things worked in the nation's capital, but they rarely had any time actually working in our office, where we had no space for them. Some of them would put in short stints in various sections of the office, then move on someplace else, but that was more of a waste of staff time than anything else—having to train these short-termers and then seeing them leave.

The first week of August, President Johnson signed the Voting Rights Bill into law. Then, about a week later, the Watts riots began in Los Angeles. While codifying voting rights for African Americans was a huge step forward, RFK seemed to be one of the few politicians who understood that there were more grievances in the Black community than could be solved by simply protecting their right to vote.

The fact was that African Americans in L.A. had been brutalized for years by the LAPD, and the unrest in Watts that summer was directly tied to that. So, when former President Eisenhower commented that the solution to the riots was "greater respect for the law," the Senator publicly called him out, retorting that there was no point in telling Black people to obey the law when, for so many of them, the law had been "their enemy"—that it had almost always been used against them. RFK was widely criticized for these comments, but mainly, I think, because so few White people in those days (and still today) recognized the injustice being done to African Americans. Later, in his book *To Seek a Newer World*, the Senator would write:

> *How overwhelming must be the frustration of this young man -- this young American -- who, desperately wanting to believe and half believing, finds himself locked in the slums, his education second-rate, unable to get a job, confronted by the open prejudice and subtle hostilities of a white world, and seemingly powerless to change his conditions or shape his future.*

At the end of August, I flew home to Los Angeles for a couple of weeks to visit my parents. A short time later, I received an 8 x 10 photograph of Mrs. Kennedy that was inscribed to me. It read: *For Donna Stanley, with best wishes, Jacqueline Kennedy*. It was a lovely remembrance of my trip to Hyannis Port, and I still treasure it. The photograph was reportedly President Kennedy's favorite of his wife.

Inscribed photograph to me from Jackie. Photo credit: Arnie Sachs

Chapter 8

The Beach Boys

Things are not always what they seem; the first
appearance deceives many; the intelligence of a
few perceives what has been carefully hidden. ~
Phaedrus

I returned to Washington in early September. In August, my
friend Judy had found an apartment in Foggy Bottom not far
from the dormitory where I'd been previously living, and I
moved in with her. It was exciting to finally feel a bit like a real adult
and to be free of the confines and rules of the university residence. I
could eat coffee ice cream directly from the carton, drink cold duck
whenever I wanted (a big mistake!), and make telephone calls without
having to hike down nine floors or wait in line for a half hour with
quarters and dimes falling out of my pockets.

I also went back to work in the Senator's office as before. I was
still taking a full complement of classes, but it seemed less taxing for
me at this point—I guess because I had adjusted to the routine. I

continued to see Gerry on my bus rides up to the Hill, and he still showed no interest in asking me out, so my social life was nothing to write home about. Not that I would have written home about my social life anyway, since my parents were already concerned about what I might be up to.

With Judy in our apartment

I don't think I ever told them about what happened later that September to me and Lois, but it's probably worth sharing here. Lois was a friend of mine from the dorm, and we used to hang out quite a lot. Just as a bit of background, she started as a cheerleader for George Washington University that fall (GW actually had a football team in those days, but 1966 would be its last season). She would travel with the team, and on September 18, they were playing against Temple University in Philadelphia. She was staying at a hotel there when she happened to run into Dennis Wilson of the Beach Boys—in an elevator, I think. The group was on tour and scheduled to perform at the DC Armory in Washington the next night. Dennis wanted to get together with her when he was in Washington, which she was excited to do—after all, he was the *cute* Beach Boy. So anyway, in the late afternoon of September 19, Lois went over to meet Dennis at the hotel where the group was staying—as I recall, it was the Shoreham. Then in the early evening, out of the blue, I received a phone call from her. She explained that she was there with the Beach Boys and that they had asked her to call a friend—that they wanted someone as a "date" for Mike Love, the lead singer of the band.

With Lois (right) and her Congressman, Rep. James Burke, at the Capitol

So, naturally, I was all in. I changed my clothes—I remember I wore my best dress—it was this yellow, sleeveless shift with a huge, bright pink flower embroidered across most of the front—very 1960s—and I headed over to the Shoreham to meet Lois and the guys. When I got there, I went up to their room. Mrs. Wilson (Dennis's mother) was there too, so we felt safe enough. Mike Love and I mostly talked about my being from L.A., and he asked me what I was doing in D.C., so I filled him in on that. After having a drink and chatting for a while, we then got into a limo with Mrs. Wilson to go to the concert. Throughout the ride to the Armory, she kept talking to us about what great guys the Beach Boys were—how down to earth they were and how they weren't affected at all by their fame—and that she was sure we would love them the way she did. She was really working hard to sell them to us, which seemed a little strange.

When we arrived at the DC Armory, we went inside, and they set up special folding chairs for us so that we could sit just below the stage. They were really going all out to treat us like VIPs.

The concert was fabulous, and Lois and I were really eating it up. When they got around to singing their hit song, "California Girls," Mike Love actually came over to the edge of the stage where I was sitting and started singing the song to me. It was quite a moment in my young life!

Once the concert was over, we headed back to the hotel with Mrs. Wilson, but she said she was tired and begged off going up to the boys' room with us. At any rate, we got up to the room—this time it was just Dennis and Mike there. They fixed us more drinks, and apparently, they figured it was time for us to repay their generosity. Once we sat down on the sofa in their suite, they were all over us.

Needless to say, I wasn't prepared to lose my virginity to Mike Love that night. Lois and I ended up running for our lives out of their hotel room. We weren't really upset at the time—I think we thought it was funny, more than anything—because I remember that we were laughing (not crying) hysterically as we ran to the elevator. Later, though, we found out that they were both married at the time. Correction—they were married or *nearly* married. Dennis had just gotten married less than two months before. And Mike Love, I learned, got hitched in October of that year—less than a month after my encounter with him—so I imagine he was at least engaged or in a serious relationship at that point.

But what was even more disturbing when we thought about it later was how Mrs. Wilson seemed to be pimping for them when we were with her in the limo. This is just speculation, but I couldn't help but wonder whether she did this all the time with young girls when the Beach Boys were on the road.

Unfortunately, it wouldn't be my last "Me Too" moment with a celebrity, but that's a whole other story.

Beach Boys poster

As for the Senator, I believe he spent that entire weekend in New York. He would frequently fly to New York City and upstate New York when there was no Senate business to keep him in D.C. In fact, on the 9th of September, he'd made headlines when he testified before a New York State legislative committee after conducting unannounced visits to the Willowbrook State School for the "mentally retarded" (as they were called then) on Staten Island and another similar school in upstate New York. The Senator described the Willowbrook school as a "snakepit," saying that he was shocked and saddened by what he saw. He said:

There are young children slipping into blankness and lifelong dependence... And there are many, far too many, living in filth and dirt, their clothing in rags, in rooms less comfortable and cheerful than the cages in a zoo—without adequate supervision or a bit of affection —condemned to a life without hope.

He charged that the State of New York had failed to take advantage of federal grants that were available for research, construction, and therapy, and he made several specific recommendations to the committee for action that the State could take to help alleviate some of the problems that he'd found in the schools. His decision to visit the facilities in the first place had been prompted by letters to our office from some of the parents of children in the schools, complaining about the conditions there. I remember reading some of them—it was horrifying to learn what was happening there.

Then, on Friday, September 18, he returned to New York City for less serious business. Mayor Wagner had declared Friday "Mickey Mantle Day," since Mantle was about to play in his 2,000th game for the Yankees. The ceremony honoring him was due to start at one o'clock Friday afternoon in Yankee Stadium. The Senator had been invited to attend the ceremony and the game afterward against the Detroit Tigers, and he decided to go. So he was among the several dignitaries gathered on the field—together with 50,000 fans in the stadium who were there to witness the event. Famed announcer Red Barber was the master of ceremonies, and Joe DiMaggio introduced Mantle, who said a few words. Whether RFK actually stayed for the game, I don't really recall.

Earlier that same week, however, something more important was happening on the other side of the country that would eventually become of great concern to the Senator. On September 16, 1965, in the Central Valley of California, Cesar Chavez and his United Farm Workers union had voted to join a strike by Filipino American grape workers against Delano-area grape growers. At that point, RFK had only met Cesar Chavez once—very briefly in 1959 at a voter registration drive in Los Angeles. But six months later, he would meet him once again. At the request of other labor leaders, the Senator's Migratory Labor Subcommittee would go to Delano in March 1966 for public hearings. While reluctant to make the trip at first, the Senator's daylong meeting with Cesar Chavez in March would change everything for him. It marked the beginning of a deep and abiding commitment by RFK to fight for migrant farmworkers not just in Delano, but throughout the country. Cesar Chavez would later say about RFK, "We loved him...it was like respect, admiration, love, and idolization. God, I can't explain it." I can't either, but that's the way I felt as well.

At the time, I thought that the Senator and Chavez had a lot in common despite coming from such diverse backgrounds. They not only shared some physical traits, but they both had a strong belief in the justness of what they were doing and a willingness to sacrifice whatever was necessary in order to achieve their aims, regardless of the risk to their own lives. Of course, they also shared a strong religious faith—tinged, perhaps, with a dose of fatalism.

More than twenty years later, in April 1988, I would meet Cesar Chavez for the first time at a symposium called "RFK Remembered" that was being held for staff and friends of Robert Kennedy in Los Angeles at Loyola Marymount University. It was about three months before Chavez would begin his longest and final fast, one that may well have contributed to his death in 1993.

I remember I was in awe of Chavez that day. I admired him so much. Of course, recent accusations about his personal behavior have come as a complete shock to me. I'm certain that the Senator, if he were alive today, would also be stunned and saddened.

Of course there was always an aura of sadness, as well as fatalism, that often seemed to envelop the Senator. It was as though he knew how short his days on the planet would be and that was why he was always in such a hurry to get things done, to challenge the status quo, to ask the hard questions, and look for answers. And so often, he was doing God's work—caring for the dispossessed and the poor, for the neglected and the powerless, for those with developmental disabilities, for the forgotten people whom no one else seemed to care about. I believe that his emotional urgency and compassion came directly from his core, from that part of him that had been irreparably ripped apart by the death of his brother, from that deep sorrow in his heart.

I think it came, as well, from his own struggles when he was a kid. Back then, even his father used to call him "the runt," and his sister Jean would later remark that nothing was easy for Bobby when he was a boy—that he was "constantly struggling to make the football team—against boys who were taller and stronger," and perhaps that was what gave him his empathy for those less fortunate. She said, "He, in some peculiar way, understood their soul."

I think she was right. The man I knew was so very different from the mythology about him that the media constantly perpetuated. Article after article would describe RFK as being ruthless and calculating, driven only by political ambition. They were always attributing ulterior motives to everything he did. Some even seemed to view the sadness that surrounded him as nothing more than stubborn sullenness. The attacks continued even into his campaign for President, up until the day he died. Perhaps reporters just didn't want the public to think that they had gone soft on him, but in writing these stories, they demonstrated instead a reckless disregard for the truth and an unmistakable bias against the Senator. In response, he would sometimes make self-deprecating jokes about his "ruthlessness," but I think it was simply a cover for the hurt and anger that he felt about that characterization.

When I knew him, he simply wasn't at all that way. He was sensitive, compassionate, and totally authentic. Yes, he could do or say things that sometimes seemed contradictory, but I think that was more a reflection of his own personal complexity rather than any sort of political calculation or ruthlessness on his part.

At his center, he had a truly gentle spirit, and he was shy—so shy that his hands would actually shake when he spoke, particularly in public. This is not to suggest that he was weak or soft, because he wasn't—he was tough and he was courageous. And he was a gifted politician as well, but he had to work at it—it didn't come naturally. So much of who he was existed below the surface—hidden in some private place that few got to see. As Adam Walinsky would say about the Senator years later, "He was a lot of things...He was sensitive, but he was a tough guy."

Still, the accusations got to him, I think. The beat poet Allen Ginsberg came to see the Senator in his office early in 1968 and, at one point, he accused RFK of being "heartless" and told him that what the country needed was "a politician who's friendly and tender-hearted"—with the clear implication that RFK wasn't. Ginsberg would later say that the Senator "really resented that."

I'm not surprised. As Adam would remark about the Ginsberg meeting, "I could see him taking umbrage...Because, remember, by the time this happens, he's had his Gethsemane and he's pretty much aware that his Calvary is ahead of him. And by that point, he's picked up and held a lot of little poor kids, who probably have pellagra all over them. So when he gets lectured on tenderness, maybe he's thinking, 'Who is this guy? Has he been where I've been?'" Adam added that he had often seen the Senator become irritable when he was completely misunderstood.

And who could blame him? It must have been extremely frustrating for him to have to continually deal with all of these firmly held misconceptions about his character, particularly when he would go out of his way to listen to people, to let them have their say, like he'd done with Ginsberg, only to have them turn around and insult him.

Chapter 9

The Fall of 1965

Few will have the greatness to bend history itself, but
each of us can work to change a small portion of
events. ~ Robert F. Kennedy

I n the fall of 1965, the administration's foreign policy continued
to be front and center on RFK's agenda. Since the U.S. invasion of the Dominican Republic in April, the situation there
had worsened—so much so that the Pope's ambassador to the island
nation had contacted the Senator to express his alarm about the
rapidly deteriorating economic conditions there.

Following their conversation, the Senator reached out to the
White House, first speaking with Press Secretary Bill Moyers, then
with the President himself on October 5, when Johnson telephoned
RFK about another matter. Of course, the Senator had publicly criticized the U.S. intervention back in May, so it was a sore subject
for LBJ.

During their conversation, Johnson became quite combative and immediately went on the defensive. The two men seemed to be talking past each other. While the Senator's focus was on the urgent need to do something about widespread starvation in the Dominican Republic, Johnson's only interest seemed to be in disarming leftists in the country to keep it from turning Communist like Cuba. LBJ did indicate that he would instruct Secretary of State Rusk to speak with the papal envoy to learn more about the situation, so they left it at that.

At the same time, across the U.S., demonstrations against the war in Vietnam were growing, particularly on college campuses, with students burning their draft cards. In early November, the Senator held a press conference at the University of Southern California, where he was asked about it. RFK equivocated. He was then asked about the rights of students to give blood to the North Vietnamese, and he responded that he thought that was a good idea, explaining that he was in favor of giving blood to anyone who needed it. As you might imagine, his comments created a firestorm of criticism within the press and the halls of Congress, with Senator Barry Goldwater saying that it was "closer to treason than academic freedom." The right-wing John Birch Society went so far as to tape-record a message for their followers that asked, "Isn't advocating the giving of blood to the enemy treason?" The Senator would later concede that it wasn't his "finest hour."

That same month, he would leave for a fact-finding tour of Latin America. During the summer, he had received an invitation to speak in Brazil during the Senate recess in November. He'd accepted the invitation but decided to expand his visit to some other Latin American countries as well—including Argentina, Chile, Venezuela, and Peru—partly because he wanted to be out of the country on November 22, the second anniversary of his brother's assassination. He would also be there for his fortieth birthday—the 20th of November. It was another painful anniversary for him. That was the day in 1963 when he had last seen President Kennedy alive. The two of them were at the White House, and JFK had wished him a happy birthday. The President left for Texas the next morning. The Senator would never talk about it, but it was during this trip to Latin America that he finally decided to stop wearing that black tie of his in mourning for his brother. He would continue, however, to wear the PT-109 tie clasp until the day he died. Sometimes, he would wear it clipped to his shirt even after he took off his tie.

When President Johnson first learned about RFK's travel plans to South America, he went ballistic. Coming on the heels of his conversation with the Senator about the situation in the Dominican Republic, LBJ was convinced that RFK would use the trip to criticize the administration's foreign policy. Not only that, but he also suspected that it might mark the beginning of the Senator's campaign for the presidency—another fear with which Johnson was becoming increasingly preoccupied. Still, there wasn't anything that LBJ could do to stop RFK from going.

So, on November 10, 1965, the Senator and a rather large entourage—including Angie and Adam from our staff—left Miami for their three-week tour of South America. Throughout his trip there, RFK generally defended the administration, but there were times when he did take some direct swipes at Johnson's foreign policy. When asked about the U.S. invasion of the Dominican Republic, he called it "a mistake," but he did challenge those in Latin America who tried to characterize it as "American imperialism."

For the most part, he was well received and met by cheering crowds. However, at a university in Concepción, Chile, he was greeted by leftist students chanting, "Go home, Bobby" and "Yankee go home." They threw eggs, rocks, and coins at him—none of which hit their mark, fortunately—and tried to kick him and spit at him. Following the incident, the Senator reportedly remarked in his usual sardonic way, "If these kids are going to be revolutionaries, they're going to have to improve their aim."

And then, in Recife, Brazil, police foiled a plot to throw acid in the Senator's face. The throwing of acid was apparently intended to be a signal to other anti-U.S. demonstrators throughout Latin America to begin their protests.

Those of us back on his Senate staff read the reports of what had happened in Chile and Brazil and felt badly about the incidents. We wanted to do something to pick up his spirits when he returned to Washington. I don't recall whose idea it was—perhaps Provi's. But we decided that we would all go out to the airport to greet him upon his return. So when he walked into the terminal at National Airport after his long flight, what he saw were our smiling faces and signs reading "Welcome Home, Senator" and "We Love You, Senator." He was truly surprised and rather touched, too, I think.

About a week after RFK got home from Latin America, he was invited to appear on *Meet the Press* with Lawrence Spivak. It was the Senator's custom to invite the staff out to the NBC studios to watch him on the program whenever it was being broadcast from D.C. Usually, some ten or more members of the Senate staff and other friends of his would go to see him when he was scheduled to appear, and I tried to be there as often as possible.

Seated with us in the studio was invariably Alice Roosevelt Longworth, the daughter of Teddy Roosevelt. Back in 1906, when she married Congressman Longworth in a ceremony at the White House, the press had dubbed her "Princess Alice." But in 1965, she was 81 years old—the same age as my grandmother. In fact, they had been born just ten days apart in 1884. For some reason, Mrs. Longworth always seemed to be present whenever the Senator did one of these interview shows. She usually would come in with Ted and sit right next to him and Ethel.

I knew that she was often a guest out at Hickory Hill as well. She would comment that at dinners there she and "Bobby" would "gossip" together. Later, her *Washington Post* obituary would suggest that, despite their age difference, they had a "thing" for each other. I assume that was tongue-in-cheek, but I do think he appreciated her intellect and her acerbic wit, and they did have a lot of fun together arguing about things in a friendly way. Quoting Kipling, Alice would remark about herself that "I carry the curse of unstaunched speech." Proving the point, in an interview on her 90th birthday in 1974, she said, "Ethel is behaving very badly these days. There's a certain brash quality about her I never liked. I liked Bobby, though, a great deal."

But the Senator always seemed to enjoy being around women who were smart...and smart-assed (as I had discovered for myself). That was probably because his own wit could be rather sharp and cutting. However, his friendship with Longworth was occasionally strained. Earlier in the year, she had privately made fun of him when he climbed Mt. Kennedy. It got back to him, and he didn't appreciate it. He could be quite sensitive, and his feelings were easily hurt, particularly if it involved someone he considered a friend.

As for the Senator's appearance on *Meet the Press*, to be perfectly honest, I never thought he did particularly well on that show or on other live interview shows, even though he would usually prepare for them pretty extensively. He would generally have Adam, Peter, and Joe, plus sometimes some of the JFK old-timers, come out to Hickory Hill and quiz him beforehand. They would throw questions at him about whatever was in the news, whatever the press was obsessed with at the time. But I never thought it helped much.

Despite the preparation, he still seemed quite nervous and a bit tentative in his responses. Afterwards, he would always ask us how he did, and everyone would usually lie and tell him that he did just fine. But I got the impression that he knew he hadn't performed all that well. He was usually pretty self-aware and often self-critical.

I think part of the problem was just his natural shyness and discomfort in those kinds of situations. He was not like most other politicians—always ready with some glib answer or false affability. He would tend towards silence, if anything—not the ideal demeanor for a *Meet the Press* appearance. On the other hand, when it came to issues for which he cared deeply, he could be very direct, impassioned, and articulate. He could also be quite funny when he chose to be. He was not one to tell jokes, but he was always good with the one-liners and sharp comebacks. So I think this inherent contradiction of personality perhaps made some people suspicious of him, thinking that he was calculating or devious, when in fact, there were just many different sides to him.

As for this particular *Meet the Press* interview, much of it naturally dealt with his recently completed Latin American trip. On the show, the Senator tried to make many of the same points that he had spoken to during his visit. He maintained that negative attitudes toward the United States in Latin America reflected a widespread belief there that American foreign policy was primarily based upon the business interests of companies like International Petroleum. He also believed that the U.S. government's obsession with anticommunism (and aligning itself with anti-communists) came at the expense of our own interests and was ultimately self-defeating.

The Senator would reiterate these points in a speech on the Senate floor the following spring, which I got to witness. In his remarks that day, he would assert that Batista was more responsible for communism in Cuba than Castro, and that so long as we allowed communism "to carry the banner of reform," the poor and the dispossessed in those countries would see it as "the only way out of their misery." As you might imagine, his comments about communism and U.S. policy in Latin America were not well received by the White House or widely applauded by American business leaders.

I was due to go home to L.A. for Christmas, but before I left, the Senator had a staff Christmas party out at Hickory Hill. Most of us had been out to the Senator's home many times—primarily in the summer months, when he would invite us to use the pool while he was out of town for the weekend. But on those occasions, we never went into the house itself. We would bring our own food, and there was a pool house that had dressing rooms, a living room area, and bathrooms, so there was never a need to go up to the main house.

Actually, the house at Hickory Hill had a lot of history, which I found fascinating. I knew that the original structure had been built in the mid-1800s and had passed through several hands and been rebuilt over the years. In fact, President and Mrs. Kennedy had lived in it before RFK and his family. Jack and Jackie had moved there in 1955, a couple of years after their wedding. JFK had actually written *Profiles in Courage* at Hickory Hill but sold the house that same year to his parents when he and Jackie moved to Georgetown.

Of course, after Ethel and the Senator moved in, they kept adding on to the house to accommodate their expanding family. On the lawn in front, the children had made their own addition: a sign that warned, "Trespassers will be eaten." This was an apparent nod to the number of animals—both domestic and wild—that resided on the five-and-one-half acres of property. But aside from the menagerie of animals and the numerous employees they had working at the house, in many ways daily life at Hickory Hill was much like that of other families in the neighborhood. On Saturday mornings (if he were in town), the Senator would even drive his trash bins down to the local elementary school for pick-up by the trash trucks, since there was no curbside pick-up back then.

As for the party that night, from what I can recall, it was an elegant affair, with all of us dressed up in our finest. Perhaps I've embroidered the memory in my mind, since my recollection about the evening is somewhat hazy, but I certainly don't remember that anything out of the ordinary occurred. So, it wasn't like some of the wild parties at Hickory Hill that reportedly took place during the Kennedy presidency. For one thing, since it was the middle of December, nobody ended up in the swimming pool fully dressed, and, as I recall, there were no games of "Sardines"* that night either. No, it was all very sedate, and everyone on staff was quite well behaved. Since I'd never entered that big red front door of theirs before, I was quite curious about what the interior of the house looked like, and I made a point of checking out all of the rooms.

We were only on the first floor, but I spent most of the evening

---

* *"Sardines" was an after-dinner game that Ethel apparently loved to play at Hickory Hill parties. It was a kind of hide-and-seek game in which whoever found the person hiding had to climb in with them, and the next person would do the same thing, and so on and so forth, until everyone was crammed in together.*

wandering around from room to room, looking at all the silver-framed photos of the Kennedy family—particularly those of the late President—as well as autographed photos of some world leaders, including Winston Churchill. There were numerous framed shots of various Kennedys—including JFK—atop a grand piano in the high-ceilinged living room, as well as on small tables scattered throughout the first floor.

On the wall, there was also an inscribed copy of President Kennedy's inaugural address (to Bobby from Jack—Christmas 1961), as well as a signed letter dated 1935 from FDR to a nine-year-old RFK, talking about the young Bobby's stamp collection and inviting him to come to the White House to see the President's. FDR had apparently sent him some stamps from his personal collection, and RFK replied to President Roosevelt, thanking him for them and for the stamp book the President had also sent him, saying that he would frame FDR's letter and keep it always.

HYANNISPORT
MASSACHUSETTS

July 19, 1935

Dear Mr. President,

I liked the stamps you sent me very much and the little book is very useful. I am just starting my collection and it would be great fun to see yours which mother says you have had for a long time.

Reply from 9-year-old RFK to FDR

I am going to frame your letter and I am going to keep it always in my room.

Daddy, mother, and all my brothers and sisters want to be remembered to you.

Bobby Kennedy

Son of Joseph P. Kennedy

Reply from 9-year-old RFK to FDR

July 12, 1935.

Dear Bob:-

Your Dad has told me that you are a
stamp collector and I thought you might like
to have these stamps to add to your collection.
I am also enclosing a little album which you
may find useful.

Perhaps sometime when you are in
Washington you will come in and let me show
you my collection.

My best wishes to you,

Very sincerely yours,

Robert Kennedy,
Hyannisport,
Massachusetts.

(Enclosure)

Letter to RFK from FDR

I would later read in one of Arthur Schlesinger's books that his son Stephen attended a Christmas party at Hickory Hill on December 19, 1965. I don't recall if that was the date of our party or if Stephen Schlesinger was actually there that night, but he apparently told his father that the Senator's mood at the party he attended was pretty gloomy because of what the administration was doing—or failing to do—in Vietnam. According to Stephen's telling, RFK singled out Secretary of State Dean Rusk for criticism because he

109

thought Rusk was the main stumbling block in efforts to begin negotiations with Hanoi.

To be honest, I don't recall what the Senator's mood was the evening of our party, but it seems to me now that he wasn't any different than always. However, the fact that I don't have a clear recollection of him that night could be a clue that he might not have been particularly social, for one reason or another.

I'm certain that Ethel, however, was her usual outgoing and energetic self. In fact, whenever I was in her presence, she seemed to be in good spirits, never displaying the volatility and unrestrained anger that some of those employed by her suggested.

The Senator did give me a present that Christmas. It was a copy of President Kennedy's book, *The Burden and the Glory*. He inscribed it: "For Donna, With Appreciation, Robert F. Kennedy, Christmas 1965."

I also received a Christmas card from him and Ethel that year.

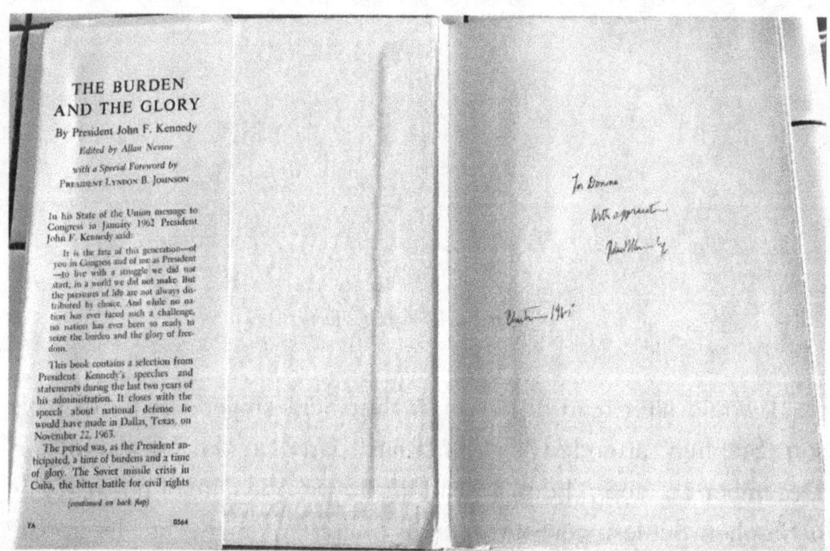

My Christmas gift from RFK

"'Twas the night before Christmas

And all through the house

Not a creature was stirring

Not even a mouse"

Bob and Ethel Kennedy

The Night Before Christmas
Clement Clarke Moore

Senator & Mrs. Kennedy's Christmas Card

Interior of Christmas Card

Chapter 10

The Senator's Staff

Think where man's glory most begins and ends
And say my glory was I had such friends.
~ W.B. Yeats

L et me take a moment to say a few words about the Senator's staff. I already talked a bit about Joe Dolan. Joe was my favorite of the professionals in our office. He was also the only political adviser that RFK had on his Senate staff.

Although his legislative aides often tried to steer the Senator in one direction or another on the issues, he generally didn't turn to them for purely political advice, even though both Adam Walinsky and Peter Edelman had worked on his Senate campaign. Instead, he would sometimes call in the old JFK advisors, and we would see them hanging around the office. These were guys like Kenny O'Donnell, Dick Goodwin, Arthur Schlesinger, and Ted Sorenson. In fact, when Sorenson's biography of JFK came out in 1965, he stopped by the office to autograph it for each of us. There were others as well, such as

John Seigenthaler and William vanden Heuvel, who had been with him in the Justice Department, as well as his old pal from earlier years, Dave Hackett—who would visit the office occasionally too.

Rarely, if ever, though, would the Senator meet with both his Senate aides and the old-timers at the same time. I don't think either group had a particularly high opinion of the other. Adam characterized the JFK advisors as "relics," and Schlesinger would call both Adam and Peter "exasperating."

But as far as in-house political advice, Joe Dolan was pretty much it. Joe's instincts about politics and people were almost always right on the mark, and because he and the Senator went back together so many years, they were able to communicate with few words. Years later, Joe would recall how—long before the 1968 campaign—the Senator had called him into his office one day, told him to shut the door, and said, "I was thinking about running for President—what do you think?" Joe turned around and began staring at the wall. Impatiently, the Senator asked, "What are you doing?" and Joe replied, "I'm looking for Candid Camera."

Remembering the incident, Joe went on to say that he didn't know how to respond to the Senator "because I had assumed that he knew that everything we did was geared to make it easy for him to run for President in '68. For example, we were the only Senate office that answered out-of-state mail, which we did because we had friends all over the country." To tell you the truth, when I was working in the office, I often wondered why we did that—it created so much additional work for us—and I never realized that there was a long-term strategy behind it. But Joe Dolan was the sort of canny political adviser who always had his eye on the future and was two steps ahead of the rest of us.

Joe would actually run for political office himself after the Senator's death. In 1974, he was a Democratic candidate for the Senate in his home state of Colorado (he had previously served in the state legislature there back in 1959–60). A former governor of Colorado, Dick Lamm, would remark about Joe that "He was probably the most significant political figure that nobody ever heard of." Unfortunately, that would spell disaster for his Senate candidacy. Gary Hart, who was much better known by Coloradans at the time, would win the Democratic primary that year. Actually, I think that 1974 was the last time I saw Joe, but more on that later.

Joe Dolan; credit: Duane Howell/Denver Post via Getty Images

During the period that I worked on his staff, the Senator had three different press secretaries. The first guy, Ed Guthman, was my favorite, but he stayed only a few months with us, leaving in the spring of 1965 to become national editor of the *Los Angeles Times*. While at the *Times*, he was honored by being named on President Nixon's "enemies list." Ed had a background as a journalist and had won a Pulitzer Prize for reporting back in 1950, when he worked for the *Seattle Times*. He became RFK's press secretary in the Justice Department beginning in 1961. In 1962, Ed had traveled to Oxford, Mississippi, during the admission of James Meredith—the first Black student at the University of Mississippi—to serve as a liaison for RFK with the federal marshals who were protecting Meredith.

Then, after working in the 1964 New York Senate campaign, he was tapped to become press secretary for the Senator. Ed was a close personal friend of his—had known RFK since the 1950s—and was a super nice guy—very approachable and down-to-earth, with a great sense of humor—who treated everyone in the office with respect, no matter his or her position. Ed would continue to provide the Senator with advice even after he left the office, particularly during the last few months of RFK's life, when he was running for President.

I would meet Ed again a couple of times out in Los Angeles after the Senator's death, first at the Loyola Marymount symposium, "Robert F. Kennedy Remembered," in 1988 and then, nearly ten years later, when he was a professor of journalism at the University of Southern California (USC). It was 1997, and my son, who was editor of his high school newspaper and was graduating that year, was considering various universities. He was planning on majoring in journalism, and USC had offered him a big scholarship to come there. We had been invited out to the USC president's home in San Marino for a party as part of the school's recruitment strategy, and Ed was there. My son, Ian, and I spent a long time talking with him, and it was great to catch up after so many years. How ironic it was, though. Here Ian was even older than I had been when I first met Ed as a college student working in the Senator's office.

Ed died in 2008 at the age of 89.

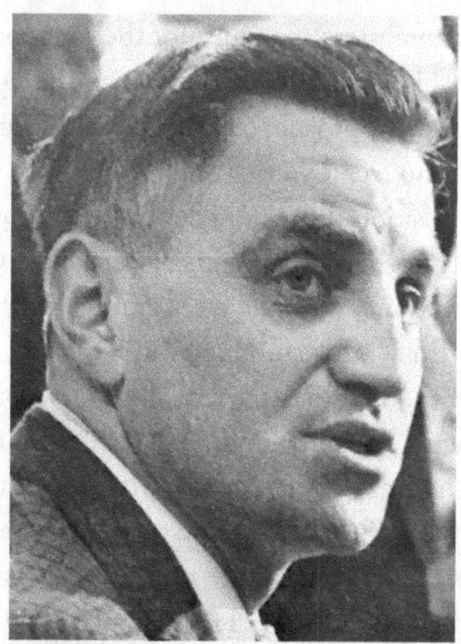

Ed Guthman; credit: AP wire photo, 1963

Ed had long wanted to work for the *L.A. Times*, but he stayed on with the Senator until he was able to find a replacement. The replacement turned out to be Wes Barthelmes. According to Wes, the only advice that Ed ever gave him on taking the job was to learn how to read the Senator's silences—to distinguish what they meant: yes or no. I got the impression that Wes never really mastered that skill; word was that the chemistry between him and RFK was just not right.

Wes also had a background as a newspaperman, and prior to coming to our office, he was working up on the Hill for Rep. Edith Green of Oregon. After he left RFK's office, he was employed by several other senators, eventually becoming Joe Biden's administrative assistant in 1974. Wes was also a good guy—very kind and friendly—but I never really got to know him as well as I had Ed Guthman. Sadly, Wes died way too young, in 1976, of a brain tumor. He was just 54 years old.

Frank Mankiewicz eventually replaced Wes. Frank didn't have a background as a journalist. Actually, he was the Latin America regional director of the Peace Corps at the time that he first met with RFK to brief him prior to his trip to Latin America in November of 1965. The Senator was apparently quite impressed with Frank during that meeting and brought him onboard as press secretary in the late spring of 1967, when Wes left.

I only really knew Frank for a very short period during the summer of that year and saw him a few times during the 1968 presidential campaign, so perhaps it's not fair for me to judge him. But he struck me as being somewhat arrogant and full of himself—maybe it was just the Hollywood connections—he was the son of Herman Mankiewicz, co-writer of *Citizen Kane* (and subject of the film *Mank*), and his uncle was the famed Hollywood director Joseph L. Mankiewicz. In my experience, he would rarely even acknowledge most of the non-professional staff who worked for the Senator, myself included. But take that for what it's worth—again, I really didn't have much interaction with him at the time. I think he did serve the Senator well, and I believe the Senator was very happy with him, so in the final analysis, that's what really mattered. And, of course, we all remember Frank from those awful days in June 1968.

Following the Senator's death, Frank ran for Congress unsuccessfully in Maryland in 1976. And, in 1984, he became a part-time adviser to Gary Hart in his unsuccessful bid for the presidency. Frank died in 2014 at the age of 90.

Angie Novello was the Senator's personal secretary and had been with him since he served as chief counsel to the Senate Rackets Committee back in 1957. Angie's brother-in-law, Carmine Bellino, was chief accountant for the Rackets Committee and a former agent-accountant for the FBI. Angie had worked as a secretary for the FBI, and it was through Carmine that RFK recruited her to be his personal secretary. She continued in that position when he was appointed attorney general and stayed with him when he went to the Senate.

You may have noticed that throughout this memoir, I always refer to Robert Kennedy as "the Senator" or "RFK." As long as I was in his office, the only person I ever heard call him "Bob" was Angie. Perhaps on a phone call from the White House, she might have referred to him as "Senator," but during all of their one-on-one interactions, it was always just "Bob." Now, I suppose that some of the other old-timers, like Joe Dolan or Ed Guthman, may have called him "Bob" or even "Bobby" when they were alone in his office, but to be honest, I never heard them do so.

The point of all this is that Angie Novello had a very special relationship with Robert Kennedy (she was also one of the few people in the office who could almost always decipher the Senator's scribbled handwriting!). I imagine if he had made it to the White House, Angie might have started calling him "Mr. President" in respect for protocol, but sadly, we would never find out.

Now, as others have noted, Angie—whom the Senator called "a saint"—was the only woman in our office who wielded any sort of power, primarily because of her closeness to the Senator and because she was the gatekeeper—the one who decided who could see him or talk to him on the telephone. This was not always the case, because there were those on staff—the professional people, primarily—who would simply barge into the Senator's office whenever they felt like it, Angie be damned. But there were real risks in doing that if you weren't one of those with unlimited access—and I never did. In the office, I always tried to be respectful of both Angie and the Senator, so if I needed to see him, I would go through her.

You have to remember that I'm talking here about the mid-1960s —a time that people like to call the "Mad Men" era. The truth is that there were few women who had any sort of power on Capitol Hill or elsewhere in Washington. Those were the days when, if a woman worked, it was generally as a secretary, a nurse, or a teacher. It was also a time when women themselves often looked upon college and the workplace not as an opportunity for career advancement but as a pathway to a trip down the aisle and an MRS degree. Unfortunately, that was the way things were in the Senator's office too.

After all, the National Organization for Women (NOW) wasn't

organized until October 1966, and even then, most women hadn't heard of it. In fact, they didn't start getting much national attention until they disrupted the Miss America competition in September 1968. So a lot of us women who were working at the time just accepted what was going on in the workplace. To be honest, we didn't feel oppressed or enslaved as NOW would have us believe. The thinking of women generally was: if you're unhappy with your job, just go find another one. I don't think we saw ourselves as fragile creatures requiring the protection of a women's movement. Of course, our attitudes were primarily the result of cultural constructs. And I do believe that if he had been elected President, RFK might well have changed all that and hired women for positions of greater importance in his administration. But back then in the Senate, it was strictly a boys' club, and nobody really talked about it. I feel rather certain that if I had marched into the Senator's office at that time and complained to him that women on his staff were not being treated equitably, he probably would have been shocked and would actually have considered making some changes. But that was something that never occurred to me.

As for Angie, unlike some on our staff, I never felt the least bit intimidated by her, despite the power that she had, and she was always very kind and friendly to me. Perhaps this was partly because both she and I shared a close friendship with Provi, or perhaps it was because she knew that the Senator liked me a lot. Angie didn't miss much. Although she and I didn't have a close personal relationship during the years I worked for the Senator, we did become friends in the years following his death. In fact, Angie would also become friends with my parents, who were the same age as she, and they would spend time with her whenever they were in Washington. The same was true for me—I would always see both Angie and Provi on my trips to D.C., but more on that later.

Anyway, when I was in the office, I had a great deal of respect for her. I don't believe anyone who was with the Senator worked harder, was more loyal, or gave up more in a personal sense in order to see the Senator succeed. Angie never did marry, and I think that was partly because she was married to her job. I'm sure the Senator trusted her completely, and no doubt she was not just the gate-keeper in his office life but also the keeper of some of his secrets. In some respects, she probably knew more about RFK than even his family—as secretaries often do. Don't get me wrong. I'm not suggesting anything scandalous here, just pointing out that personal secretaries probably spend more time with their bosses than their families do.

Angie Novello (Cropped) – Photo Credit: William J. Smith/AP

Following the Senator's death, Angie worked for a brief time as secretary to the U.S. Ambassador to Denmark, Angier Biddle Duke.

The "young Turks," Adam Walinsky and Peter Edelman, who were in their late twenties, were among the most important members of the Senator's staff. Even though the two were probably equally talented, they had very different personalities and strengths, as well as approaches to dealing with the Senator and other staff. Both had attended Ivy League law schools—Adam went to Yale and Peter to Harvard. Neither one of them went way back with RFK or had any political experience to speak of. They had both worked briefly in the

Department of Justice but secured their Senate jobs through their efforts during RFK's 1964 campaign.

When I was in the office, I used to refer to Adam as RFK's "alter ego." But, in looking back on his role, the term *alter ego* wasn't quite right either. Adam was more like the Senator's "evil twin." He always seemed to be the one pushing RFK in whatever direction he, meaning Adam, deemed was the right one (particularly when it came to the war in Vietnam), regardless of what the Senator actually thought. He would also try to insert statements into RFK's speeches that he hadn't first cleared with the Senator—positions that reflected his own, not necessarily the Senator's viewpoint. As a result, RFK would sometimes have to set Adam straight. It was common knowledge in the office that he found it necessary to remind Adam on several occasions who the Senator of New York actually was...and that it was *not* Adam Walinsky.

Rumor had it that the Senator had even yelled at Adam on one or two occasions. The Senator never, ever raised his voice with anyone on staff, so this was highly unusual and out of character for him. I never did find out what Adam's offense might have been to prompt that sort of response, but it must have been something really bad to get a rise like that out of RFK. He was normally very quiet about his displeasure when someone screwed up—more like a parent telling a child, "I'm disappointed in you." There would be exceptions now and then, though. He was very clear that staff shouldn't speak *for* him to the press unless they cleared it with him first. If he saw a newspaper article where it said that an aide to RFK said this or that regarding what the Senator's thinking was...and it wasn't true, that would really get his blood boiling. Or even if it were true and the person hadn't asked the Senator beforehand, there would be trouble. Adam, however, had a huge ego, so I don't think it bothered him much if he was yelled at, even if it was by the Senator.

In his defense, Adam was also super-smart and an extremely talented speechwriter. There was no question that he was particularly adept at crafting a speech in just the way that the Senator spoke, invariably coming up with some wonderful turn of phrase that was pure RFK—and, for the most part, I think the Senator really valued his contribution. He probably even liked being pushed by Adam on occasion. But sometimes Adam would press the Senator a little too hard to speak out—particularly on the war, in a way that would undoubtedly be perceived as an attack on Johnson—and RFK would be extremely reluctant to do that.

Another thing: like the Senator, Adam did not suffer fools gladly. And, in Adam's case, he could also be arrogant and abrasive, meaning that he had a special knack for rubbing people the wrong way. Another staffer on the Hill once described him as "nasty and brilliant, in that order." This tendency would get the Senator himself into trouble sometimes, particularly when the people that Adam was rubbing the wrong way were part of the press corps or other Senators or members of the Johnson administration. But, despite his shortcomings, RFK obviously felt that Adam's positives as a wordsmith outweighed the negatives, and he kept him on. However, that meant that he would frequently have to edit out the little tidbits that Adam would try to slip into his speeches.

After the Senator's death, Adam became the 1970 Democratic candidate for Attorney General in the State of New York, but he was defeated in the general election. Sadly, he died in November 2023 at the age of eighty-seven. As Joe Klein would write in May 2024, "There was, amazingly, no *New York Times* obituary for Adam Walinsky, so I didn't know that he died last November." I didn't either. There was no obituary in *any* U.S. newspaper, and I only happened upon Klein's blog post by chance.

Peter was very different from Adam in personality. He was a nice guy, for one thing, and he wasn't strident or brash as Adam could sometimes be. He also seemed to better understand RFK's boundaries and was appropriately deferential to the Senator (unlike Adam, who was deferential to no one). Peter was an excellent writer as well, but his strengths seemed to be more geared toward the academic—researching an issue and getting all the details and nuances right. A self-described "policy wonk," Peter's specialty was more in drafting bills and putting together legislative initiatives, while Adam was better suited to strictly speechwriting. The two of them made for a good combination, however, ensuring that the Senator had both bases covered.

Peter would be involved in all the mechanics of getting a bill or an amendment to a bill through, including drafting the text of it, working with the staff of other Senators, letting RFK know which Senators he should talk to personally about it, working with the Senate floor managers on the timing, preparing all the background that the Senator would need, and sitting next to him on the Senate floor to answer any questions when it came up for consideration. Then, if the bill passed, he would do the same sorts of things when the bill went to conference with the House. These were the nuts and bolts of a legislative assistant's job in Congress, and Peter was very good at it. I'm not sure Adam had the patience or the temperament to do this as well as Peter, or to work as effectively with the staff of other Senators to get it done, since his strengths were elsewhere.

Peter could also be quite passionate about the issues. He was the one who accompanied the Senator to the Mississippi Delta in 1967, and they both returned from that trip shaken by what they saw. Peter would eventually marry the woman who was their guide throughout the trip—Marion Wright. She later served as President of the Children's Defense Fund, and both she and Peter would act as real advocates in the field of social welfare after the Senator's death. Peter was appointed Assistant Secretary of the Department of Health and Human Services under President Bill Clinton. However, in September 1996, he resigned his position in protest of Clinton's signing of the welfare reform act that same year, saying that it destroyed the social safety net.

RFK with Adam (right) and Peter (center). Credit: New York Times/George Tames/Redux

Jerry Bruno headed up the Senator's office in Syracuse. He also had a long history with the Kennedys. Prior to joining RFK's Senate staff, he had worked as an advance man for JFK, beginning with his 1960 campaign for President and extending throughout his time in the White House. In fact, it was Jerry who planned President Kennedy's fateful trip to Dallas. By Jerry's own account, he felt guilty for years afterward. He would say that he had trouble believing the conspiracy theories about the assassination, though, since the motorcade route that day in Dallas (unlike those on the other Texas stops) wasn't known until a day or two before the President's visit. According to Jerry, there was some uncertainty about where the President's luncheon speech would be held that day. Apparently, there were two options, and after much weighing of the pros and cons, it was finally decided that JFK would give his speech at the Dallas Trade Mart. Jerry would later note that if the other luncheon location had been chosen, the President's motorcade would have traveled "two blocks farther away from the School Book Depository—and at a much faster rate of speed"—so it would have been nearly impossible for a sniper in the Depository to shoot him. Bruno had argued for the second option but was overruled. He would later blame himself for not fighting harder for it. But nobody could have foreseen what a difference it would make.

While heading up RFK's upstate New York office, Jerry also did the advance work whenever the Senator traveled. I didn't know him well when I was working in the office, since he spent most of his time in New York and would only occasionally come down to our office in D.C. I would get to know him better in October 1966, when the Senator came to Berkeley, and during the campaign, when Jerry traveled with RFK in California. Although Jerry was with the Senator throughout the 1968 primary campaign, he wasn't with him in the Ambassador kitchen. That night, Joe Dolan had insisted that Jerry fly on to New York to get things rolling for the big primary coming up there, so he'd jumped on a flight out of LAX at 10:30 p.m. He was informed of the shooting by the pilot of the airplane in which he was traveling and had to get off the plane in Cleveland and return to Los Angeles.

Jerry died in 2015 at the age of eighty-eight and, like the Senator, was buried at Arlington.

Finally, there was my dear friend, Providencia Paredes. As I mentioned, she had a long history with the Kennedy family, serving as Jackie's personal assistant before, during, and after her time at the White House. Provi was originally from the Dominican Republic and had first come to this country back in the late 1940s, when she was working for the Dominican Ambassador to the U.S. It was during that time that she met JFK, who was a young Congressman. When he became Senator, he asked her to come work for him in his household. Once he wed Jackie, Provi would become her personal assistant.

She was very close to the President and the First Lady and frequently traveled with them. She joined Jackie on many of her solo foreign trips as well, including to India, Pakistan, Cambodia, and

Thailand. In fact, the trip to Dallas was one of the few times that Provi did not accompany the President and Mrs. Kennedy on Air Force One. She had begged off because it was so close to Thanksgiving.

In her role as personal assistant, Provi would track Jackie's engagement calendar, as well as take care of all the preparations for the First Lady, both in the White House and while traveling—getting her packed, choosing outfits to wear, and making sure that everything was in perfect order. She once told me that she even ironed Jackie's stockings. And it was Provi who, at President Kennedy's request, chose that bright pink Chanel suit and matching hat that Jackie wore in Dallas.

She was also there at the White House to comfort and attend to a shaken and grieving First Lady when she returned on that awful day in November 1963. Provi would later recount how a tearful Jackie had called her just hours after JFK died, saying that she needed a change of clothes—that her pink suit was covered with the President's blood. Provi had laid out a blue outfit for the First Lady, who returned to Washington before sunrise the next morning. Provi stayed with Jackie throughout the rest of the day, trying to keep busy, not wanting to leave her side. Jackie confided to Provi how scared she had been. "They could have killed me too," she said to her, crying. Jackie's sister, Lee, told Provi, "Maybe if you'd been on this trip, it wouldn't have happened."

Later, when Mrs. Kennedy moved to New York City, she asked Provi to join her there. Not wanting to uproot her young son, Provi decided not to make a permanent move from Washington. Nevertheless, she and the former First Lady remained close for the rest of Jackie's life, and Provi would always be there to help out if she or her children needed anything. Jackie would remember Provi in her will, leaving her $50,000. Those of us who were familiar with everything that Provi had done for the First Lady and the President over the years felt that Jackie could have been more generous to Provi, particularly considering her wealth and Provi's limited financial means. But

I never heard Provi say a bad word about either Jackie or the President.

I think she was particularly fond of President Kennedy, who loved spending time with her as well. The President and Provi would frequently joke around together, and she told me how the two of them would regularly watch the television show *Maverick*. Sometimes, when they were alone, JFK would ask her opinion of certain women in whom he'd taken an interest. Provi was extremely loyal and could always be counted on for her discretion.

President Kennedy used to quip that Provi was smarter than his Secretary of State. He said it so often that Jackie actually had a throw pillow made up with this embroidered on it: "Provy, you're smarter than Dean Rusk! J.F.K." (for some strange reason, Jackie always managed to spell Provi's name wrong!). I used to see the pillow sitting on Provi's sofa every time I went over to her apartment.

Provi and President Kennedy Credit: Cecil Stoughton/White House Photo/JFK Library

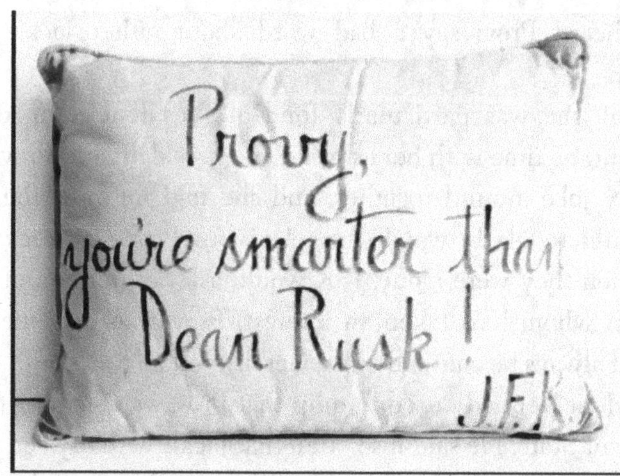

Pillow from Jackie

Then, for Christmas in 1967, RFK gave Provi a copy of his book, *To Seek a Newer World*. It was inscribed by him this way: "And what Pres. Kennedy said about you and Secty Rusk is correct."

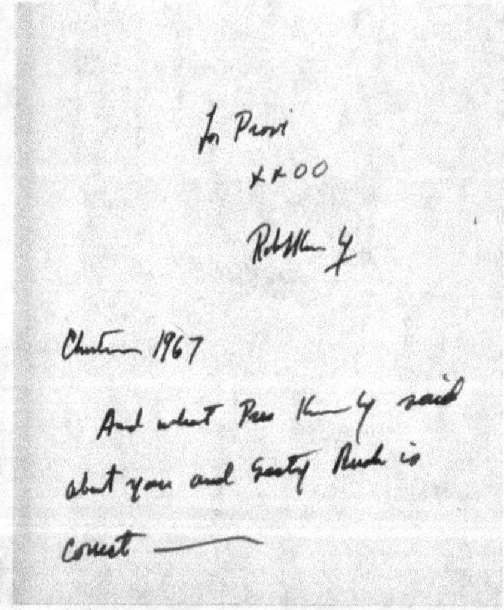

RFK inscription to Provi in his book, To Seek a Newer World

I'm not sure why the Kennedy brothers had so little confidence in

Dean Rusk. Perhaps it was because—as some books about the period have pointed out—Rusk failed to speak up much or express his thoughts in cabinet meetings early on in the Kennedy administration. Following the President's assassination, RFK had even pressed Johnson to remove Rusk from his position and replace him with Bill Moyers. And, as Senator, he would continue to voice his concerns about Rusk's competence to the President and others.

But, as for Provi, she had such a magnetic personality and was always so much fun to be with. I suppose that's why I was immediately drawn to her as well, despite the difference in our ages—she was 40 and I was just 18. Her son Gustavo would later say that I was like a daughter to Provi. But she was more than a mother figure to me— she was also my best friend and confidante. Lord knows I shared things with Provi that I would never have dared tell my own mother. Actually, both my mother and my father would also become close friends with Provi, and throughout the years following the Senator's death, they would fly her out to L.A. or visit her in Washington or up on the Cape.

During one of the visits my parents made to see Provi, my mother took several photos of Jackie's house in Hyannis Port. This must have been in the late 1960s or early 1970s.

Later, I will talk more about my relationship with her during the years following the Senator's death.

This was Caroline's bedroom, with photos of her father.

In this photo, you can see the small refrigerator in the corner. Jackie had the habit of stashing pints of peach ice cream there so others wouldn't take it...and she would walk around eating directly from the ice cream container with a spoon.

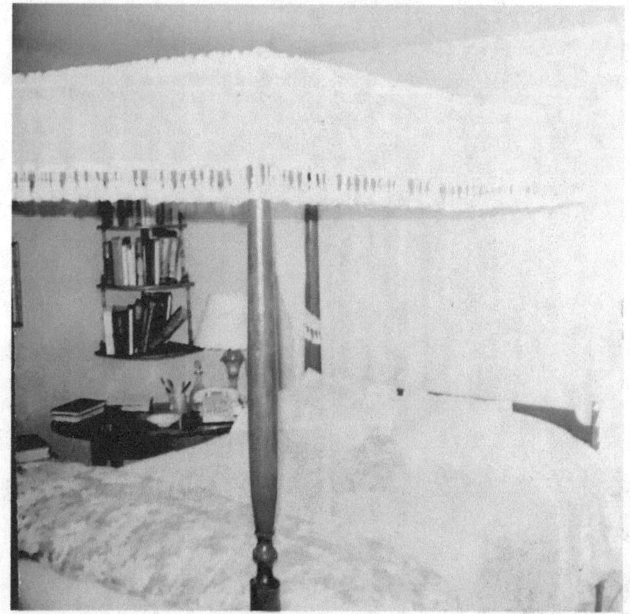

Jackie's bedroom

Jackie's bedroom

Jackie's house at Hyannis Port

Chapter 11

The New Year, 1966

Experience is simply the name we give our mistakes.
~ Oscar Wilde

After spending the Christmas holidays in Los Angeles, I returned to Washington, D.C., and the Senator's office in January 1966. It was also in January that I lost my virginity. If you think I'm about to recount some romantic story of teenage love, you're wrong. The truth is I didn't actually "lose" my virginity—it was stolen from me.

As the Planned Parenthood website points out, "the definition of virginity is complicated." And so is my story. Technically speaking, I only lost my hymen, not my virginity, but boys back then always seemed to equate the two, so forevermore I would no longer be considered a virgin—thanks to a Capitol Hill policeman by the name of Chuck. During the COVID pandemic, I went online looking not just for Gerry McGowan, but for Chuck as well...and lo and behold, I found him.

It was his obituary.

It's hard to describe the mixed feelings I had seeing the photo of Chuck that was printed with his obituary—still looking handsome and grinning from ear to ear. He was immediately recognizable to me, even in his 70s. The obituary said that he'd died in 2018 due to brain cancer. He was 72 years old.

I try not to feel joy over the death of another human being. For one thing, I figure it's probably bad karma, unless that person happens to be Adolf Hitler himself. Still I have to admit that, even after all these years, I felt an odd sense of peace knowing that Chuck was no longer with us on the planet.

But back in the late fall of 1965, Chuck was very much alive. He was on the Capitol Hill police force, and the first time I met him, he was operating an elevator in the New Senate Office Building. In those days, the Capitol Hill Police were in charge of the elevators throughout the Capitol complex. Chuck's elevator was one that I had to use all the time.

"Well, hello there, little lady," he said to me that first day, doing his best imitation of John Wayne in one of his B-westerns while giving me the once-over. I said "Hello" and smiled at him, which was my first mistake. Chuck wasn't as tall in the saddle as Wayne, but he was handsome in a Nordic cowboy sort of way, if there is such a thing. He had blond hair and blue eyes and was noticeably bow-legged—he always looked like he'd just gotten off a horse. He was a year older than I was, and he was taking a course or two at GWU in addition to working on the Hill. He was also a big flirt. He had the gift of gab and could be quite charming. In fact, he would have made a great used-car salesman or even a politician. As I soon learned, he was from Bismarck, North Dakota, and managed to get his job from one of the two Senators from that state.

Now, back then, a good number—perhaps all—of the Capitol Hill policemen were patronage positions, meaning that senators or congressmen were able to dole out the jobs to constituents or others. I think that system was eventually done away with. But just to be clear,

Chuck was not a professional cop and hadn't graduated from a police academy of any kind. As he would proudly tell me, though, he had attended the Coast Guard Academy the previous year. I gathered he had been kicked out for bad behavior. But his time there still seemed to be a source of great pride to him. In fact, he had this denim half-zip jacket from the Coast Guard Academy that he loved to wear whenever he wasn't working. His first initial "C" and his last name were printed across the front of it.

Anyway, after meeting him and chatting him up quite often at work, Chuck and I started dating. He didn't have a lot of money, so it usually involved going for a beer at a local watering hole or making dinner—usually pasta of some sort—at his place. He had a couple of roommates, and they all lived in an old Victorian house not far from the Capitol, as I recall. I was still a virgin and had no desire to lose my virginity to him, so whenever he got too sexually aggressive with me, I would let him know that I wasn't ready to take the next step. For some reason, his comeback was always, "I don't believe you." It was really amazing to me how many guys back then seemed *not* to believe that young women could still be virgins. And this was before all the "free love" and "sexual liberation" of the late 1960s.

Anyway, one evening after we'd made dinner at his place, we went up to his bedroom. We were lying on his bed smooching when his hand began to move up my leg. I clamped my hand over his and stopped it from going any further.

I said, "I told you. I'm a virgin, and I don't want to do that."

Again, he said, "I don't believe you. Prove it."

He shoved me back on the bed, restraining me with the weight of his body while he pulled my underwear halfway down my thighs and forced his fingers inside me. I was struggling the entire time and crying, even though it wasn't all that painful. What hurt me was the sense of complete violation. I couldn't believe what he was doing. When he'd finished, he smiled and said very casually, "Oh, I guess you really were a virgin," using the past tense. At this point, I was sobbing. It felt like rape.

"How could you do that to me?"

He was indignant. "Why are you making such a big deal out of it?" he asked, as if the real problem was my attitude. "Who cares?"

"I care," I replied, with tears streaming down my cheeks.

I should have known better than to be with this jerk. When I first met him, he would brag that he had slept with the wives of various senators. I thought it was simply swagger on his part—I never took him seriously. Still, I suppose it was partly that "bad boy" side of him that appealed to me in the first place. That's on me.

I was still crying when I finally managed to climb out of his bed, head down the stairs and out of the house. Before I left, though, I spotted his precious Coast Guard Academy jacket tossed over the back of one of the dining room chairs. I grabbed it and ran out the door and down the block. Frankly, taking the jacket was the only thing that made that experience bearable.

I saw him up at the Capitol just once more after that. I would go out of my way to avoid running into him, and he eventually got himself moved to another part of the Capitol complex. But I did see him that one time, and he was his usual cocky self, as if nothing untoward had happened between us. Except he did ask, "When are you going to return the jacket that you stole from me?"

I looked him straight in the eyes and said, "I'll give it back to you when you return what you stole from me."

I never saw Chuck again. The jacket still hangs in my hall closet. And he's dead.

Not long after that last night with Chuck, "The Blizzard of 1966" rumbled through Washington, D.C. Nothing made the dysfunction of the nation's capital more palpable than when a snowstorm hit the city. This one was particularly bad. It eventually dropped nearly 14 inches of snow in just a couple of days.

Now, there were some advantages to not having a television set in our apartment or even bothering to tune in to the news on the radio occasionally. It gave us more time to lounge around on our couches with our legs propped up against the wall and listen to the latest

Stones album or gab excitedly about Judy's date the night before with the Ambassador from Sierra Leone (I kid you not—he even picked her up in a long black limousine). But keeping up with the weather forecast was not one of them.

So it was that one night at the end of January, we decided to go out to see a movie. Roman Polanski's psychological thriller *Repulsion*, starring Catherine Deneuve, had just been released in the United States in the fall, and it was playing in D.C. at a theater up near Connecticut Avenue. Judy and I and another friend threw on our wool coats and our fur-lined boots and headed out after eating dinner.

When we got inside the theater, we were surprised to find it empty. We thought, "That's weird," but chalked it up to the fact that the movie had gotten mixed reviews—and with the controversial subject matter, it probably turned a lot of people off. Indeed, it was a disturbing film, but we managed to sit through the whole thing. What was even more disturbing, though, was what we discovered when we left the theater—the streets and sidewalks were completely deserted and covered with snow. There was not a soul around and no one even working in the lobby of the theater.

The lights on the marquee had been turned off, and every business up and down the street was also shrouded in darkness. We tried reopening the door to the theater, and it had apparently locked behind us. It was probably about ten or eleven o'clock at night by this time, and our plan to catch a taxi home obviously wasn't going to work. But hey, we were tough cookies, so we thought, "Well, we'll just have to walk home."

We started to trudge down the sidewalk, but with each step we took, our boots sank deeper and deeper into the snow. It came up past our knees. Not only that, but a freezing, wet wind was whipping into our faces. Anyone who's been to Washington in the winter knows how bone-chilling the wind off the Potomac can be. There are not enough clothes you can wear to protect yourself from it.

Bottom line, it was a complete nightmare. Somehow, we were

able to make it to the corner—I forget what the cross street was. When we got there, we looked at each other with panic on our faces. The direness of our situation was finally beginning to sink in. Hiking all the way back to the apartment was out of the question. We would die before we got there, and our bodies wouldn't be found until the next morning, if then, since they would probably be covered with a foot of snow.

The only hopeful thing was that the cross street looked pretty clear in both directions—a snowplow must have come through earlier. Still, there were no cars on the road. We stood there at the corner, shivering for a few minutes, trying to decide what the hell to do. We didn't have cell phones back then, and with all the businesses closed, there was no way to call for help. Then, all at once, we saw the lights of a police car, and it was heading our way. We started waving at them like crazy. They drove up, stopped, and the officer in the passenger seat rolled down his window.

"What are you doing out here, girls?" he asked. He said it in such a casual way that it almost made me laugh. I'm thinking—*Oh, we're just out for a late-night stroll.*

We explained to them how we'd been in a movie theater watching a film and had no idea that it had snowed while we were inside. We asked if they could drive us home.

"Sorry, it's against policy. We can only let you in the car if you're under arrest."

At this point, arrest seemed the preferable option to dying in the snow like some pathetic characters in a Tolstoy novel.

We begged and pleaded. We told them that if they left us out there, we wouldn't make it. Finally, they gave in, and we climbed into the back seat of the patrol car. So that's how we got home that first night of Washington's 1966 blizzard. I have no excuse for our dim-wittedness. I can only say, with some embarrassment, that it wasn't the stupidest thing I did that year.

For the next few days, the entire city was shut down. No work. No school. Only building snowmen and having snowball fights down on the National Mall in front of the Lincoln Memorial. What a way to begin the New Year.

The Senator had a far more productive start to 1966. After spending New Year's in Sun Valley, Idaho, with his family, RFK flew to Los Angeles for a few days. He took his children to Disneyland and met with some civil rights leaders, as well as other people, regarding the JFK Library. Upon his arrival at LAX on January 4, he was questioned by local reporters about the situation in Vietnam.

Just before the holidays, in response to a Viet Cong proposal for a 12-hour Christmas truce, the Senator had called upon the Johnson administration to explore all possibilities for a negotiated pause in the fighting, "because we are getting into a more dangerous situation for all mankind." Surprisingly, on December 18, President Johnson had actually agreed to a Christmas truce that was to run through the end of January.

So when reporters in Los Angeles asked him about Vietnam, RFK said that he commended President Johnson for his efforts to find a peaceful solution there. A few days later, he would send the President a handwritten note telling him basically the same thing, and the President would respond on January 27, thanking the Senator for his "warm letter." This rare rapprochement between the two of them wouldn't last long, however.

On January 12, RFK was back in New York meeting with Mayor John Lindsay—looking for a way to end the 12-day subway strike in New York City. He urged both the transit workers and the Transit Authority to accept the findings of the mediation panel to end the walkout. Of course, he and Lindsay never really liked each other. When Lindsay was in Congress, he'd criticized RFK as Attorney General, so it went back a couple of years. But the Senator's trip was successful, and the transit strike ended the next day. RFK's last-minute intervention would cement Lindsay's view of the Senator as nothing more than a publicity hound, particularly after some journalists gave RFK credit for the settlement.

Following his meeting with Lindsay in New York, the Senator

immediately flew back to Washington for the President's State of the Union address that evening. In his speech to Congress and the nation, Johnson claimed that the country could afford both "guns and butter," but RFK wasn't so sure. In the Senator's view, the Johnson administration seemed far more interested in funding the Vietnam War than the War on Poverty.

RFK was determined to keep the issue of poverty alive. So in January 1966, he gave three consecutive speeches in New York about the plight of the poor in urban areas, with an emphasis on housing and the creation of jobs—"an effort that we know is the only real solution." In one of his addresses, he proposed an innovative neighborhood redevelopment initiative—the establishment of community development corporations that would be under the control of the area's residents. This was followed by a walk through the Bedford-Stuyvesant area of Brooklyn in early February, where he met with community activists. It marked the first steps in what would become a yearlong effort by the Senator to create the Bedford-Stuyvesant Restoration Corporation. He continued to press Johnson to do more to address the problems in urban areas, and later that year the Senator would fight unsuccessfully for an additional $750 million appropriation for the War on Poverty.

Also in January, the Senator spoke out about the mass killings of alleged Communists by the government of Indonesia. Between October 1965 and the early months of 1966, an estimated 500,000 to 1.2 million people were killed (some estimates went as high as 2 to 3 million). The CIA later described it as "one of the worst mass murders of the 20th century." The release of declassified documents in 2017 would reveal that the U.S. government had knowledge of and supported the Indonesian army's extermination campaign. But in January 1966, Robert Kennedy was the only U.S. official talking publicly about it.

He said, "We have spoken out against inhuman slaughters perpetrated by the Nazis and the Communists. But will we speak out also against the inhuman slaughter in Indonesia, where over 100,000 alleged Communists have been not perpetrators, but victims?" His question was greeted with a deafening silence.

Then, on January 31, the Johnson administration resumed bombing in Vietnam, with President Johnson making this statement:

> We do not regret the pause in the bombing. We yield to none in our determination to seek peace. We have given a full and decent respect to the opinions of those who thought that such a pause might give new hope for peace in the world.
>
> Some said that 10 days might do it. Others said 20. Now, we have paused for twice the time suggested by some of those who urged it. And now the world knows more clearly than it has ever known before who it is that insists on aggression and who it is that works for peace.

In response, RFK rose on the Senate floor to criticize the administration. In his speech, he said, "If we regard bombing as the answer in Vietnam, we are headed straight for disaster."

RFK Outside the New Senate Office Building—January 1966

Chapter 12

Guns vs. Butter

If America's soul becomes totally poisoned,
part of the autopsy must read Vietnam.
~ Martin Luther King, Jr.

On February 4, 1966, the Senate Foreign Relations Committee began hearings on the Vietnam War. The committee was meeting in a room on the fourth floor of our building, and in subsequent weeks the Senator would become a regular at the hearings, sitting in the back of the room (he wasn't a member of the committee because he lacked seniority). When he didn't personally attend the televised hearings, he closely followed them from his office.

They lasted for two weeks, and on the final day Chairman Fulbright called Secretary of State Dean Rusk to appear before the committee. RFK was in his usual seat at the back of the room, watching the proceedings. He didn't trust Rusk anyway, but he grew particularly frustrated as he listened to the doves on the committee throwing softball questions at the Secretary. The Senator wanted to hear what the administration's position was on a negotiated peace—specifically what concessions they were willing to make and what role North Vietnam's National Liberation Front (NLF) would play. But none of the Senators on the committee were asking those hard questions or pressing the administration for details on what a negotiated settlement would look like.

Since nobody else was talking about it, he decided that he would. When the meeting adjourned just after five in the evening, RFK rushed back downstairs to our office on the first floor and told Adam that he wanted to release a statement the next morning. It seemed an impulsive move...and one he would no doubt come to regret. Adam, of course, was happy to comply. He'd been urging the Senator for weeks to speak out about the war and had actually been working on such a statement.

So, the next morning, just before leaving for a President's Day weekend ski trip to Vermont, the Senator held a press conference and read a seven-page statement about the war in Vietnam. In it, he criticized the administration's approach of calling for peace talks without offering even a hint of any concessions, pointing out that it didn't provide the North Vietnamese with any incentive to come to the negotiating table. He said, "A negotiated settlement means that each side must concede matters that are important in order to preserve positions that are essential." He went on to say, "There are three things you can do with such groups [as the National Liberation Front]: kill or repress them, turn the country over to them, or admit them to a share of power and responsibility." He believed that the last option—allowing the National Liberation Front to participate—was "at the heart of the hope for a negotiated settlement."

The Senator didn't expect that his statement would generate a lot of pushback. If he had, he probably wouldn't have immediately flown off to join Ethel on the ski slopes. But he'd seriously miscalculated. His words instantly drew harsh criticism from the Johnson administration and many others. Throwing both his "politics of joy" and caution to the wind, Vice President Humphrey fired the opening salvo, saying, "It would be like putting a fox in the chicken coop."* A *Chicago Tribune* editorial dubbed the Senator "Ho Chi Kennedy."

RFK rushed back to Washington from Vermont to try to quell the uproar. He went on several television shows defending his position and continued for a few weeks to publicly press for a negotiated settlement, but the damage had been done. It was obvious that his position was not a popular one. Interestingly, Dr. Martin Luther King, Jr., was one of the few people who came out in support of the Senator's statement. On March 2, he said, "Your great brother carried us far in new directions with his concept of a world of diversity; your position advances us to the next step which requires us to reach the political maturity to recognize and relate to all elements produced by the contemporary colonial revolutions."

MLK had been speaking out against the war since March of 1965, saying that it was "accomplishing nothing" and, like the Senator, calling for a negotiated settlement. In August 1965, Dr. King had urged that the bombing of North Vietnam be stopped and had asked that the United Nations step in to mediate. Throughout late 1965 and 1966, however, King had become less vocal in his opposition to the war after being roundly criticized by members of Congress, the press, and even his own colleagues in the civil rights struggle, who feared that his comments might harm the movement. So King's support of the Senator's statement in February 1966 was unexpected.

Although the Senator and Dr. King did not interact much during the first couple of years of RFK's Senate term, William vanden Heuvel, who was close to both of them, would sometimes act as a go-between. Also, their joint opposition to the war in Vietnam brought

---

* Four years later, Humphrey would concede that at the time he "was being a little cute" and that he never felt that the Senator was "irresponsible in his attacks" on the administration's Vietnam policy or that they were politically motivated. He would also acknowledge that the President eventually came around to the Senator's position supporting participation of the NLF through the elective process.

them closer. As Adam put it, "They didn't have to sit down and strategize. They couldn't have been more directly going down the same path if they'd spent an hour on the telephone every day." Andrew Young—a close associate of Dr. King—would later write that the relationship between Robert Kennedy and King was "a distant camaraderie that needed no formal tie or physical link—a bridge across lines of race, class, and geography which nevertheless led them to common faith, hopes, and at last a common tragic destiny..."

As for the Senator's February 1966 Vietnam statement, RFK would later concede that the way it was originally written was "a little confusing," that what he meant to say was that the National Liberation Front should be allowed to participate in the political process—meaning negotiations—not necessarily participate in the government. After receiving such strong criticism, the Senator became more cautious about making public statements about the war. Although he would speak out on the Senate floor in April against escalation of the conflict, he wouldn't release any more official public statements on the issue for some time. Peter Edelman would later say that the Senator's reluctance came from the fear that Johnson "was so insane that he would literally prolong the war" simply because RFK was against it.

On March 16, the Senator traveled to Delano, California, for hearings on the farmworkers' strike. During the hearing, the Senator was appalled at how local law enforcement was treating the striking migrant workers. In an exchange with a local sheriff, he discovered that picketing workers were being arrested simply because they looked "ready to violate the law," not because they had actually committed any crime. RFK famously suggested to the Sheriff and the District Attorney that, during the luncheon break, they should "read the Constitution of the United States."

It was this sort of personal exposure to injustice that always lit a fire under the Senator. His trip to the Mississippi Delta in 1967, where he witnessed the abject poverty and hunger there firsthand, would have an even more profound effect upon him.

But after his trip to Delano, the plight of farmworkers would become an ongoing concern for the Senator. The following year, he would visit a migrant workers camp in upstate New York and be disgusted by the conditions in which they were forced to live. He discovered that some of the migrant workers and their young children were being housed in an abandoned bus where the seats had been torn out and replaced with dirty mattresses. Enraged by what he saw, RFK told the owner of the camp, "You are something out of the nineteenth century. I wouldn't put an animal in those buses." He would call for labor leaders to organize the migrant workers and demand that the Governor of New York conduct an investigation of health conditions in the camps.

I should note here, as someone who actually knew Robert Kennedy and was able to observe him up close, that his deep and abiding compassion and concern for the poor, the hungry, and the needy was not part of some phony act perpetrated in order to advance his political career or to grab headlines. This was not just some politician paying lip service to grandiose liberal ideals, either.

The intense pain that he felt for the hungry child with a bloated belly living in filth—whether in a New York ghetto or in the Mississippi Delta—for the migrant farmworker being mistreated by law enforcement or the neglected Native American boy living without hope on a reservation in North Dakota—all of it was very real. Helping them was the calling of his life. He was, by nature, a reformer. He knew that we could do better. And if he had lived, he would have made damn sure that we did something about these problems.

There have been those who've suggested that he was motivated by ambition and by a desire for media attention when he went on fact-finding trips or when he spoke out on these issues. That is so far from the truth. After all, concern for the poor and the dispossessed has never been a vote-getter. He wasn't out there calling for middle-class tax cuts. Sadly, these issues were not foremost in the minds of most Americans. No; in fact, if anything, solutions to the national shame of hunger and poverty in this country would have likely required massive amounts of additional spending and higher taxes. For RFK, these trips were not political stunts.

The same was true with his stance on the Vietnam War. In fact, every time he spoke out against the war, his poll numbers would go down. So no, he wasn't saying what people wanted to hear. He wasn't currying favor or tailoring his speeches to please a particular audience. He was saying what was truly in his heart.

If you take away only one thing from this memoir, I hope it is this: Robert Kennedy was authentic; he was the real deal. And the people in these places he visited immediately recognized that and sensed, on some level, that he actually felt their pain—that he really did care. And because of that, they trusted him.

Another fact about the Senator—he was never fearful of facing potentially hostile audiences. On March 18, 1966, he accepted an invitation to address students at the University of Mississippi Law School. Four years earlier, as Attorney General, he had directed U.S. Marshals to accompany James Meredith when he registered as the first African American to attend the university. The Marshals were attacked, and President Kennedy had to send in federal troops to restore order. Given this history, RFK expected that the students there would not be glad to see him. But he was wrong. Despite some protests on campus beforehand, his speech before a crowd of 6,000 was well received.

He began with some of his usual self-deprecating humor. Making a not-so-veiled reference to Hubert Humphrey's criticism of his Vietnam statement the month before, he quipped, "I know that there was some controversy about my coming, and someone down here suggested that it was like putting a fox in the chicken house, and elsewhere, some of my friends said that it was like putting a chicken in the fox house." This drew laughter and seemed to break the ice. The speech itself was primarily focused on the idea of creating a society in which Black people would "be as free as other Americans—free to vote, and to earn their way, and to share in the decisions of government which will shape their lives."

That same day, the Senator also spoke at the University of Alabama, where less than three years earlier Governor George Wallace had stood in the doorway of the university to prevent its integration. RFK was again greeted warmly, this time by a crowd of 4,000. *The Birmingham News* reported that "Northern reporters were amazed to hear the Alabamians applauding Kennedy's statement that he thinks his invitation to speak here means, 'We can talk now, not as Americans from different parts of a single nation, but partners in a common future.'" His experience at both schools served to reaffirm RFK's belief that the bigger challenge when it came to race relations was in the Northern cities.

At the end of March, our office began to make plans for the Senator to visit South Africa in June. For a bit of history—back in the fall of 1965—the Senator had received an invitation from the anti-apartheid student group, the National Union of South African Students (NUSAS), to speak at their annual Day of Affirmation, so in February the Senator had applied for a visa to visit South Africa. On March 22, the South African government approved the application. This was somewhat surprising, since just the year before they had refused to grant a visa to Martin Luther King, Jr.

Throughout the spring, though, the war in Vietnam continued to weigh heavily on the Senator's mind. On the afternoon of April 14, he and Adam, together with Dave Burke—Ted Kennedy's chief of staff—met privately with Philip Heymann, who was the State Department's Administrator of Security and Consular Affairs. The Senator wanted the Johnson administration to increase its efforts to secure the release of American soldiers being held as prisoners of war in Vietnam. The administration, however, continued to be reluctant to meet with the National Liberation Front about anything, even if it involved our prisoners of war. They felt that the negative consequences of such a meeting were more important than any benefits we might secure from it, so the meeting went nowhere.

On April 19, the Senator made a speech in upstate New York at a civic dinner criticizing proposed cutbacks in domestic spending in Johnson's budget. He said that spending on the war in Vietnam didn't justify a reduction in social welfare programs, particularly those aimed at helping the poor. The next day there was immediate push-back by Johnson surrogates, including Vice President Humphrey, White House Press Secretary Bill Moyers, and Democratic Rep. Joseph Resnick,* in whose district the dinner had been held, the latter accusing the Senator of "talking like a demagogue."

Then on April 26, after an incident in which American jets engaged with Soviet-designed MiGs over North Vietnam, the Johnson administration repeated a warning first delivered back in July of 1965. They declared that there would be "no air sanctuary" for Chinese-based or other foreign aircraft involved in the Vietnam War.

The next day, the Senator, who was growing restless about remaining silent on the war, rose on the Senate floor to deliver a brief speech with his own warning about further escalation in Vietnam, but without ever mentioning Johnson's name. He was the only Senator to publicly state his concern about the administration's "no air sanctuary" policy. Still wary of being accused of simply harboring a personal grudge against Johnson, he did not go further in expressing his disagreement with administration policy. That would come months later.

---

* *Resnick would later push his way into the funeral services for RFK despite Jerry Bruno's best efforts to keep him and other RFK detractors (like L.A. Mayor Sam Yorty) out.*

Chapter 13

The Senator and I

Yours is the light by which my spirit's born: yours is
the darkness of my soul's return— you are my sun,
my moon, and all my stars ~ *e.e. Cummings*

Some of the most memorable times that I spent with the Senator were after work. I would frequently leave the New Senate Office Building at the same time that he was departing for home. I became attuned to his routine, and sometimes I would deliberately stay in the office a little longer than I had to just so that I could run into him on the way out. As Senator, he rarely put in the twelve-to-fourteen-hour days that he was known for when he was Attorney General. So he would often leave the office at six or a little later, and if he saw me, he would invariably ask if I wanted a ride home. I suppose you can guess what my answer was.

The Senator's car at that time was a convertible. I'm not sure what make it was—something American, perhaps a Ford—but nothing fancy. His driver, Jim Boyd, would always be parked right outside the front door of the building on Constitution Avenue, and in the warmer months he would have the top down. In his early days at the Senate, when RFK used to bring Brumus to work a lot, that big old bear of a dog would ride in the back seat of his convertible, and the two of them would make quite the sight driving around the Capitol. But fortunately, Brumus was never with him when I was in the car. I love animals, but Brumus was just too huge and, given half a chance, he probably would have slobbered all over me.

The Senator always rode in the front seat with Jim, whether he had passengers or not. The car had just two doors, so the Senator had to open the door for me and stand outside while I climbed into the back seat. Sometimes Provi and I would be leaving at the same time, and he would ask both of us if we wanted a ride. Since I was usually the first to get out, if Provi was along she would climb in before me and sit behind Jim while I sat directly behind the Senator.

We would occasionally pass by the back of the White House on the way home. In those days, the streets running directly behind and in front of the White House were still open to traffic. Anyway, one time in particular sticks out in my mind when Provi and I were both in the Senator's car heading home. It was a beautiful, warm evening in Washington, probably around six-thirty at night—the time of evening when the light is just beginning to fade. We had laughed and talked all the way from the Capitol. The Senator had swung his body around so that his back was up against the passenger door, one knee up on the seat, and he had turned his head to look at us. In my mind's eye, I can still picture him—that shaggy hair of his tousled by the wind. It kept falling into his face, his fingers continually brushing it back out of his eyes.

But then, as soon as we approached the White House, his body tensed a little—it was palpable—and he immediately faced forward again, as if he wanted to be alone with his thoughts. As we drove past the South Portico, I remember that he didn't move an inch—he was like a stone statue. He just stared straight ahead. The car suddenly became quiet, and nobody said a word. I could only imagine what he was thinking in those moments. Provi, too. Both of them had spent so much time inside that house; they had left so much love there. Jim—sensing his boss's discomfort—accelerated, and a few moments later the White House was out of view. In a complete transformation, the Senator turned toward us again and was back to joking around, just like before.

And then, when it came time for me to get out, Jim would bring the car to a stop at the curb—most often he would let me out on Pennsylvania Avenue—either at 19th Street when I was still in the dormitory or at 21st Street the following year when I was living in the apartment. Once, though, he actually drove me all the way to the corner of 19th and F Streets, where my dorm was located.

After Jim stopped the car, RFK would open the door and climb from the front seat onto the sidewalk so that I could get out. And then...I have to admit that even after all these years I'm reluctant to share this next bit. But here it goes.

The Senator stood next to the car on the sidewalk as I climbed out, and he started to say goodbye. And this was how I responded—from that very first lift home and every time thereafter. I looked him directly in the eyes, and then, with a coy smile, I said, "Aren't you going to kiss me good-bye?"

That first time I said it, he looked a little startled. But good sport that he was, he simply chuckled, leaned in, and gave me a kiss on the cheek. Picture it. Here was one of the most well-known politicians in the world standing there in full view on Pennsylvania Avenue kissing this young blonde on the cheek. And the one time that he dropped me off at the dorm, he kissed me there, too. I have no idea how many people actually witnessed our good-byes, but I'm sure that if they did, it came as something of a shock. After that first time, I didn't have to say anything, but I usually did. Other times, I would just tap my index finger against my cheek and he would kiss me there. It became a routine. But for me, it never felt routine. I can't deny it—it was exciting.

Now, I have no defense for my behavior. That was simply the

way I rolled in those days...and, to be honest, I'm not that different now. But, in the Senator's defense, I can only say that I believe he understood that this was not Donna trying to seduce him, but rather Donna being her usual outrageous self. It was more like me daring him to do it in public, and I don't think he was one to back down from a dare. I assumed that he didn't mind, since he continued to offer me rides home. But he had a certain playful, childlike quality that seemed to show itself whenever I was around him. On more than one occasion, he would stick his tongue out at me, and I would do the same to him. We were like a couple of kids. While Gore Vidal would talk about "Bobby's Holden Caulfield contempt for the adults," I always saw it simply as his way of unleashing what Jung would call his "inner child." After everything that the Senator had been through, I figured he deserved a little silliness every now and then. And, of course, silliness was my specialty.

But spending that time with him was one of the coolest things ever—and I'm glad I asked for those kisses. What I wouldn't give for a photo of one of those moments!*

---

* Just as a postscript to this story, I have to admit that I also ran into Jimmy Carter in the basement of the Los Angeles Biltmore Hotel once when he was running for President, and I asked if I could kiss him for good luck. He also didn't back down. But who knows—maybe he was just "lusting in his heart." When I met Bill Clinton a couple of times years later, I figured that he was probably lusting for real, so I didn't ask if I could give him a kiss.

Bill Clinton in 2016—the second time I met him

In the warmer months, I had the habit of often eating my lunch or taking afternoon breaks out on the grass behind the Capitol. If it were a pretty day, a lot of the staffers up on the Hill would do the same thing. In addition to enjoying being out in the sunshine, I liked to get a bit of a tan, so I would position myself under a tree where my face was in the shade but my legs were still exposed to some sun. I rarely wore any sort of hose or leg covering when it got hot. Instead, I would wear sandals that I could kick off whenever I felt like digging my toes into the grass. I kept a towel at work that I would sit on to avoid getting grass stains on my clothes. I did have an ulterior motive for taking my breaks out on the lawn, however. Naturally, it involved the Senator.

When RFK first came to the Senate, he was surprised to find that the windows in his office were sealed shut. He was quite upset and made a big deal out of it, but soon discovered that there was no way to get them open. And even though there was an underground passageway to the Capitol that Senators could use, he would, more often than not, just walk outside from his office over to the Senate chamber in order to get some fresh air.

As someone who always took every opportunity to run into him or catch a glimpse of him when he was outside his office, I would sit as close as I could to the sidewalk he used or where he would cut across the grass. He would sometimes be with his brother Ted when he walked over to the Capitol. If he spotted me, he would always wave, and I would wave back...or, if I were feeling particularly naughty, I would throw him a kiss. He seemed to get a kick out of that, and Ted would as well.

If he weren't in a big hurry, he would often come over to say hello. I would be sitting on my towel, leaning up against a tree, my sandals off and my legs stretched out strategically in the sun, and he would stand there, looking down at me.

"What are you doing out here, Donna?"

It was always that question, even if he had asked me the same thing a couple of days before. I tried to make my answers amusing and new each time. "Waiting for a bus," I would say, or "Teaching ants how to sing," or simply, "Looking for love." It became one of our little games. He would chuckle or just nod his head and reply, "I see," nothing more. Then he would continue on his walk to the Capitol. I loved that he was willing to be so playful with me, and I relished those moments of odd intimacy between us.

Many people have commented that in private the Senator was shy and a man of few words. As I mentioned before, I experienced him the same way when I worked on his Senate staff, even though he always seemed at ease around me personally. But in the company of others, he was most comfortable (and most himself) around children. Perhaps it was because he had that little-boy quality. Children seemed to recognize and appreciate it in him. They always wanted to get close to him, to touch him, to climb on his lap and hold onto his hand. And he too would become very tactile with them—tenderly ruffling their hair, stroking their cheeks with his fingers, crouching down with his knees bent so he could talk to them face to face.

But with adults he didn't know, he could be uncomfortably shy. I remember my parents coming to visit me in Washington—I think this was during the summer of 1967, possibly earlier—and I took them into the Senator's office so that they could meet him. I introduced them to him, and after shaking hands he just sort of stood there awkwardly and said nothing. Finally, he jokingly commented, "You know Donna runs the entire office," to which my mother retorted, "Well, she certainly runs our lives, but I had no idea she ran your office too."

That seemed to ease the tension, and we briefly exchanged a few more pleasantries before making our escape. My parents told me afterward how shocked they were at his shyness—he was certainly not a typical politician. He wasn't one to engage in glad-handing or speaking in platitudes.

I knew that it wasn't just his shyness at play in those moments. The Senator also hated to make small talk and would rarely engage in it. Not that he was purposely being rude; I don't think that would be fair to say—although some might have interpreted his reticence to speak as rudeness. I think instead that it was just a reflection of his sense that there were only so many hours in the day and that his time on the planet was limited. So why waste it on small talk? Most of us who knew him or worked for him were well aware of his feelings on the subject and would never prolong a conversation with meaningless chitchat.

A few weeks after that meeting with my parents, an inscribed photo arrived at their home. It read, "For Mr. and Mrs. Stanley—Best Wishes and my appreciation for Donna—Robert F. Kennedy." That was so typical of him—he could be extremely thoughtful and caring to those of us on his staff, even if he would rarely let us know it in words.

I do think he got better at interacting with people he didn't know when he was running for President, however. When he was on a rope line shaking hands, there was little need for small talk. Just a "thank you for coming out" or a "nice to meet you" would suffice. And in speeches, he generally stuck to the issues, except for a few joking remarks at the beginning to warm people up.

He seemed to get better at delivering speeches as well during the Presidential campaign. He at least gave the appearance of being self-assured and confident, with his voice sounding stronger, even though he would occasionally stammer and his hands would often shake.

RFK's inscribed photo for my parents—Credit: Phillippe Halsman—official Senate photo

I don't remember exactly when it was that I first started thinking about leaving Washington, but perhaps it was shortly after my near-death experience during the blizzard of 1966. I believe my roommate Judy was the first to talk about moving on. At some point, she mentioned that she was considering going back to Chicago in the fall. She wasn't particularly happy with her job in D.C., and she longed to return to the Art Institute there, where she'd worked. Then my friend Lois started making noises about possibly transferring to the University of Colorado at Boulder. She was an avid skier, and the idea of being able to ski all winter long appealed to her.

And finally, like some virus, the change bug infected me too. I started thinking that maybe I would transfer to the University of California at Berkeley. Not only was Berkeley the center of the free speech and anti-war movements, but I would also be close enough to my family to go home occasionally on the weekends. Earlier that year, I'd applied for a transfer to the University and had been accepted, so that sent the idea into overdrive.

Now, perhaps it seems counterintuitive that I would even consider moving back to California when I'd achieved my dream of working for Robert Kennedy. To this day, when I tell people how I decided to leave D.C. back then, they simply don't get it—they view it as some sort of aberration. But here's the truth—as much as I loved being around the Senator, the reality was that it was simply a dead-end job. After all, I was planning on getting a university degree and do what—work in a mailroom? Plus, I had established a good enough relationship with RFK that I knew I could always come back if I wanted to. Like everyone else in his office, I figured that he would eventually run for President—but probably not until 1972, when LBJ was finally gone. And when that happened, I would have my degree plus more work experience under my belt, and I could rejoin his staff, hopefully in some higher-level position. At any rate, that was my thinking.

Besides, my social life in Washington had produced no permanent boyfriend, and back in those days, that was pretty important for a young woman of nineteen. There was one guy from Georgetown University whom I dated for a while that spring by the name of J.J., but by the summer, our relationship had fizzled out. I'd met him at the Whisky A Go Go club, which had just opened in Georgetown that year. My friends and I would go there regularly to dance and drink. (As an amusing side note, the owner of the club, Jacques Vivien, actually offered me a job as a go-go dancer there, but I declined, figuring that even a job in the mailroom was preferable to that.)

Anyway, there was an immediate attraction between J.J. and me. He was tall and handsome and a star on Georgetown's rowing team. I remember one of his friends describing him as "a cross between a Greek god and Billy Budd." I wouldn't go that far, but he was quite good-looking...and a nice guy, to boot.

At this point, I was still a virgin (without a hymen), and J.J. told me that he was too. But after several weeks together, he and I began pushing the envelope when it came to sex. So it was that one night, we were together in his room at the house he shared with some other Georgetown students, and things were getting pretty hot and heavy. I asked him if he had any protection. He didn't have anything on him, so he excused himself and left the room. Naturally, I thought he was going to get a condom. Well, he was gone for a good ten minutes, and by this time, I was beginning to cool off. Finally, he returned. And what was he holding in his hand? Not a condom, but a box of Saran Wrap.

I asked, "What are you planning to do with that? I don't think there will be any leftovers when we're done."

He looked at me, and he was totally serious when he said, "I was planning to use this as protection...you know—wrap it around."

Well, I couldn't help myself. I burst out laughing. I might have been a virgin, but I wasn't an idiot. Needless to say, we didn't go through with what we'd been planning to do that night, nor did we ever. It was probably just as well. Not too long after that, I broke up with him. However, I did begin to wonder if I would ever lose my virginity—at least in the right way.

Chapter 14

Leaving Washington

If you think adventure is dangerous, try routine – it's
lethal. ~ Paulo Coelho

In June 1966, I was preparing to leave Washington to study
archaeology in Oxford, England. Science had never been my
strong suit, but incredibly, I was the top student in my Geology
class at GWU. As a result, my professor had recommended me for a
summer program at Oxford. Although it meant that I would be gone
from the office for most of July and August, I was looking forward to
my first trip outside of the United States.

The Senator was also planning to travel overseas. The first week
in June, RFK would fly to Johannesburg, South Africa. His trip came
at the height of South Africa's apartheid oppression and, even though
he'd been granted a visa, he was not welcomed by the government.
When the Senator arrived in Johannesburg, the authorities refused to
give him any security or allow the U.S. government to provide any,
either. So his visit there was at great risk to himself and to those who

were traveling with him. He was accompanied by his wife, Ethel, as well as two members of our staff—Adam and Angie. Interestingly, members of the American press were refused visas to cover his trip.

RFK would give four speeches while in South Africa, but the most memorable and inspiring was delivered at Cape Town University on its Day of Affirmation—June 6, 1966—exactly two years to the day before the Senator's death. In that speech, he famously said:

> *Few will have the greatness to bend history itself; but each of us can work to change a small portion of events, and in the total of all those acts will be written the history of this generation...*
>
> *Each time a man stands up for an ideal, or acts to improve the lot of others, or strikes out against injustice, he sends forth a ripple of hope, and, crossing each other from a million different centers of energy and daring, those ripples build a current which can sweep down the mightiest walls of oppression and resistance.*

The next day, the Senator spoke to Afrikaner students at Stellenbosch University and then went on to Durban to address students at the University of Natal. When he flew from Cape Town, he asked the pilot to tip the wing of the plane toward Robben Island, where Nelson Mandela was imprisoned—as a gesture of respect. We later learned that the pilot, who did as RFK asked, was subsequently banned by the South African government from ever flying again. That's how oppressive they were in those years.

On the final day of his stay in South Africa, RFK visited Soweto, the township in Johannesburg originally built by the white apartheid government to house its Black labor force. Wire fences surrounded the township, and the inhabitants could only enter or leave by showing their identity cards. It was extremely rare for white people to visit Soweto, but RFK didn't hesitate. Thousands turned out to see him, and he climbed onto the hood of his car to speak to them. In the years following his visit, many of the inhabitants of the township would honor him by naming their children "Robert Kennedy" or simply "Kennedy."

When he left Johannesburg, RFK also visited Kenya, Tanzania, and Ethiopia, followed by a stop in Rome on June 18, where he met privately with Pope Paul VI for thirty-five minutes to press the Church to take a clear position on apartheid. The meeting, according to the Senator's telling, was not entirely satisfying, but the Pope did urge RFK "to continue speaking on the moral aspects" of the issue. In their meeting, the Senator also talked about the war in Vietnam, and the Pope encouraged him to continue efforts to find a peaceful solution.

The Senator would write about his experiences in South Africa in an article published in the August issue of *Look* magazine. It was entitled, "Suppose God Is Black," and it recounted an interaction he had with a student there.

In part, it read:

> *During five days this summer, my wife Ethel and I visited South Africa, talking to all kinds of people representing all viewpoints. Wherever we went...apartheid was at the heart of the discussion and debate.*
>
> *Our aim was not simply to criticize but to engage in a dialogue to see if, together, we could elevate reason above prejudice and myth. At the University of Natal in Durban, I was told the church to which most of the white population belongs teaches apartheid as a moral necessity...*
>
> *"But suppose God is black," I replied. "What if we go to Heaven and we, all our lives, have treated the Negro as an inferior, and God is there, and we look up and He is not white? What then is our response?"*
>
> *There was no answer. Only silence.*

Look *Magazine Cover Credit: Stanley Tretick/Look Magazine/Library of Congress*

When the Senator returned to Washington from his trip to South Africa, I went down and asked Angie if I could speak to him privately —that it would only take a few minutes. She had no problem with it and told me to go right in. I peeked around the corner and knocked softly on his door. He waved me in. He looked rather tired from his recent overseas trip, but he greeted me warmly. He asked me how I was doing, and I told him that I was fine, but that I had to talk to him about something. I think he must have picked up on my nervousness, because he immediately looked concerned. "What is it—is anything wrong?" he asked.

The rest of the conversation went something like this:

"Well, I just wanted to let you know that I'll be leaving the office in July," I responded.

He looked surprised.

"For good?"

"Well, I hope not...but for the time being, anyway."

"Why? Is there a problem? Why would you want to leave?"

I couldn't believe how hurt he seemed. It was as though I had betrayed him somehow. To this day, that's the main thing I remember from my meeting with him that afternoon—that look of hurt on his face. It was devastating.

"No—nothing like that. It's just that I got accepted to study in Oxford, England, this summer, and I'm planning to transfer to UC Berkeley in the fall."

"Really? Don't you like it in Washington?"

"It's not that...but I am a bit homesick for California." At that moment, it felt like a shameful admission, something more appropriately confessed at an AA meeting. I quickly added, "Plus, Berkeley is a much better school, so..."

"I never pictured you as a radical." There was that cryptic smile of his again.

I chuckled. "I'm not really...but if we're going to stop this war, it's the place to be, isn't it?"

He shrugged. "Well, I hate to see you go. I hope you'll return. You know you have a job waiting for you here whenever you want to come back. In fact, if you want to work here next summer, we'd love to have you."

"Oh, thank you, Senator. That's very sweet of you."

"Just let Angie know if you're coming, and she can arrange it. Is there anything I can do for you?"

"As a matter of fact, there is something. I would love to have a photo of you and me together."

"Of course—I'll have Angie set it up and let you know. Again, I'm disappointed that you're leaving."

"I'll really miss you, you know."

He looked a little embarrassed. "Well, you have to do what's right for you."

I didn't want to take up any more of his time, so I got up to leave. As I was walking to the door, he said softly, "I'll miss you, too."

I turned around and smiled, but I felt like crying.

The next day, Angie called me to say that the Capitol Hill photographer would be coming that afternoon to the Senator's office.

I think the photo of both of us turned out well, and without a doubt, it is my most prized possession.

The Senator inscribed it:

"For Donna, With appreciation, and I hope you will come back. Robert F. Kennedy"

Inscribed photo of the Senator and me in his office; credit: U.S. Senate Photo

Then, a couple of days later, he threw a goodbye party for me in his office. It was during the workday, so there were no alcoholic beverages—probably just as well. But there was a beautiful cake and some coffee. I'm sure Provi was the one who arranged it all. The Senator presented me with some goodbye gifts—a sterling silver letter opener with my initials engraved on it that the staff had bought for me. He also gave me a limited edition, privately printed copy of President Kennedy's Inaugural Address that had been presented to friends of the President. It was beautiful—in a white slipcase with the Presidential seal embossed in gold on the cover. When I was at her apartment, Provi showed me the copy of the Inaugural Address that she had—it was personally inscribed to her by JFK. I considered asking the Senator to inscribe mine, but as always, I was a bit reluctant to talk with him about anything that had to do with his brother.

Also, he reached into his pocket and presented me with about ten PT-109 pins and tie clasps. I'd already received a pin from him when I first joined the staff, but I think he wanted to give me something that day that was more personal and just from him. Over the years, I've doled out a few of them to other people who loved RFK and President Kennedy, but I still have some tucked away in a jewelry box.

Gift from the Senator — bound copy of JFK Inaugural Address

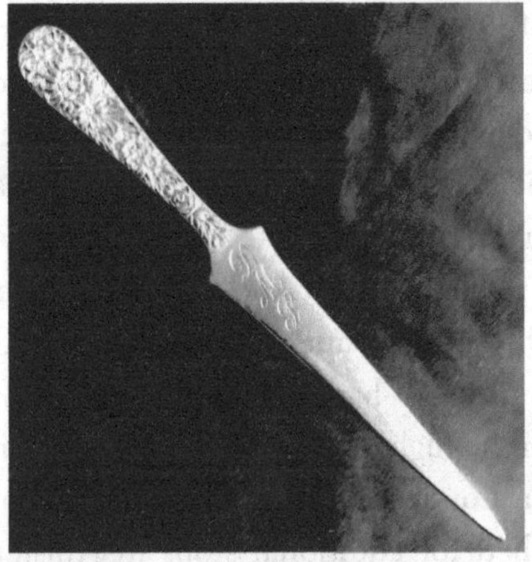

Gift from the Senator — an engraved silver letter opener

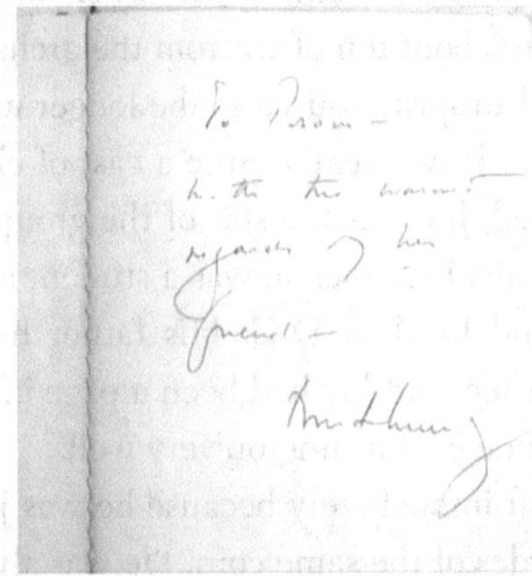

*Provi's copy: "To Provi, With the warmest regards of her friend—
John F. Kennedy"*

The day I left Washington, I was really quite sad. Frankly, I wondered what I was doing, but I had this feeling that I would be back.

The group that would be studying archaeology in Oxford was to travel to England on a chartered plane out of New York. Unfortunately, it wasn't the Boeing 707 jet that I was used to flying on from D.C. to Los Angeles. In fact, it wasn't a jet at all, but an older turboprop. Well, most people these days have never flown on a turboprop plane—and hopefully not on one like we were on. First of all, it was going to take some thirteen hours from New York to London, plus a stopover in Gander, Newfoundland, to refuel. Secondly, all of the seats on this particular plane were configured backward, so that when you took off, you would be thrown forward, and when you landed, the same. And I'm glad I didn't know it at the time, but apparently the company that built the plane—I think it was headquartered somewhere in Eastern Europe—had a history of crashes.

Most of us on the flight had purchased an add-on tour of Europe, so after landing in London, we got on another plane to Copenhagen. Our itinerary called for additional stops in Amsterdam, Hamburg, and finally, Paris. We would stay overnight in a couple of the places, and they had arranged tours to some of the key sights in each city.

I think there were about ten of us from the archaeology program who were doing the European tour, and the longer we were together, the closer we became. It was really quite a cast of characters, but as far as I was concerned, Jay was the star of the group, and we would become lifelong friends. Like me, he was a student at George Washington University and lived in D.C. His father had worked on a congressional committee, and Jay had been a page in Congress, so he knew the political scene in Washington very well.

He and I hit it off immediately because he was just as crazy as I was. We were two sides of the same coin. He was always ready to go along with my harebrained schemes, and he had a few of his own that I embraced. While we were overseas, I couldn't figure out why there was no sexual tension between us. We could stay in the same hotel room without any problem. We were like brother and sister. It was only much later that he would come out to me and tell me that he was gay.

One of the more memorable experiences we had during our European tour was in Hamburg, Germany. Since we were there on the Fourth of July, the American Embassy invited us to come to their Independence Day celebration in the evening for hot dogs, beer, and fireworks. The embassy was housed in a beautiful white colonial-style structure, as I recall—it looked more like a country estate than a government building. And it was surrounded by lush greenery, so that we could all sit out on the grass.

Well, it was just starting to get dark, and the fireworks display hadn't yet begun. We were stretched out on the lawn enjoying our food and drinking beers when, all of a sudden, demonstrators began to appear outside the gates of the embassy. They were young Germans protesting U.S. involvement in the Vietnam War. They were all holding signs and chanting anti-war and anti-American slogans. It didn't really bother us—frankly, most of us were against the war too and were used to protests. But then, about a half hour into the demonstration, the German police showed up. When they couldn't get the crowd of protesters to disperse, they brought out the German Shepherds and turned on the fire hoses.

I was horrified. For one thing, it brought back awful memories of "Bull" Connor and his police brutalizing demonstrators during the peaceful Birmingham marches of 1963. I was so upset watching it unfold that I burst into tears. It was just appalling to witness these young people being attacked by dogs, and then falling down and being pushed along the asphalt by powerful bursts of water from the fire hoses.

I think we remained at the embassy for the fireworks, but I certainly didn't feel like celebrating anything that night. To this day, it's hard to shake those awful images from my mind.

In Paris, there would be other disturbing images that would continue to haunt me all these years. On the first day of our stay in Paris, Jay and I decided to take the Métro to Montmartre. In earlier times, it had been a gathering place for artists, some of them quite famous. After checking out the open-air cafés and the works of street artists scattered throughout the area, we climbed up to the beautiful Sacré-Cœur Basilica, which was at the top of Montmartre.

Just beneath the church was a grassy hillside with stunning views of Paris, where one could stretch out, so we headed down there. Shortly after we sat down on the grass, this rather attractive young man dressed in jeans, with dirty-blond hair, came over to us and plopped down right next to me. He started talking to us. His name was Benny, and he said that he was from Yugoslavia and had lived in Montmartre for several years. He looked to be in his late twenties. He claimed to be an artist. He seemed very nice, and we chatted for a while. He spoke perfect English.

Benny offered to show us around Paris, and I thought it would be great to have a tour guide. Jay, however, thinking that he was becoming a third wheel, begged off and left.

Benny and I continued to talk for several more minutes. Then we got up and walked toward the closest Métro station to begin our city tour. When we arrived there, Benny turned to me and said, "Hey—I just remembered—I have a couple of Métro passes we can use. They're back at my place, which is just around the corner. It won't take us more than a minute to grab them. It'll save us a few francs."

I believed him, so I said, "Okay."

He was right. His apartment was very close to the Métro station. When we got there, I said that I would wait down on the street for him, and he started up the stairs alone. But then, halfway up, he stopped, turned around, and said, "Why don't you come up for a minute—you can tell me what you think about my artwork."

Well, at this point, I had no reason to imagine that Benny was anything other than a nice guy and a starving artist. I also believed what he was telling me.

Boy, was I wrong.

His apartment was really just one decrepit room with a bed in it and no works of art anywhere to be found. The minute he opened the door and we went inside, he shoved me down on the bed, which was only a few feet from the door. I screamed, and he clamped one hand over my mouth while he tried to pull down my underwear. He wasn't having much success because I was squirming around, trying to get free of his grasp. I started crying hysterically and screaming—for my mother, of all people (she was many thousands of miles away)—and begging him to stop, but he seemed determined.

He kept saying, "If you don't shut up, I'm going to hurt you real bad."

I didn't care what he said—I wasn't about to give in to this creep. So I continued to cry and scream—"Please, please don't do this." At the same time, I was struggling with him as hard as I could, trying to work myself out from under his body, trying to get free.

Then suddenly, my guardian angel appeared, and miraculously, Benny just stopped. Apparently, he'd had enough of my crying. He rose from the bed and shouted, "Get the hell out of here!"

I jumped to my feet, opened the door, and ran all the way to the Métro station. My heart was pounding, and my entire body was shaking as I climbed onto the subway train and headed for my hotel. "The City of Love" was nothing but a nightmare for me.

I didn't go to the police because I didn't want the trip to be all about those terrible few moments with Benny. Besides, I didn't think my eighth-grade French was good enough to carry me through a police interrogation, and I figured that no damage had been done anyway. In fact, I wouldn't get really angry about what had happened to me in that awful little room in Montmartre until years later. But that day in Paris, all I felt was an unbearable sadness. So far, my "love life" had consisted of a sexual assault, a failure to launch, and an attempted rape. Could it get any worse?

Of course, it could.

Chapter 15

The Summer of 1966

> I am a part of all that I have met; Yet all experience is
> an arch wherethro' Gleams that untravell'd world
> whose margin fades For ever and forever when I
> move. ~ Alfred, Lord Tennyson

School started in Oxford on July 11 and was scheduled to run until July 30, followed by a two-week archaeological dig somewhere in England. When we arrived at the college, there was an orientation for new students, where they talked about the rules of the school and went over the hours of the classes, which were to be held six days a week.

The head of our summer program was a Brit by the name of Bernard Wailes. He was an anthropology professor from the University of Pennsylvania and was quite well known in his field, but a guy who, it seemed to me, had something of a stick up his behind—very, very old-school British.

The rest of the teaching staff were also from Penn, but British as well. They explained that we would be expected to attend classes each day from 8 in the morning until 6 at night—Monday through Saturday—with an hour break for lunch.

What??

Jay and I looked at each other, rolling our eyes. We couldn't believe that this was what we had signed up for during our summer vacation. Part of the trouble was that we'd gotten a taste for traveling during our tour of Europe, and now, sitting around in classes all day long listening to these professors drone on sounded like a real drag. We immediately started plotting how we might escape from the school.

First off, we agreed—the dig had to be scrapped. We were told that if we failed to show up for it, we wouldn't get any credits for the course. But we figured—what the hell? The fact was that this course wasn't part of our required studies anyway, and frankly, we didn't want to squander our time overseas digging through dirt in some God-forsaken English field. We didn't know when we might get back here again, if ever. I have to admit it: Jay and I were troublemakers from the start.

The only thing that somewhat tempered our eagerness to escape the confines of the college was the arrival a few days later of a group of French students who had come to the school to study English. Jay immediately set his sights on the most beautiful girl in the group— Catherine, I believe her name was. All the other American boys were interested in her too, so the competition was going to be tough. But my man Jay was up to it.

As for me, I was rather attracted to one of the French guys by the name of Jacques. He wasn't all that good-looking, and like most French men, he was a bit short, but there was something about him that appealed to me. He resembled that French actor, Jean-Louis Trintignant, who starred in the film *A Man and a Woman*, which had just been released that same year. At any rate, he appeared very French, and there was that accent—always a turn-on. Jacques and I would exchange long, adoring looks across the room whenever we were in each other's company.

So Jay and I immediately put our escape plans on hold and instead began to look for romance. I won't go into all the gory details, but will start out by saying that Jay's efforts bore fruit, and mine were far less successful. By the end of our time at Westminster College, Jay had himself a French girlfriend... and I had myself—for a short time, anyway—a French boyfriend who, I one day discovered, liked boys better than girls. Strike three or four or five for me? By then, I had lost track.

Naive young thing that I was, I must say that I was rather shocked that morning when I found Jacques in bed with his "best friend" Marc. At my tender age, I had never imagined such a thing in my wildest dreams—how could he be attracted to me and have a boyfriend too? But there it was—in living color. I had gone up to Jacques' room early in the morning for some together time before class, and when I opened the door, there the two of them were— naked, their arms wrapped around each other in bed. I later found out that Jay was pretty much in the same position with the lovely Catherine. Well, boys will be boys, I suppose. So, anyway, that was that. We were finished. It was just a summer romance, anyway—but what a disappointment.

However, as you might expect, romance wasn't the only trouble that Jay and I got into at school. We would cut classes and hitchhike to London every chance we got. And then there was our final triumph. The school had a large tower that sat in the center of the campus, and up at the top of the tower was a bell that they would ring at noon each day. From the first moment that we arrived at the school, I'd proposed to Jay that somehow we find a way to get up to the top of that tower and ring that bell. At some point, we became so obsessed with the bell that ringing it became our sole purpose in life, aside from romance, of course. The question was when? Well, the logical answer was the night before we were to leave—not that we were thinking logically in those days, but somehow, when it came to the bell, we considered all the angles. We figured since we weren't planning to go on the dig anyway, what could they do to us? It wasn't as if we were committing some crime, right?

So it was that on that last night of classes, Jay and I bucked up our courage with several glasses of wine, then climbed to the top of the tower at three in the morning and rang that bell like there was no tomorrow. Jay would tell you that there was a look of sheer madness on my face as I pulled and pulled on the rope, and the bell rang loudly over and over again. I think it may have damaged my hearing for life, but hey—it was worth it.

Naturally, it woke up everyone in the residences on campus. It was the distinguished Bernard Wailes himself who had to pull us off the ropes. He was spitting mad as he marched up to us in the tower that morning, dressed in his matching Marks & Spencer robe and slippers, ready to hang us from those very same ropes. Naturally, he gave us a first-class chewing-out, but we couldn't stop laughing the entire time, which made him even angrier.

So that was our grand send-off from Oxford. For the time that we were supposed to be on the dig, Jay decided to travel to Italy, and I was headed to Sogndal, Norway—my grandfather's place of birth. I don't regret for a moment that I didn't complete the archaeology course. That particular trip to Norway was a once-in-a-lifetime event for me.

When I returned to England, I went directly to London, where I was reunited with Jay and the other students from our archaeology course. We would all be bunking in dorms at the University of London for the final week of our stay. But on the day of my arrival, Jay and I decided that we had to have a hamburger—it had been far too long without one. So we took the Tube to a "Wimpy Bar," one of the few places that sold hamburgers in London back then. Although Wimpy's was originally an American chain of restaurants, in the U.K. they still hadn't figured out how to cook a burger right. It was awful—barely edible. But Jay and I were prepared to have a good time anyway, so we were really whooping it up, sharing with each other the highlights of our respective trips to Italy and Norway.

We were sitting on stools at the counter, and I had swung around to face Jay. My handbag was atop the stool next to me, apparently wide open. While we were engaged in talking and laughing, somebody reached into my bag and stole my wallet. Unfortunately, I didn't realize it until we got ready to pay. So there I was in London for another week without a penny to my name. Fortunately, room and board at the University of London were pre-paid, but I had no money to do anything else. Plus, Jay and the other students didn't have enough that I could borrow from them to cover the entire week. What was I going to do?

As luck would have it, my parents were on an ocean liner about to complete a transatlantic crossing from New York to Southampton, and they were due to arrive the next day. I borrowed money from Jay to send a telegram to the ship. It read something like this: "I lost my money. Meet me in Trafalgar Square at 12 noon tomorrow. I will wait."

So, just a little after noon, there I was sitting on a bench below the statue of Lord Nelson, thumbing through an old issue of *British Vogue* that I'd found in the University of London dorm when I heard the unmistakable, mellifluous tones of my father's voice. He said, "Well, who do we have here?"

I jumped up and ran into his arms. I've never been so happy to see anyone. To be honest, I was ready to go home.

But first, my mother, English teacher that she was, was intent that I learn something about England's finest Lake Poets, starting with William Wordsworth. She had planned a tour for the three of us that included Tintern Abbey, where Wordsworth had written his famous poem of the same name. On the way there or the way back—I can't remember which—we would stop off at Cambridge, make a trek to Wales, and also go to Runnymede, where the Queen had dedicated a memorial plaque and an acre of land to President Kennedy. My mother, as always, had planned their tour of England down to the last detail. Fortunately, it didn't require much adjustment as a result of their detour to London to pick up their delinquent daughter.

After all the craziness I'd been a part of during the last month, I had to admit that it felt good to be in the protection of my parents once again. I was ready to be a real child for a week.

I will never forget the three of us sitting beneath the ruins of Tintern Abbey and my father reciting these beautiful words that the great poet had penned some 170 years before:

> Therefore let the moon
>> Shine on thee in thy solitary walk;
>> And let the misty mountain-winds be free
>> To blow against thee: and, in after-years,
>> When these wild ecstasies shall be matured
>> Into a sober pleasure; when thy mind
>> Shall be a mansion for all lovely forms,
>> Thy memory be a dwelling-place
>> For all sweet sounds and harmonies; oh! then,
>> If solitude, or fear, or pain, or grief,
>> Should be thy portion, with what healing thoughts
>> Of tender joy wilt thou remember me
>> And these my exhortations!

Frankly, listening to the poem, I began to think he must have written the words for me. But I did not know then, on that beautiful August day, as we sat on the banks of the River Wye, what pain and grief would be my portion less than two years later. In those awful days of June 1968, I would turn again and again to these words for some comfort. And, in September of 1968, this passage would also be recited at my wedding ceremony.

One of the other highlights of the time I spent with my parents in England was our trip to Runnymede, which overlooks the River Thames, where King John signed the Magna Carta in 1215. Although the Senator had been present at the Queen's dedication of the memorial in May 1965, I was glad to finally be able to see it for myself. My father took a photo of me there, standing in front of the memorial plaque to JFK.

At Runnymede—August 1966

In Cambridge—August 1966

After our tour of England together, my parents dropped me off in London in time to catch the plane back across the pond with my fellow students. When I arrived in New York, I immediately jumped on a flight to Washington. My friend Mo, who lived in D.C. and worked for the International Monetary Fund, had kindly offered me the use of his apartment for a few days while he was off on a business trip to Afghanistan.

Once I arrived in Washington, I immediately went down to see my friends at the office and to say a last goodbye to the Senator. He and I had a fairly lengthy conversation by his standards—maybe ten or fifteen minutes. He asked me about my trip, and I described how I had visited the Runnymede memorial to President Kennedy. I told him that it reminded me of when I used to walk over to Arlington several times a week. He didn't say anything, but he looked at me for a long time, and I sensed his discomfort. That melancholy was back, and his hands shook a little as he fidgeted with a piece of paper on the desk.

I quickly changed the subject, recounting the incident at the American Embassy in Hamburg. He seemed surprised to hear how horribly the German police had treated the peaceful demonstrators.

I also told him how I'd met up with my parents in England—how my dad had read Wordsworth's poem to my mother and me at Tintern Abbey.

He asked, "Who's your favorite poet?"

I thought for a moment and then said that there were several, but that one of my favorites was E. E. Cummings. And Yeats, of course.

He said, "I like the Greeks...and Emerson. Have you read any Emerson?"

I replied, "Yes, he's one of my mother's favorites. She actually has a framed portrait of him hanging in our house. She's an English teacher. I don't think I've read any of his poetry since high school, though."

"You should," he said. Then, to my astonishment, he started

reciting a few lines of an Emerson poem from memory—I don't recall which one.

"I'm sure my mother has a book of his poems at home somewhere—I'll read it when I get back. I'll have to tell her about your shared love of his poetry."

He again reminded me about returning to work for him the following summer and said he hoped he would see me before then. He ended the conversation with the same question as always—"Is there anything I can do for you?" When I said, "No, thanks," he got up from his chair at the same time that I rose from mine. But then I stopped and said, "Well, there is something...can I kiss you goodbye?" He just smiled and moved closer. So I kissed him.

As things worked out, just two months would pass until we saw each other again. This time it was in Berkeley.

I started the fall semester at Berkeley in September. It was required that all new students undergo a full physical examination. The university had contracted with a local military base for the exams to be handled by their Army physicians. A handsome, young doctor in a khaki uniform conducted my exam, and I was found to be fit...or at least fit enough for Berkeley.

However, a day or so later, I was up in my dorm room when I was informed that there was someone downstairs waiting to see me. I immediately headed to the lobby. At first, I didn't recognize him because he was in civilian clothing. Then, as he began to talk, it hit me. This was the same Army doctor who had performed the examination on me just a few days before. I asked why he had come to see me.

"I thought we might go out for a cup of coffee."

I looked at him in stunned silence for a moment. This "doctor" had given me a breast examination and had seen me half-naked. Fortunately, a pelvic exam wasn't part of the procedure, but I figured that it wouldn't have made any difference to this guy. I suddenly felt sick.

I was furious. "You're asking me out on a date?? Do you have any idea how unethical this is?"

He looked confused. "I don't understand. There's nothing wrong with us going out for a cup of coffee, is there?"

I couldn't believe it. I said, "Look, doctor. I suggest you leave right now and never come back. If I ever see or hear from you again, I will report you to the Army's medical board for disciplinary action. Understand?"

He just stared at me like I was crazy.

Then I turned around and headed for the elevator. I suppose I should have been flattered, but the whole thing creeped me out. Not a great way to start my new life at Berkeley.

Chapter 16

The Pleasure of His Company

I have spread my dreams under your feet.
Tread softly because you tread on my dreams.
~ W.B. Yeats

I n October of 1966, the Senator campaigned tirelessly all across the country on behalf of Democratic candidates who were up for election, including Pat Brown, Governor of California, who was facing the Republican Ronald Reagan in November. In conjunction with his trip to Northern California, RFK had been invited to address UC Berkeley students on October 23 as part of the University's Civil Rights Speaking Series. I had just started there the month before and was excited to learn that the Senator would be coming to the Berkeley campus on the final day of his campaign swing through California.

I recruited one of my new friends from the dorm to accompany me to the outdoor Greek Theatre, where the Senator was scheduled to speak. We got there early so we could stand just beneath the stage.

Fortunately, my friend brought her camera along so that she could take some photos.

Earlier in the day, the Senator had been at Sacramento City College when he was asked during a question period if he would be running for President. He responded with his usual fatalism, saying that he didn't know what the future would bring. He said, "I think that one cannot plan that far in advance. I'm going to continue, as long as I'm around on this globe—I'm going to continue in public life in some way. I don't know where that man way up there is going to take me."

When the Senator came into the Berkeley Greek Theatre, he got a huge ovation and waved to the crowd of more than 20,000 students. The President of the Intrafraternity Council introduced him, and he headed over to the podium to speak. There was another long round of applause, during which he looked around at the crowd and spotted me. He mouthed "Hi" and smiled, and I blew him a kiss.

He opened his talk by saying that he was pleased to be in Berkeley—"the first college to become a major political issue since George III attacked Harvard for being a center of rebellion and subversion." He took a jab at candidate Ronald Reagan, remarking tongue-in-cheek that if Reagan were elected, he felt confident that he'd grant him "a visa" to come back to California again. Then, as was his custom, he recounted a funny story, this one dealing with his brother, Ted. Apparently, much of the political class had left Washington for the campaign trail in anticipation of the upcoming November elections. The Senator pointed out that also absent from D.C. were both President Johnson and Vice President Humphrey. He quipped that he had just "received a rather disturbing telegram" from Ted telling him that in view of the fact that nobody was in Washington, he had "seized control." That got a huge laugh.

Finally, he talked about his "warm feelings" toward California, pointing out that the first settler in the Golden State had come from New York, and that later, New York had sent us the motion picture industry, the Dodgers, and the Giants, and that we were "kind enough" to send them Richard Nixon (Nixon had relocated to New York after losing the California governor's race in 1963).

Once he finished the warm-up, he launched into his formal speech. The substance of it dealt with civil rights and the right to dissent. He began with this:

> We dissent from the fact that millions are trapped in poverty while the nation grows rich.
>
> We dissent from the conditions and hatreds which deny a full life to our fellow citizens because of the color of their skin.
>
> We dissent from the sight of most of mankind living in poverty, stricken by disease, threatened by hunger, and doomed to an early death after a life of unremitting labor.
>
> We dissent from the willful, heedless destruction of natural pleasure and beauty.

He then went on to talk about distinguishing the difference between the right to dissent and how we chose to exercise that right, admonishing that it wasn't enough to justify our actions simply because they were legal or constitutionally protected. Basically, he was making the point that dissent for dissent's sake was not enough, and that violence, in particular, was counterproductive in achieving our goals. He stressed that dissent had to be followed up with concrete, practical action in order for it to be meaningful.

He closed his speech with the following:

> You live in one of the most privileged nations on earth. You are the most privileged citizens of that privileged nation, for you have been given the opportunity to study and learn, to take your place among the tiny minority of the world's educated men and women.
>
> By coming to this school, you have been lifted onto

a tiny, sunlit island, while all around you lies an ocean of human misery, injustice, violence, and fear.

You can use your enormous privilege and opportunity to seek purely private pleasure and gain. But history will judge you, and, as the years pass, you will ultimately judge yourself, on the extent to which you have used your gifts to lighten and enrich the lives of your fellow man.

In your hands, not in presidents' or leaders', is the future of your world and the fulfillment of the best qualities of your own spirit.

When the Senator was done speaking, the students gave him another rousing ovation. Following the speech, there was a brief question-and-answer period. It was mostly a friendly exchange, but he was booed once when he said that he planned to support the Johnson-Humphrey ticket in 1968. Then, when the Q&A was finished, he came over to the edge of the stage where I was standing, leaned down, and asked if I wanted to join him and his entourage for the rest of the day. Naturally, I was delighted to do so. He called over someone to help lift me up to the stage, and we went on our way.

It was late afternoon, and we headed to Oakland for a Democratic fundraising event. Just one week earlier in Oakland, the Black Panther Party had been founded by Huey Newton and Bobby Seale. Stokely Carmichael would come to Berkeley the week following the Senator's speech to give his own address at a Black Power conference there.

On our way from Berkeley to Oakland, there was a rather scary incident. I wasn't aware of it at the time, but later learned about it from Jerry Bruno (advance man for the Senator). Apparently, the police had passed along a report to Jerry about a threat on the Senator's life. The suspect was described as a white man with a beard who had allegedly told a hitchhiker he picked up earlier that day that he was going to buy a rifle to kill Robert Kennedy. Our motorcade to

Oakland was moving very slowly, so when a car with three men—one of whom matched the suspect's description—pulled up alongside us, Jerry jumped out of his vehicle and into the front seat of the Senator's car, squeezing in next to him in order to block any potential gunshot.

According to Jerry's account, RFK didn't say a word but gave him "that look": the cold, blue eyes, the look that said, "Something funny's going on here and you guys don't want me to know about it." In the meantime, Joe Dolan and another advance man raced over to the suspect's car, pulled the keys out of the ignition, and threw them into the bushes. Then we all went on our way. I think it was later determined to be a false alarm.

At any rate, we didn't stay too long in Oakland. After RFK made a brief appearance at the fundraising event, we headed to San Francisco's Fairmont Hotel, where the Senator was staying, for a party in his suite. He seemed in high spirits.

During the gathering in his hotel room, I talked with him at length. He wanted to know how I liked Berkeley and what I had been up to. One of the things he asked me about was a controversial play called *MacBird!*, which had been written by an anti–Vietnam War activist from Berkeley and was getting a lot of press notice at the time. I had heard about it, but I hadn't actually read it.

The satirical play superimposed the assassination of JFK onto the plot of Shakespeare's *Macbeth*. In it, JFK was "John Ken O'Dunc," LBJ was "MacBird," and Lady Bird Johnson was "Lady Mac Bird." MacBird was eventually defeated by Robert Ken O'Dunc (RFK). The plot was also driven by the "Three Witches," representing students, Blacks, and leftists.

The Senator told me that he wanted to read the play, but that it was available at that time only in Berkeley, and given his shaky relationship with LBJ, he didn't want anyone in the press to find out about his interest in it. So he asked me to purchase it and send it to him via Adam, who was also there that night. Angie and Joe Dolan were traveling with him too, but as I recall, the three of them were the only ones with him from RFK's Capitol Hill staff (aside from Jerry Bruno, who worked out of our Syracuse office).

We were all drinking in his suite, and I still hadn't eaten anything, so I was feeling a bit high, as most of us were. The Senator was probably the most sober one among us. As was his usual practice, he'd had only one or two drinks. The party lasted about an hour or an hour and a half—it must have been getting on to about eight o'clock or a bit after by then. The Senator had to meet some political people in San Francisco for dinner, but at one point he pulled me aside and asked if I could come back to his suite when he returned. I told him I would. This was the last stop on his trip to California, and he was flying out the next day.

Anyway, the party was breaking up, but before I left, I went to use his bathroom. I remember walking into the bedroom, and William vanden Heuvel was sitting on the edge of the bed talking on the telephone in hushed tones. I believe that he was accompanying the Senator to his dinner meeting that night. So I used the bathroom, then came out of the bedroom and shut the door behind me. By this time, everyone else had left his suite. It was just the Senator standing there all by himself.

I said, "I wish you weren't leaving."

He replied, "I'll only be gone for a couple of hours. I should be back by around 10."

I said, "I'll miss you anyway."

He asked, "Will I see you later?"

I said, "Of course. Angie said that I could go down to her room and hang out until you return."

He looked me directly in the eyes. "Good. I'll call when I get back." His voice was gentle.

We were face to face at this point, the lights of San Francisco behind us. I was about to take off, but then I couldn't help myself. I asked him, "Aren't you going to kiss me good-bye?" He looked at me again for what seemed like a long time, and then he moved in closer, took my face in his hands, and kissed me. This kiss was very different from the others—for one thing, it was on the lips. Afterwards, he held me close in his arms for a few moments. We exchanged some more words, and I left his suite.

I headed down to Angie's room. There were a couple of other people there who'd been at the party—I don't remember exactly who. I do recall that Adam was there, possibly Joe and Jerry too. We ordered some food—finally—and continued to drink, which wasn't a very good idea. By this time, I was feeling no pain. I wasn't used to so much booze, particularly hard liquor. I remember that we sat around on the floor and talked and laughed. We were really having quite a good time.

At a certain point, Angie and I had a long, private talk about the Senator; I was starting to have second thoughts about seeing him later. I was conflicted. Although I was madly in love with him—we all were—my feelings about him were also very complicated. I don't mean that I was in love with him in a purely romantic sense, even though that might be hard to believe given how I sometimes behaved. But it was different. I admired him so much, and he was the embodiment of everything I believed in, too. So it was difficult for me to look at him as just another man.

I asked Angie, "Do you really think he'll call when he gets back?"

"If he told you he would, he will."

I said, "I don't understand him." She laughed.

"Few people do."

But I was serious.

"Why would he risk everything?" I was in my head now and struggling to make sense of what was happening.

Her face softened. "I don't know...he's a man," she said.

I figured that Angie probably understood this particular man better than almost anyone else, so I was looking for answers. But that night, she was unable or unwilling to help me find them. And as well as she might know him, I imagine that there was a lot he didn't share with her. As Adam would later say, "he was a very secret man in many ways."

I realized that, to a large extent, I had brought this situation upon myself with all my flirting, but on some level I couldn't believe that it had actually come to this. I suspected that, as usual, I had probably bitten off more than I could chew.

Not long after my heart-to-heart with Angie, I began to feel a little sick to my stomach and had to use the bathroom to throw up. I'm not sure whether my upset stomach was the result of drinking too much or anxiety over the circumstances in which I found myself. Probably a combination of both. But, as one does, I felt a bit better afterward. My trip to the bathroom also helped me make up my mind. I had purged myself of any lingering doubts about what I should do. For better or worse, I decided that I would not go back up to the Senator's suite that night. I knew what would likely happen if I did, and I worried about how it might change our relationship forever.

So, after some more conversation with Angie and the others, I stood up—it must have been around 9:30 by then—and announced with some regret that I was going to get a taxi and head back to Berkeley. Adam offered to share a cab with me. He said he was staying in Oakland that night—I don't remember why.

Anyway, he and I went downstairs and hailed a taxi. From the time that we climbed into the back seat and started going over the Bay Bridge, Adam became a bit frisky. Normally, I suppose I would have pushed him away, but the fact was I was too high—not just from whatever I'd been drinking that night, but from having spent most of the afternoon and evening with the Senator. In particular, those few moments of intimacy that we'd shared in his suite had taken me to new heights, and I just didn't want to ruin the sense of euphoria that I was feeling by creating some scene in the back of a taxi in the middle of the Bay Bridge. Plus, I didn't really blame Adam anyway. He'd had too much to drink that night as well. And who knows? Maybe by that time, he looked pretty good to me. After all, he was the Senator's evil twin—better than nothing, right? I jest. Honestly, I don't recall exactly what I was feeling about Adam. But finally, we arrived at my dorm, and he went quietly on his way to Oakland. No harm done.

I immediately headed for the showers when I got inside. I just stood under the hot water and got soaked from head to toe. Once I stepped out of the shower and got dressed again, I ran down to the telephones in the lobby of my dorm in panic mode—with my hair still dripping wet.

Shaking, I pushed a couple of coins into the public telephone and called Angie in her room at the Fairmont. Everybody in the lobby of the dorm stared at me like I had just been released from a state hospital for the criminally insane. But I didn't care. I felt really badly that I had bailed out early on the Senator, so I had to talk to her. By now, my head had cleared and, to be honest, I also kind of regretted that I had left. I asked Angie to tell him that I was really sorry. Thankfully, she sounded completely cool with it. She said—no problem—and assured me that she would pass along the message to him and that he would understand. So that was that. But that afternoon and evening had to be one of the more memorable times I ever spent with the Senator. Unfortunately, I wouldn't see him again until the following summer.

I did obtain a copy of the *MacBird!* play that he had asked for and forwarded it to Adam at the office, with a message telling him rather coyly that it was a pleasure to see him again. I immediately received a note back that read:

> *Dear Donna—*
> *Many thanks for the MacBird—it was as requested.*
> *The pleasure was all mine; Thank you.*
> *I look forward to seeing you back with us next*
> *summer.*
> *Again, with all the best,*
> *Adam*

I had to chuckle when I read the words, "The pleasure was all mine; Thank you," with the "you" underlined. I guess he wasn't too drunk to remember our taxi cab ride.

RFK at Berkeley's Greek Theatre

RFK at Berkeley's Greek Theatre

𝔘nited 𝔖tates 𝔖enate
WASHINGTON, D.C.

Dear Donna —

Many thanks for the MacBird — it was as requested.

The pleasure was all mine; thank you.

I look forward to seeing you back with us next summer.

Again with all the best

Adam

Note from Adam Walinsky

So, did I make the right decision that night? As I sit here today nearly 60 years later, I wonder how returning to the Senator's suite might have changed me. Honestly, I don't know. If the circumstances had been different, if I had been different, perhaps everything might have been fine. Yet, in retrospect, I can't help but wonder whether my 19-year-old self was emotionally equipped to deal with it all. At the time, the irrevocability of crossing that line in our relationship frightened me. It would not have altered the course of RFK's life—of that, I'm quite certain. But mine, I'm not so sure. In any event, I'm not one who likes to think about the could-haves and should-haves of life. And in a lot of ways, it's beside the point. There is no going back for a do-over. Someone once said, life is not a dress rehearsal. So we have to make the best choices we can with what we've been given. I made my choice that night and moved on. That was all I could do. At least that's what I told myself.

As for the Senator, the next morning he left California to continue campaigning for Democratic candidates across the country. Within the next two days, there would be two more credible threats against his life—one in Wyoming and another in Montana. Fortunately, both turned out to be false alarms, but according to Jerry Bruno, the staff took them seriously and instituted various precautions, such as using a closed car instead of a convertible and taking the Senator out through back doors instead of letting him wade through crowds in the front. The Senator soon realized what was going on, and he became furious.

In Casper, Wyoming, RFK had finally had enough. He called Jerry and the others traveling with him into his hotel room to chew them out and to demand that their attempts to keep him away from the crowds stop. He said, "If someone wants to kill me, they're going to kill me. I do not want to live from day to day with this constant threat. I want to make it clear to you, I want it to stop right now." Jerry said that he thought it wasn't so much anger on the Senator's part, but his way of telling them that although he understood that he was in danger, he "couldn't live his life in fear."

Jerry would later conclude that perhaps RFK's instincts were more on target than his own—that the Senator had a better sense of what he should be doing. Tragically, the night he was killed, he was shot not while going through a crowd as he liked to do, but by taking a shortcut through the kitchen of the Ambassador Hotel in order to avoid going through the crowd of people gathered in the hotel's ballroom.

But, as a lot of us who were close to him believed, it was probably inevitable that an assassin's bullet would eventually find him. If not that night, then some other night. I think that, on some level, he believed it as well and was driven, at least in part, by that awful sense of inevitability. During his 1968 campaign, he was asked about the danger to him by reporters on his plane, and he responded, "I just don't worry about that. There's no sense in worrying about those things. If they want you, they can get you" and "There's nothing I could do about it anyway."

As for the November 1966 election, it did not go well for the Democrats. I volunteered for Governor Brown's campaign, getting out the vote on Election Day, but it didn't make any difference. Ronald Reagan was elected the next Governor of California. In fact, the Democrats did poorly throughout the country, and the Republicans managed to pick up 47 seats in the House, three in the Senate, plus eight governorships.

The Senator was featured on the cover of the November 18 issue of *Life* magazine and was the subject of several articles inside. They pointed out in one of the write-ups that most of the candidates he'd supported in the midterm elections had gone down to defeat, as if that was somehow his fault. Of course, President Johnson had been chastised by many in the Democratic Party for not doing more to help out in the off-year elections, while RFK campaigned from one side of the country to the other, "drawing record crowds and collecting political IOUs."

Life magazine also speculated about whether the Senator would run against Johnson in 1968. They examined a few possible scenarios under which he might mount a challenge to the sitting President. But none of them anticipated what actually happened, with LBJ choosing not to run again.

Shortly after seeing the Senator in San Francisco, I was set up on a blind date with a foreign student from Argentina. I would eventually marry him. It was not a match made in heaven. Despite his European Jewish heritage, Norberto was as macho as any other red-blooded Argentinian man. Back then—perhaps even to this day—they pretty much felt that women should be barefoot, pregnant, and in the kitchen. I might be exaggerating a bit. Norbie, as he liked to be called, was somewhat more modern in his thinking, but he still held to the maxim that a man's home was his castle...and he was king. Why I ever thought the relationship might work is a mystery to me now. But at the time, he seemed mature for his age, he could be quite charming when he wanted to be, he was handsome, and most importantly, he adored me. So what's not to like? At any rate, from the moment we went out on that first blind date to a Cal football game, we spent virtually all of our free time in Berkeley together. In December, I went home to L.A. for the holidays. My sister was getting married on Christmas Eve, and I was to be the Maid of Honor.

In Berkeley—1967

Chapter 17

1967 Begins

The arc of the moral universe is long but it bends
toward justice. ~ Martin Luther King, Jr.

As the New Year began, I returned to school in Berkeley and the Senator took off at the end of January on an overseas trip to England, France, Germany, and Italy. During his time there with foreign leaders, there was much discussion about the war in Vietnam. The French and Germans in particular were adamant in their opposition to American involvement in the war.

While in a meeting in Paris that RFK attended with an official from the American Embassy, the French passed along a tip about a change in the North Vietnamese position on negotiations, indicating that the North was willing to waive any preconditions so long as the U.S. bombing stopped. Since the talk was in French, the Senator apparently didn't pick up on the fact that this was a significant change in position by the North Vietnamese. However, the American Embassy official, who spoke fluent French, did and immediately sent a cable off to Washington, which someone in the State Department apparently leaked to a *Newsweek* correspondent. The day after the Senator returned home, on February 5, *The New York Times*, which had received an advance copy of *Newsweek*, led with a story about the "Kennedy peace feeler."

President Johnson was livid. He had been upset that RFK was making an overseas trip in the first place and suspected that the Senator himself had leaked the story about the peace feeler. On February 6, RFK went to the White House to meet with LBJ. To say that the meeting was contentious is an understatement. According to Frank Mankiewicz's account, the President told RFK that the war would be over by June or July and that he would destroy the Senator and every one of his dove friends, adding, "You'll be dead politically in six months." RFK would afterwards tell a friend that LBJ had been "abusive" and "seemed very unstable."

The meeting with the President marked a turning point for the Senator. After being falsely accused by Johnson of something he hadn't done and treated with abuse, there no longer seemed any point in not speaking out on the war.

As for Johnson, he had no intention of pursuing a peaceful solution in Vietnam. Eight days later, on February 14, the President ordered the resumption of bombing. Perhaps it was his Valentine's Day gift to the Senator. By this time, the President had committed more than 400,000 American troops to the war.

Less than three weeks later, on March 2, the Senator rose in the Senate Chamber to denounce the administration for the resumption of bombing. Some old friends and his brother Ted had pleaded with him not to do it. In fact, the morning of his speech, the Senator reportedly quipped to Ethel that Ted had told him to be sure that "they announce that it's the Kennedy from New York." Newspaper columnist and friend Joseph Alsop had gone so far as to warn RFK in his column that if he went ahead with the speech, he would never become President. He was right about the Senator never becoming President, but for the wrong reason.

In his address, RFK proposed a three-part approach to ending the war. First, bring the bombing to an unconditional halt and call for negotiations. Second, ask for international assistance in preventing an escalation of hostilities. And third, replace American and Viet Cong fighters on a phased-in basis with international troops. He said, "We are not in Vietnam to play the role of an avenging angel pouring death and destruction on the roads and factories and homes of a guilty land. We are there to assure the self-determination of South Vietnam."

As always, Adam and Peter had urged RFK to go even further in his speech, but the Senator was still worried that he would be seen as simply trying to undermine Johnson. Peter would later recall that after he read the draft that the Senator had decided to go with, RFK asked, "Am I dove enough for you?" and when Peter answered, "No," the Senator said, "That's good."

Even so, his position was still an unpopular one, not just with the Administration, but also, according to polls, with the public in general. The media continued to frame his disagreement with Johnson as part of their ongoing feud. RFK tried to play down that perception at every turn, but they didn't seem to take him seriously. For the most part, the press viewed his widening break with the administration simply as more evidence that he might be planning to vie for the nomination in 1968.

The week before his address to the Senate on Vietnam, the Senator delivered what I think was one of his most memorable speeches. It was at the 20th Annual Roosevelt Day dinner of the Americans for Democratic Action (ADA) in Philadelphia. During his second year as a Senator, RFK had been one of only four Senators to receive a perfect score on his voting record from the liberal organization. It was ironic because the Senator was not one who believed in traditional liberalism, in a top-down approach. What he believed in was the empowerment of people. Yes, government could provide the tools for the disadvantaged to achieve their potential, but he thought that, in the end, it was really up to the individual to do for himself.

RFK spoke that night from the same podium in the same ballroom that his brother, John F. Kennedy, had addressed the ADA in 1959. The extraordinary speech that he delivered got very little press coverage at the time, and even to this day, it is difficult to find mention of it anywhere. However, shortly afterward, word spread on college campuses about the speech, and our office received hundreds of requests for copies of it from students around the country. Even when I returned to the Senator's office in June, we were still getting letters requesting copies.

Fortunately, RFK's Democratic colleague from Pennsylvania, Senator Joseph Clark, who was with him that evening, asked that the full text of the Senator's address be printed in the *Congressional Record*, and that is, I believe, the only place where one can still read it in full. The subject of the speech was "Youth," but it dealt more specifically with the widening gap between generations, the disaffection of America's young people not just with the war in Vietnam but with society in general.

I have quoted large sections of the speech below because I think it provides some real insight into exactly who the Senator was and what he believed. No one else was talking about these things. No politician other than RFK dared speak about distrust of all those institutions that older Americans held dear. But I think his speech addressed more than just the disenchantment of young people. It was really about his own disenchantment as well.

Throughout, he spoke about the way that "they" saw the world, but in virtually every instance, it was, in fact, how he also viewed the issues of the day. And when he talked about young people feeling "remote from the decisions of policy," he was also expressing his own frustration with being unable to influence the country's direction—not just in Vietnam, but on social issues as well—frustration that would ultimately play a role in his decision to run for President.

He opened his speech by talking about how young people viewed the war:

 However the war may seem to us, they see it as one in which the largest and most powerful nation on earth is killing children (they do not care if accidentally) in a remote and insignificant land.

We speak of past commitments, of the burden of past mistakes; and they ask why they should now atone for mistakes made before many of them were born, before almost any could vote.

They see us spend billions on armaments while poverty and ignorance continue at home; they see us willing to fight a war for freedom in Vietnam, but unwilling to fight with one-hundredth the money or force or effort to secure freedom in Mississippi or Alabama or the ghettos of the North.

And they see, perhaps most disturbing of all, that they are remote from the decisions of policy; that they themselves frequently do not, by the nature of our political system, share in the power of choice on great questions which shape their lives.

He went on to say, "It would be tempting—but it would be wrong and self-deluding to trace to the war all the problems of our disaffected youth." He then talked about how young people also felt disconnected from the American business world—in part because corporations played "so small a role in the solution" of the country's problems, such as civil rights, poverty, unemployment, health, and education. He added that they were disenchanted with liberal institutions as well—that they viewed labor unions as "sleek and bureaucratic with power," even "corrupt and exploitative," "a force not for change but for the status quo."

In education, he warned that we seemed headed for "a standardization of the mind, what Goethe called 'The deadly commonplace that fetters us all.'" He maintained that student protests were "surely a protest of individuality against the university as corporate bureaucracy," against a "dull sameness."

He talked about it this way:

> The non-recognition of individuality—the sense that no one is listening—is even more pronounced in our politics. Television, newspapers, magazines are a cascade of words, official statements, policies, explanations, and declarations; all flow from the heights of government down to the passive citizen; the young must feel, in their efforts to speak back, like solitary salmon trying to breast the Grand Coulee Dam.
>
> The words which submerge us all too often speak the language of a day irrelevant to our young. And the language of politics is too often insincerity—which we have perhaps too easily accepted, but which to the young is particularly offensive.

He closed with this:

> Whatever their differences with us, whatever the depth of their dissent, it is vital—for us as much as for them—that our young feel that change is possible; that they will be heard; that the cruelties and follies and injustices of the world will yield, however grudgingly, to the sweat and sacrifice they are so ready to give.

Less than six months later, the Senator would tell Lawrence Spivak of *Meet the Press*, "I am dissatisfied with our society. I suppose I am dissatisfied with our country."

This is who Robert Kennedy was. This speech was not just about young people; it was about him—about his own disenchantment with what was happening in our country. Why this speech has been mostly lost to the dustbin of history is beyond me.

A little more than a month later, on April 10, 1967, the Senator traveled to the Mississippi Delta with fellow members of the Senate Labor Committee's Subcommittee on Poverty. He wasn't satisfied with just holding hearings there; he wanted to see the conditions for himself. The other senators on the subcommittee couldn't be bothered, so just RFK and Senator Joseph Clark actually visited people in the area.

His tour of the Delta would affect him deeply. He couldn't believe that this sort of thing actually existed in the United States. As described by one of those who accompanied him, they went into "a dark, windowless shack" where "the odor was so bad you could hardly keep the nausea down." There was a small child with open sores sitting on the floor of the shack with "his tummy...sticking way out just like he was pregnant."

Bobby looked down at the child, and then he picked him up and sat down on that dirty bed. He was rubbing the child's stomach. He asked, "How can a country like this allow it?" Then tears streamed down his face as he held the child close.

That was what the Senator was all about. He felt things in his heart and in his gut. It was part of the empirical learning process upon which he always depended. He wasn't some high-brow intellectual who sat around systematically weighing all the aspects of an issue like poverty. And he didn't look at it through a political lens either. He felt it physically and emotionally. Seeing a child suffering was a punch to the gut, and it pained his heart. Only when it came to taking action to fix these problems would his intellect and his political savvy kick in.

After visiting the Mississippi Delta, he was determined to do something, and for the rest of his days on the planet, the issue of poverty would be front and center on his agenda. When he returned to Washington, he appealed to the Secretary of Agriculture in an attempt to get free food stamps for the poorest of the poor, but to no avail. By then, poverty was no longer a top priority for the Johnson

Administration. But the Senator would return to the issue again and again for the rest of his life.

The following month, on May 15, the Senator participated in a CBS program called *"A Town Meeting of the World."* He had agreed to do the program only because Frank Mankiewicz had strongly urged him to. As designed, it was supposed to be a debate between Governor Ronald Reagan and RFK on the topic of the war in Vietnam, with the two men sitting in different studios and a group of students in a third studio in London. However, once it started, the program devolved into a series of anti-American rants by the students. So, instead of being able to present their own positions on the war, both Reagan and Kennedy were put in the position of having to fend off extremely hostile and unrelenting questions from the foreign students.

By most accounts, Reagan fared much better than the Senator. RFK was not only unhappy with his own performance but angry that he'd been talked into it in the first place. He would never let Frank forget it.

Two days later, on May 17, the Reverend Martin Luther King, Jr. came to Berkeley to deliver a speech in front of some 7,000 students. The month before, MLK had led an anti-war demonstration in New York City and had spoken at the Riverside Church there, calling for our withdrawal from Vietnam and reparations for the Vietnamese. His remarks at the church that day made even his strongest supporters uncomfortable. In his speech, he called the United States "the greatest purveyor of violence in the world today," and he equated testing our latest weapons on the Vietnamese with Nazi Germany's testing of new medicines and tortures in their concentration camps. Following King's speech, the NAACP had distanced itself from his remarks, releasing a statement saying that King's speech was a "serious tactical mistake." Black students at Berkeley apparently agreed with the NAACP and decided to boycott his speech.

But I was among those gathered to hear Dr. King talk on that sunny day in May. His address to Berkeley students would prove to be far less controversial than the Riverside Church speech the month before.

The audience was packed tightly together in the plaza below the steps of Sproul Hall—the site of the Free Speech rallies just a couple of years before—with the overflow crowd sitting on the rooftops of buildings overlooking the plaza. Many students carried signs that read, "King-Spock '68." At the time, Dr. Spock—a pediatrician—was a well-known anti-war activist. Ironically, he was the first one from the peace movement to urge the Senator to run against LBJ for president. He had approached RFK in 1965 and then again in the fall of 1966, telling him that he was "the only person who could lead the country back to peace and decency."

In his address, King called Berkeley students the conscience of the nation and said that the chief moral dilemma that the country suffered from was a "poverty of spirit." He said that despite all of our advancements in technology, we had "not learned the simple act of walking the earth as brothers and sisters." He went on to talk about the twin evils of poverty and war.

He said that many poor people had lost hope and had "concluded that life is a long and desolate corridor without exit signs." Linking poverty to the war in Vietnam, he maintained that the Johnson administration was "more concerned about winning an unwinnable war in Vietnam than about winning the war against poverty here at home." He reminded us that "a great nation" must be a "compassionate nation" and that "we should not be conscientious objectors in the war against poverty," that we needed a reordering of priorities. In an observation that still rings true to this day, King said that the U.S. should not see itself as "the peacekeepers of the world."

Reiterating a point that the Senator had made on several occasions, MLK warned that the Vietnam War had diverted attention from civil rights and was standing in the way of social programs. He urged us to "escalate our protests against the war," that we needed a kind of "creative discontent" in our country.

King closed by saying, "I still have a faith that keeps me going through these difficult days," that he could still sing "We Shall Overcome" because "the arc of the moral universe is long, but bends toward justice." He added that the 17th-century philosopher Thomas Carlyle was right when he wrote that "No lie can live forever." Quotes from Dr. King's speech that day would later be etched into his memorial in Washington, D.C.

He spoke for some fifty minutes, then answered questions, one of which was whether he would be a candidate for president in 1968. He quipped, "I don't feel that I'm Presidential timber," then added that he had no ambitions in that area and that he had "sense enough to know" that he couldn't win.

It was quite an extraordinary day.

I later learned that, following his address, King did meet privately with a large group of the Black students who had boycotted his speech, and he was shaken by it. According to one of the Berkeley students who was driving him around that day, Dr. King "came out of the meeting with the Black students upset. Very upset—he felt like they were polarized. Like they didn't have an investment in the university." Apparently, Dr. King had told the Black students that day, "You can't disengage; you've got to be involved."

As the Senator had suggested, I'd written to Angie earlier in the year to ask about returning to the office during the summer. She had responded to my letter quickly and positively, telling me that while they hadn't made definite plans for summer help yet, there would be no problem where I was concerned.

So, at the beginning of June, after finishing up final exams in Berkeley, I headed back to Washington.

ROBERT F. KENNEDY
NEW YORK

United States Senate
WASHINGTON, D.C.

February 13, 1967

Dear Donna:

I talked to Joe Dolan about your wanting to

come back to work this summer and he

said although no definite plans have been

made for summer help as yet, that he

is sure there would be no problem where

you're concerned. Just let us know when

you plan to come East and we'll work it

out from there.

It's always nice to hear from you!

Sincerely,

Angela M. Novello

Miss Donna Stanley
2650 Haste - D513
Berkeley, California

Angie's note to me

Chapter 18

My return to Washington

It is not in the stars to hold our destiny but in
ourselves... ~ William Shakespeare

It might have been the "Summer of Love" out in San Francisco's
Haight-Ashbury, but I was glad to be back on the East Coast
and working for the Senator again. Shortly after I arrived, I
managed to get into his office to say hello.

True to form, he threw out most of the questions, and I did most
of the talking. First, he asked me what I'd been up to since he last saw
me (neither one of us mentioned what had happened in his Fairmont
Hotel suite back in October).

I skipped the generalities and immediately got down to specifics.
I told him how Dr. King had come to Berkeley just a few weeks
before to speak to the students. From his reaction, I gathered that the
Senator hadn't heard about it. That wasn't surprising to me since, for
some strange reason, the speech had received very little press coverage, even in the Bay Area. I knew that RFK hadn't commented

publicly about MLK's controversial Riverside Church speech in April, so I really didn't expect him to say much to me about the Berkeley speech either.

I did tell him that Dr. King seemed a bit chastened by the harsh reaction to his Riverside speech and that his remarks seemed to be much more measured at Berkeley. I said that I found it interesting how King's focus, however, continued to be almost entirely on the war in Vietnam, but added that the Senator and MLK seemed to be pretty much on the same page—not only when it came to the war but also on the issue of poverty.

"He brought up some of the same points that you've been making," I said—"that it costs half a million dollars to kill every enemy soldier, while we spend only $53 a year for every poor person."

The Senator asked what kind of reception the students had given King. I told him that there were about half as many people there to see MLK as there had been at his own speech back in October, but that the response was extremely positive, although the crowd was almost entirely White. He looked surprised.

"Oh, really—why was that—do you know?"

"As I understand it, the Black Student Union actually boycotted his speech—they were apparently upset that Dr. King was turning away from civil rights and toward the Vietnam War. They felt that he was abandoning 'the dream' before it was finished."

He folded his arms across his chest and thought about that for a moment, then said, "That's interesting."

I told him that I thought it was ironic that, other than King, those in the Black community who seemed most opposed to the war were the more militant elements. I said, "Stokely Carmichael—you know, came to Berkeley to speak right after you did in October*—it was just

____

* *At the time of his Berkeley speech, Carmichael was still Chairman of the Student Nonviolent Coordinating Committee (SNCC), but he would step down in May 1967 and join the Black Panther Party in 1968.*

a week later—and he talked about the war being immoral and said that any Black men fighting in it were no more than mercenaries since they couldn't vote in their own country."

The Senator asked me if I had seen Carmichael speak, and I told him no—that I'd just read about the speech in the school's newspaper.

I also mentioned to the Senator how some students were holding up hand-written signs urging King to run for president, and that after the speech MLK had been asked whether he was interested in running.

At that point, the Senator smiled and started tapping his front teeth with his fingernail. It was a nervous habit of his. He asked, "How did he respond?"

"He said that he knew he couldn't win."

RFK chuckled but didn't say anything. I took his silence as an invitation to speak.

I shared my view that the anti-Vietnam War sentiment on campus was growing stronger every day and that the students there—at least the White students—were very supportive of anyone who opposed the war. The Senator seemed interested, but he just listened, not commenting. He asked if I could get him a copy of Dr. King's speech and of Carmichael's speech as well, and I said I wasn't sure that any transcripts of the speeches were available—but that I would reach out to my contacts at the university and ask them. I added, "If not, I can at least get you copies of the student newspaper articles that talk about the speeches." He smiled again and said, "That's fine."

We talked a bit more—I can't remember about what specifically—and then he asked me how long I would be staying in Washington. I told him that I would be there for the whole summer, and he seemed delighted. As I left, he said, "Hope to see you again. Come by any time." I said I would.

That was one thing about the Senator that was pretty unique, I think. He had an open-door policy—you never had to make an appointment to see him. If you could get past Angie, he always seemed interested in talking to you—no matter who you were. He was genuinely curious and quite open-minded. He always seemed to welcome different points of view from all kinds of people, no matter their station in life, and was willing to hear you out even if you were expressing an opinion that was vastly different from his own. That's why he would meet with people like Tom Hayden or Allen Ginsberg or even a young staffer like me and listen intently to what we had to say. Not that he was quick to change his mind—he could be quite stubborn in that regard—but he was always eager to learn something new and prepared to take in other opinions on just about any subject.

As for my return to the office that summer, things really hadn't changed much since I'd left the year before, except for a few new faces. We were still getting loads of mail—more than a thousand letters on most days, particularly whenever the Senator spoke out about the war in Vietnam. There were often organized writing groups—those letters were always immediately apparent because they were generally written in exactly the same language and, in many cases, were just mimeographed copies with different signatures. As mentioned before, we were still getting a lot of requests from students around the country for the ADA speech that he'd delivered in February.

We continued to receive "nut mail" and hate mail as well. I could usually tell if the correspondence was from disturbed people just by looking at the envelope. Often, the address would be written in different colors of ink—usually red and blue or red and black. The lettering was also a giveaway—some words written in all caps, others not.

If the hate mail was threatening, I would immediately bring it to Joe Dolan's attention, and it would be referred to the FBI for investigation. If it was just gibberish, we would generally file it away.

I remember one woman who had been sending hand-written love letters to the Senator every day since he was first sworn into office. Some days, she would even send two or three. She had developed an entire elaborate fantasy life with the Senator, calling him "sweetheart" and "darling," and would go into great detail about their dinner together the night before, how he had brought her flowers and jewelry, and how loving he had been to her—it was like a romance novel. Provi and I would get a kick out of reading the letters, but it was really kind of sad.

Unfortunately, we eventually had to refer her to the FBI as well when she started complaining about how Ethel was becoming a problem and preventing her and the Senator from fully realizing their true love. It started with the woman asking him in her letters when he was going to leave his wife, as he'd promised. That evolved into what sounded more and more like threats of actual violence toward Ethel. So we had no choice but to ask the FBI to check her out to make sure she wasn't a real threat.

I never did hear what the result of their investigation was, and I often wondered what happened to her. But the letters did stop coming. I imagine it was something of a shock when the FBI actually showed up on her doorstep. My hunch was that she was harmless, but we couldn't take any chances.

We occasionally got threats from outside the United States as well. I remember that just a month before the Senator was due to leave for South Africa in June 1966, we received two letters just a few days apart from England—one sent to Hyannisport and the other to our office in Washington. Contained in one of the envelopes was a political cartoon with a clearly threatening message handwritten along the border. In the other, there was an angry letter that, while less threatening, was from an obviously disturbed person.

With the 2025 release of FBI documents surrounding the Senator's assassination, these two pieces of correspondence surfaced again, and it was chilling for me to see them for the first time in nearly sixty years. They'll give you an idea of the kind of hate letters that I often came across as I sorted the Senator's mail. In this case, one of the individuals wrote the following on a political cartoon from the *New York Herald Tribune*, Paris:

"Don't worry Lindon [sic] there is another Oswald already

waiting in the wings only this time it may be a different method The Kennedy promotion is pathetic—even disgusting—'dead or alive' vastly overdone"

Threatening words on the cartoon

The other letter was mostly rambling—talking about how certain foods and drugs were responsible for mental disorders—but also expressing anger with the Senator because "you consult psychiatrists and turn my letters over to them." He demanded that RFK call off "any watchdogs interfering in my letters."

After I brought this hate mail to Joe Dolan's attention, he referred both letters to the FBI—in part because he suspected they might be from the same person and wanted the Bureau to compare the handwriting on the envelopes. They analyzed the two and concluded that the handwriting was not a match. Still, since the Senator was going to be in England for a brief stop during his South African trip, Joe also made sure to touch base with Scotland Yard.

ROBERT F. KENNEDY
NEW YORK

United States Senate

WASHINGTON, D.C.

May 5, 1966

Mr. Harold Reis
Office of the Attorney General
Department of Justice
Washington, D. C.

Dear Harold:

The enclosed cartoon and handwriting seem to
warrant our taking care to learn the where-abouts of
the writer while the Senator is in England. The
cartoon letter is anonymous. The other enclosure also
came from England and has a post-mark and first name.
Can you get the Bureau to tell us if it was written by
the same person? If so, we'll send it to the English
police.

Sincerely,

Joseph F. Dolan
Administrative Assistant

OFFICE OF THE
RECEIVED
MAY 9 1966
ATTORNEY GENERAL

ENCLOSURE

Joe's letter to the FBI

On June 5, Israel launched a pre-emptive strike against Egypt,
which became known as the Six-Day War. At the time, the Senator
commented, "We can welcome the United Nations call for a cease-
fire, but a cease-fire is not enough. We must deal with the causes of
the conflict by ensuring a permanent and enforceable guarantee of
Israel's right to live secure from invasion..." Nearly a year later,

during his 1968 presidential campaign, RFK would propose that the U.S. send fifty Phantom jets to Israel in furtherance of this guarantee. He would mention this proposal again when he debated Senator McCarthy in California on June 1, 1968, just four days before he was shot. Nobody could have imagined the tragic impact that his proposal would have on the Senator's life. On June 5, 1968—the first anniversary of the Six-Day War—we would find out.

But back to the summer of '67. At the end of June, the Senator headed out West to spend the July 4th weekend. He took a four-day rafting trip ninety-one miles down the Colorado River with members of his family and friends, including George Plimpton, Art Buchwald, mountain climber Jim Whittaker, and Andy Williams. Always one to tempt fate, the Senator decided to shoot some of the early rapids using only an air mattress. At one point, he also jumped into the whitewater rapids wearing just a life jacket, despite warnings from the guides that the water was too rough.

Then, on July 3, he and others hiked seven miles in 117-degree heat from the floor of the Grand Canyon up to the rim. It took them more than five hours to reach the top. Some members of his party—but not him, of course—became victims of heat exhaustion during the arduous climb and had to be airlifted by helicopter out of the canyon.

In a column published shortly after the trip, Art Buchwald would recall, tongue in cheek:

> Every morning after breakfast, Bobby would look up at a mountain and ask Mt. Everest climber Jim Whittaker, "Do you think it's tough to climb?"
>
> If Whittaker said no, Bobby would look at another mountain. "What about that one?"
>
> If Whittaker said, "It's impossible," Bobby would call the party together and say, "That's the one we're going up," and pretty soon Ethel, mother of ten, the Kennedy children, and the rest of the group would be scrambling up the mountain in 110-degree heat.

George Plimpton would remember the trip from the floor of the Grand Canyon this way:

> "...the rest of us would gather under a shelf of rock, just to rest and get out of the sun, and we knew we couldn't stay there for too long because leg cramps and so forth were a possibility—you had to keep going.
>
> So the Senator would haul himself out from under the ledge and stand facing us—this motley, dusty group, who wished we hadn't come—and he'd recite the St. Crispin's Day speech from *Henry V*.
>
> ("We few, we happy few, we band of brothers. For he today who sheds blood with me shall be my brother...")
>
> We'd stare at him, popeyed, and then we'd groan and push ourselves up; and we'd follow him for another brutal half an hour or so. That was the procedure at each rest stop: a peppermint drop, a slug of warm water, and inspirational verse from the Senator."

God knows there were many of us on his staff who were relieved never to be invited along on one of those trips. It was so much nicer lying on an inflatable lounge in the Senator's pool out at Hickory Hill. The pleasure of his company did have its limits.

It was over that same July 4th weekend that I actually did spend time out at the Hickory Hill pool. My parents were in Washington, and we decided to go there for a picnic and pool party with Provi and other friends. The pool house had just about everything one would need. I hadn't brought a bathing suit to Washington—but no problem. In the women's dressing room, there were a number of bathing suits in various sizes available to borrow for the day.

At first, I was a little reluctant to put on a swimsuit that someone else had previously worn, but I got over it. I assumed that they had all been laundered...and I thought—What's the worst that can happen?

So I slipped on a suit that Jacqueline Kennedy once wore. Actually, I imagine Jackie wouldn't have been caught dead wearing a bathing suit that wasn't her own, but that was what I told myself.

The pool house also had a jukebox, so we could listen to all the great sounds of the sixties. And there was touch football, in the Kennedy tradition, and tennis for anyone who was interested.

My mother and father spent a great deal of time that day talking to Mary Jo Kopechne's parents, who were also out at the Senator's pool house. I remember my mother telling me what nice people they were—Polish background, I think. Of course, Mary Jo and I were acquainted from the office, but she was seven years older than I and worked on a different floor, so we weren't really good friends at the time.

Naturally, I was shocked and saddened when the whole Chappaquiddick tragedy happened later. I also couldn't help but imagine that it might easily have been me who drowned that night. As for all the theories that Ted Kennedy and Mary Jo were sexually involved, I never believed them—I don't think anyone in the office did; it was ludicrous. At the time, my sources from RFK's office said that after the Senator died, Ted was more like a father figure to those boiler-room girls. I was also told that Mary Jo was seriously involved with another man at the time—I think he was a reporter.

Anyway, although I don't know for certain what happened at Chappaquiddick, I thought it was disgraceful the way the media portrayed Mary Jo. She was a sweet young woman when I knew her —rather plain in appearance and always very modestly dressed, with little or no makeup—not at all how the press talked about her—and I really doubt that she and Ted were involved in any scandalous way. Just my two cents, though.

As for our July 4th pool party at Hickory Hill, fortunately, my father had a camera with him that day, so he took some photos of us. After all these years, I often look back and wonder why I didn't just buy myself a camera. Today, we take snapshots of everything that happens to us since we have our smartphones with us at all times. But in the 1960s, cameras tended to be large and bulky, so people rarely carried them around except on special occasions.

I also wish that I had thought to keep a diary during those years. It's amazing to me that I'm able to remember as much as I do. Following the Senator's death, I did put together a scrapbook, but even then, there were lots of memories that were already beyond my mind's grasp. When you're living something, you just don't think to write it all down, and when you go to work every day and see someone all the time, it's hard to keep track of every little thing that happens.

But I wish that I had. With Robert Kennedy, even the small things were often noteworthy.

At Hickory Hill—my friend Mo, me, Mel (a volunteer in the office), Provi, my mother, and Gustavo (Provi's son)

With Provi and my mother at Hickory Hill—the back of the house

My mom, my dad, and me in front of the spool/pool house at Hickory Hill

The summer of 1967 was tragic in many ways, however. Amid rising racial tensions, 158 riots erupted across the country. When it was all over, some 7,200 people had been arrested, 1,200 had been injured, and 43 people were killed. Dr. King had warned in a speech just a couple of months before that the cities were potential "powder kegs." The Senator himself had issued the same warning as early as 1965.

The worst of the riots that summer were in Newark and Detroit during the last week of July. Following the Detroit riot, some reporters caught up with the Senator and asked him about it. Speaking in general terms about urban unrest, RFK told them, "It's rapidly becoming the greatest national crisis that we've faced in a hundred years," and "the time for speeches has pretty much passed." By then, the Senator had given up on President Johnson doing much of anything to address the riots. The administration's sole focus continued to be the war in Vietnam.

Although RFK quickly condemned lawlessness and violence as unacceptable, he was most interested in coming up with solutions that would deal with the root causes of the unrest, telling reporters that he had already introduced legislation earlier that month that would provide for low-cost housing, low-interest loans to renters, and $3.3 billion in federal money for urban areas.

He said, "When unemployment is going steadily up in the ghetto, when the school system is inadequate and unsatisfactory, and where the housing is dilapidated and deteriorated—getting worse every year instead of better—I don't think you can consider that satisfactory."

During his 1968 presidential campaign, the Senator would come back to these issues, continuing to walk a fine line between supporting "law and order" on the one hand and recognizing the kind of systemic problems that led to riots on the other. Following the murder of King, he would speak about another kind of violence—"the violence of institutions; indifference and inaction and slow decay."

It was later during the summer of 1967 that the Senator came up with the idea of a Poor People's Campaign to get the attention of Congress, telling Marion Wright that the only way to secure change was to make it "more uncomfortable [for Congress] not to act than it is for them to act." Wright would pass along RFK's suggestion to Dr. King, who embraced the idea, seeing it as the next phase in the struggle for equal rights. According to Marion Wright, MLK was planning to endorse RFK in the presidential race in 1968.

In August, the Senator appeared on the cover of the *Saturday Evening Post*. In the accompanying article, RFK talked at length about the alienation and disaffection of people—young people, in particular. It was basically a continuation of the thoughts he'd expressed in the ADA speech back in February.

According to the reporter, his words seemed to pour out almost in a stream of consciousness when he spoke about the struggle of the individual in society. In part, he said, "It is an effort today, in trying to manifest the importance of the individual, to show that the individual does count in a society where he actually appears to count less and less. Many of our young people—and older people as well—feel that they have no control over what happens in government and what happens in their country, and in the world—a world that we now have the ability to destroy, along with all mankind, through the use of atomic weapons. The individual feels he has no role to play."

In the interview, the reporter also asked whether the Senator would run for President in 1968, and he confirmed that he would not challenge LBJ head-on. Then he was asked about 1972, and the Senator demurred, saying, "I don't think I can plan for it. It would be foolish. I don't know if I'm going to be here."

My boyfriend, Norbie, was spending the summer at home in Buenos Aires and, in our regular telephone calls, he would continually urge me to fly down to meet his parents. He kept bugging me about it, and I kept putting him off, until one night when he called and announced that he had gone ahead and bought me a round-trip airline ticket from New York to Buenos Aires in August. I was actually a bit annoyed that he hadn't bothered to clear it with me first. That was the sort of thing that macho Latin American men did. It was hard to stay mad, however. To be honest, I was rather excited at the prospect. I had never been to South America before.

There was one big problem, though. I had told the Senator that I would be in the office the entire summer. Not that I was a vital part of his operation—hardly. But still, I hated to go back on my word. I knew I would have to tell him personally—I didn't want him to hear it from someone after the fact. I decided to wait, though, until we were closer to the date of my actual departure.

There were a couple of other people that I also had to break the news to: my parents. To say that they were unhappy would be a gross understatement. In fact, they were furious—particularly my father. First of all, they still hadn't met Norbie. Secondly, my father had this crazy idea in his head that if I flew to Argentina, I might never come back. It really was a ridiculous notion—that possibility never crossed my mind. Once I finally managed to convince them that I had no intention of permanently absconding to Argentina, they finally gave me their blessing. So I began making plans to fly to New York and then on to Buenos Aires.

I was able to get in to see the Senator briefly in early August to tell him of my plans. Again, he looked as though I had betrayed him. I felt terrible, but what could I do? I tried to explain the situation to him, and he seemed to understand, but he still looked hurt.

Friday, August 11, was my last day in the office. Provi arranged for a little send-off party, and then I was gone.

On my return from Buenos Aires, I stopped in Washington for a couple of days and managed to see the Senator again. He seemed most interested in my impressions of the country. At that time, there was a coup d'état in Argentina about every other week. In fact, the most recent coup had been just a couple of months before. As a result, Norbie's father had lost the factory he owned to nationalization several times in the last couple of years and had to start all over again, building from the ground up. Inflation was running rampant too, at about 30 percent. So I told the Senator—even though it was a beautiful country, no, it wasn't a place I would want to live, but that at least I'd been able to practice my Spanish.

He said that he'd been in Buenos Aires for just forty-eight hours when he was in Latin America, so he didn't get to see much. I remarked that I remembered that it was there that he'd received probably the warmest welcome of his entire Latin American trip.

"They really loved you in Buenos Aires—I recall that someone there said that you could be elected President of Argentina! They still talk about you there."

He seemed a bit embarrassed by my comment and said softly, "Yes, they were very nice to me," then chuckled and quickly added, in his usual self-deprecating way, "That might be the only place where I could be elected President."

I laughed and said, "You know that's not true."

Our conversation in his office was quite brief. As always, he asked if there was anything he could do for me, and when I said, "No," he wished me good luck. I told him that I would miss him, and then, as I got up to leave, I turned and said, "Let me know if you get back out to San Francisco." He smiled, and we exchanged—what seemed to me— a knowing look.

Unfortunately, it would be another eight months before we saw each other again. By then, his life (and mine) would be far more complicated. I didn't mention it to the Senator during our talk, but when I was in Argentina, Norbie had asked me to marry him, and I'd accepted.

In mid-September, the Senate Finance Committee met to consider the Senator's proposed housing legislation, and in hearings, then–head of HUD Robert Weaver (whose appointment RFK had opposed) would call the Senator's efforts "superfluous." Some three weeks later, President Johnson would announce his own housing bill —basically just a watered-down version of the Senator's legislation.

At the time, RFK was livid, asking, "How can they be so petty?" Adam and Peter had spent six months putting together the Senator's legislation, and Johnson didn't even bother to give him a heads-up before announcing his competing bill. Peter Edelman would attribute it to Johnson's continued animosity toward the Senator, remarking that LBJ had convened a whole task force of Administration officials to discredit the Senator's proposed legislation "just because they were Kennedy bills."

In a way, Johnson's continued attempts to thwart RFK's legislative agenda in 1967 served an unintended purpose—it fueled the idea that the Senator should run for President in order to get some of these things done. Frank Mankiewicz would remark that Joe Dolan and he, as well as others, responded to LBJ's obstruction by telling the Senator how important it was that he run for President. "Nothing was going to get accomplished if that didn't happen."

Chapter 19

The Decision to Run

The lights begin to twinkle from the rocks:
The long day wanes: the slow moon climbs: the deep
Moans round with many voices. Come, my friends,
'Tis not too late to seek a newer world.
~ *Alfred, Lord Tennyson*

Throughout the fall, the pressure continued to mount on the Senator to run for the Democratic presidential nomination in 1968. There seemed to be no stopping LBJ in Vietnam, and meanwhile, the domestic agenda was languishing. The riots over the summer were just one symptom of that. The fact that Johnson had rejected the findings of the Kerner Commission, which blamed "white racism" for the unrest, was further evidence to RFK that not only was the administration not going to do anything about the war, but it was "not going to do anything about the cities either."

Even so, the Senator was torn, and he continued to vacillate. In November, he appeared on *Face the Nation* and was asked if, given his opposition to the war, he would run for President against LBJ. The Senator said that, if he did, it would simply confirm the view of many that his opposition to the war was just an effort to "build up a political following," and he felt that his running "would not strengthen the dialogue" about the war but actually weaken it. It was quite apparent in the interview that he was still bothered that many—particularly in the press—saw him merely as "an overly ambitious individual" in a personality struggle with President Johnson.

And although he said that he would support the President if he were nominated, he went on to call the war in Vietnam immoral. He said that our moral position and what we stood for as a country were being seriously undermined by the war. He was asked by one of the panelists how, if he felt that way, he could then support Johnson in his bid for another term. It was a good question—and one that the Senator had difficulty answering. The pressure was getting to him, and he felt frustrated. In response, he said that he didn't know what else he could do "other than try to get off the earth in some way." The reporter seemed alarmed at his comment. "Senator, nobody wants you to get off the earth, obviously...Nobody is trying to put you on the spot..." But the Senator was the one who had really boxed himself in. After all, how could he—in good conscience—support a President who was waging an immoral war?

Behind the scenes, RFK continued to meet with various members of his inner circle about the possibility of mounting a challenge to Johnson. Then, on November 30, Senator Eugene McCarthy declared his candidacy for the Democratic nomination. He had been recruited to run by Allard Lowenstein, head of a Dump Johnson movement. At the end of the summer, Lowenstein had approached RFK to run, but he had turned him down. Now, hearing that Lowenstein was backing Eugene McCarthy, the Senator was discouraged.

At the time of the announcement, LBJ suspected that McCarthy was in collusion with Kennedy, but that was ridiculous. RFK had never been particularly impressed with McCarthy based upon their dealings in the Senate, and his candidacy actually put the Senator into even more of a bind. He also felt that McCarthy was the wrong man to take on Johnson—he didn't trust him, and he thought he was not competent enough to be President. In fact, in 1968, RFK would tell Jerry Bruno that if he were unsuccessful in his own presidential bid, he planned to support Hubert Humphrey. Actually, he quite liked Humphrey, and the feeling was mutual (despite the attacks that the Vice President had made on the Senator over his Vietnam remarks). Adam, however, wasn't quite so forgiving. He would later characterize Humphrey as "the Dagwood Bumstead of politicians" and as "a fool and opportunist."

In December 1967, the Senator again met with some of his advisers at his apartment in New York City to discuss whether he should enter the presidential race, but he remained ambivalent, and those closest to him continued to be split on the issue. For RFK, it was not just a political question. He felt passionately about the issues and believed that LBJ would keep putting poverty and civil rights on the back burner so long as his obsession with winning in Vietnam continued to consume him. But he still wondered whether his candidacy would actually accomplish anything.

Adam and Peter continued to press the Senator to make the run, as did Ethel, while some of the old-timers from JFK's administration cautioned that challenging Johnson would be seen as part of a personal vendetta and would simply tear the party apart. His brother, Ted, thought that if RFK lost in the primaries to Johnson, it would destroy his chances of success in 1972. The Senator, however, questioned whether he would be any stronger in 1972 than he was in 1968 and quipped that Johnson would prefer to "die and make Hubert [Humphrey] President rather than let me get it." Of course, if the result of taking on Johnson in '68 was—God forbid—a Nixon presidency, all fingers would point to RFK as the culprit.

As 1968 began, both public and private pressure intensified. During a speech at Brooklyn College, a sign was raised by the students that read, "Bobby Kennedy: Hawk, Dove or Chicken?" That really hurt. Of all things, the Senator deplored being called a coward.

He knew that he had to make a decision soon. Still, his advisers remained divided on the question, and the polls were not encouraging—a January Gallup poll showed that Democrats preferred Johnson over McCarthy by 71 to 18 percent and Johnson over RFK by 52 to 40 percent. The Senator felt he had nobody to whom he could turn for definitive political advice.

He was on his own.

He told Peter Edelman, "My problem is that I don't have anyone to be for me what I was for my brother."

Then, at the end of January, a United States Navy intelligence ship and its crew were captured by North Korea in international waters. In response, LBJ called up 14,000 reserve troops. Just a week later, the North Vietnamese launched their Tet Offensive with a surprise attack against the U.S. Embassy in Saigon.

The Tet Offensive was a turning point for a lot of people in this country. It showed that the Administration's assurances about our military success in Vietnam were merely propaganda—that, in fact, we were losing the war. Many who initially supported the war effort now turned against it. Even servicemen fighting in Vietnam began to write the Senator, expressing their support and asking him to continue to speak out.

On February 8, RFK addressed an audience in Chicago, saying that dreams of a military victory in Vietnam were gone and that "Half a million American soldiers with 700,000 Vietnamese allies, with total command of the air, total command of the sea, backed by huge resources and the most modern weapons, are unable to secure even a single city from the attacks of an enemy whose total strength is about 250,000." He said that the Viet Cong's ability to strike at will across Vietnam had "finally shattered the mask of official illusion" that a military victory was in sight.

Mayor Daley was in the audience and welcomed the Senator's speech. He told RFK that he'd tried to warn LBJ that he couldn't hope to be re-elected unless he changed his Vietnam policy. The Senator replied that he thought winning the war had become a matter of honor for President Johnson, and Daley responded, "There comes a time when you must put your honor in your back pocket and face realities." In his conversation with the Senator, Daley also proposed setting up a presidential commission on Vietnam that would seek peace in the region and restore Democratic Party unity.

On February 10, the Senator wrote an op-ed piece for *The New York Times*, in which he again raised the issue of individuals feeling that they had no control over the events that affected them. He said that "we have far too little to say or do about these issues, which have swallowed the very substance of our lives...We seek to recapture our country...And that is what the 1968 elections must really be about."

In early March, RFK doubled down on his criticism of the administration's policy in Southeast Asia, calling out the corruption of the South Vietnamese government and declaring that Johnson's never-ending escalation of the war would not save the Saigon government from itself. Although he didn't state it publicly, by this time the Senator had privately concluded that the only answer in Vietnam was withdrawal. At this point, it seemed impossible that the Senator could support another term for Johnson, given their differences on not only the war but also domestic issues like poverty that were so important to RFK. Adam and others on his staff were now threatening to resign if the Senator agreed to campaign for LBJ.

On March 10, the Senator flew to Delano, California, to be with Cesar Chavez when he broke his twenty-five-day hunger strike. According to Peter Edelman, Chavez had refused to break the fast until Robert Kennedy came out to break it with him. In moving remarks that day, the Senator expressed his admiration for Cesar and his followers:

> "And when your children and grandchildren take their place in America—going to high school, and college, and taking good jobs at good pay—when you look at them, you will say, 'I did this. I was there, at the point of difficulty and danger.'

> "And though you may be old and bent from many
> years of labor, no man will stand taller than you when
> you say, 'I marched with Cesar.'"
> 'Viva la causa.'"

It was on the flight to Delano from Los Angeles that RFK told Peter and Ed Guthman that he had finally decided to run for President. If he were to have any control over the direction of the country, it was the one choice—the only choice—he could make.

Later, many would claim that the Senator only entered the race after the March 12 New Hampshire primary, where McCarthy managed to pull off a close second to Johnson. This was not true. Although RFK didn't formally announce his candidacy until March 16, he decided to run on March 10, two days before the New Hampshire primary. In fact, some of those close to the Senator believed he had actually made up his mind at a March 5 meeting in his Capitol Hill office with his brother Ted, Kenneth O'Donnell, and Fred Dutton.

At Ted Sorensen's urging, the Senator did make one last-ditch effort during a March 14 meeting with Secretary of Defense Clifford to get President Johnson to accept Chicago Mayor Daley's proposal to create a commission on Vietnam that would seek a path to peace there. Such a commission, RFK suggested, would obviate the need for his candidacy. But LBJ flat-out rejected the commission idea and then, contrary to the administration's agreement to keep the Senator's meeting with Clifford confidential, Johnson leaked word of it to the press, falsely telling them that Kennedy had issued an "ultimatum" to him.

Angered by the President's biased version of events, the Senator released his own statement, saying, "This incident reveals in the sharpest possible terms why the American people no longer believe the President...and why it is clear that the only way we are going to change our policy in Vietnam is to change administrations in Washington."

Actually, going into the meeting with Clifford, the Senator had very little hope that Daley's commission idea would be accepted by LBJ—or even work if it were accepted—but he had agreed to the meeting just to show that he had done everything he possibly could to change administration policy.

So, the die was cast.

After finally making the decision to run, the Senator would tell a friend, "I don't know what's going to happen, but at least I'm at peace with myself."

On March 16, 1968, standing in the same Caucus Room in the Russell Senate Office Building where his brother had announced his candidacy for President eight years earlier, the Senator stated:

> "I do not run for the Presidency merely to oppose any man, but to propose new policies."
>
> "I run because I am convinced that this country is on a perilous course and because I have such strong feelings about what must be done, and I feel that I'm obliged to do all I can."
>
> "I run to seek new policies—policies to close the gaps between black and white, rich and poor, young and old, in this country and around the world."
>
> "I run for the Presidency because I want the Democratic Party and the United States of America to stand for hope instead of despair, for the reconciliation of men instead of the growing risk of world war."
>
> "I run because it is now unmistakably clear that we can change these disastrous, divisive policies only by changing the men who make them. For the reality of recent events in Vietnam has been glossed over with illusions. The report of the Riot Commission has been largely ignored. The crisis in gold, the crisis in our cities, the crises on our farms and in our ghettoes, all have been met with too little and too late."

I had heard from my former colleagues in the Senator's office that the announcement was coming, but it was still a shock to the system to hear him actually commit to running. I was both excited and terrified. From the start, I had a terrible feeling of foreboding, but I tried to dismiss it from my mind. I've always been a worrier about things both large and small, so I chalked it up to my own neuroses rather than anything based in reality. There was always that danger, particularly for a Kennedy, but I assumed that the Senator had adequate security to protect him.

Little did I realize how wrong I was.

Office of

SENATOR ROBERT F. KENNEDY

New York

STATEMENT OF SENATOR ROBERT F. KENNEDY
Washington, D. C.
March 16, 1968

I am announcing today my candidacy for the Presidency of the United States.

I do not run for the Presidency merely to oppose any man, but to propose new policies. I run because I am convinced that this country is on a perilous course and because I have such strong feelings about what must be done that I am obliged to do all I can. I run to seek new policies--policies to close the gaps between black and white, rich and poor, young and old, in this country and around the world. I run for the Presidency because I want the Democratic Party and the United States of America to stand for hope instead of despair, for the reconciliation of men instead of the growing risk of world war.

I run because it is now unmistakably clear that we can change these disastrous, divisive policies only by changing the men who make them. For the reality of recent events in Vietnam has been glossed over with illusions. The report of the Riot Commission has been largely ignored. The crisis in gold, the crisis in our cities, the crises on our farms and in our ghettoes, all have been met with too little and too late.

No one who knows what I know about the extraordinary demands of the Presidency can be certain that any mortal can adequately fill it. But my service on the National Security Council during the Cuban Missile crisis, the Berlin crisis and the negotiations on Laos and on the Nuclear Test Ban Treaty have taught me something about both the uses and the limitations of military power, about the value of negotiations with allies and with enemies, about the opportunities and dangers which await our nation in the many corners of the globe to which I have traveled. As a member of the Cabinet and a member of the Senate I have seen the inexcusable and ugly deprivation which causes children to starve in Mississippi, black citizens to riot in Watts, young Indians to commit suicide on their reservations, and proud, able-bodied families to wait out their lives in empty idleness in Eastern Kentucky. I have talked and listened to the young people of our nation and felt their anger about the war they are sent to fight and the world they are about to inherit. In private talks and in public, I have tried in vain to alter our course in Vietnam before it further saps our spirit and our manpower, further raises the risks of wider war, and further destroys the country and people it was meant to save.

I cannot stand aside from the contest that will decide our nation's future. The remarkable New Hampshire campaign of Senator Eugene McCarthy has

RFK's announcement that he was running

For purely selfish reasons, I was also afraid that his entry into presidential politics would mean that those of us on his Senate staff who had been close to him for one reason or another would lose him —and that special relationship we had with him—amid the tumult and demands of a national campaign. We had been such a small group in his Capitol Hill office. He knew all of our names. We saw him on a daily basis when he was in Washington. We weren't just employees to him. We were his friends and his trusted allies—his support system.

But now, there would be a cast of thousands working for him across the country—people trying to grab a piece of him, longing to take our places. Would there be any part of him left for those of us who had loved him first? So I felt his announcement that day as a strange kind of loss—the loosening of my bond with him somehow. Three months later, I would feel this again even more intensely as thousands of people I had never met gathered to bury him.

President Johnson would write in his memoirs that he wasn't surprised by the Senator's announcement—that he was expecting it. The truth, of course, was that LBJ had been expecting it for the last three years. His paranoia about RFK knew no bounds.

Surprisingly, the reaction to the Senator's announcement was pretty bad and all too familiar—both in the press and in the public. It brought to the fore all the old accusations of opportunism and ruthlessness. Supporters of Eugene McCarthy were particularly harsh in their criticism of the Senator, reacting as if McCarthy had gained the exclusive right to run against Johnson simply because he was the first to announce.

RFK addressed the criticism the next day when he appeared on *Meet the Press*: "I don't think there is any question that if I had gone into the race at an earlier time that it would have been felt by the press and by others that this was a personality struggle between President Johnson and myself."

His skepticism about how the media would have treated his earlier entry into the presidential race was understandable. Throughout his public life, the Senator had always had something of a love-hate relationship with the press. Some journalists, who got to know him better during the presidential campaign, would eventually develop admiration and even affection for him, but for others, it seemed that he could never do anything right.

In particular, *The New York Times* had been a constant thorn in the Senator's side. From the moment that he became JFK's campaign manager back in 1960, they had attacked him for being "too immature and inexperienced for the job." They raised the same criticisms when President Kennedy appointed him Attorney General, and they refused to endorse him when he ran for Senator from New York, saying that he inspired "an uneasiness that is no less real because it is elusive and difficult to define." What did that even mean?

The *Times* seemed to view everything that RFK did through their preconceived notion that he was "ruthless and calculating." Following the June 1 McCarthy-Kennedy debate in California, a *New York Times* editorial argued that RFK lost the debate, saying that he "was less at ease because he seemed to be reining in his native aggressiveness and trying to be deliberately low-keyed."

He just couldn't win with these guys. At one point during the presidential primaries, he would quip that if he were really that ruthless, he would figure out a way to get even with *The New York Times*. But the reality was that he was damned if he did and damned if he didn't, so he decided to move ahead with the campaign and stop trying to explain himself to those who wouldn't be satisfied with anything he said or did.

Still, the road to the White House wasn't going to be easy for him, and he knew it. As he told Ted Sorensen, "I'm the only candidate who has ever united business, labor, liberals, Southerners, party bosses, and intellectuals. They're all against me!"

Chapter 20

The Campaign

Some men see things as they are, and say why. I
dream of things that never were, and say why not.
~ Robert F. Kennedy

MARCH

On March 18, the Senator delivered back-to-back maiden campaign speeches in Kansas—first at Kansas State University, followed by the University of Kansas. He was nervous about the kind of reception he would receive from what he anticipated would be a conservative crowd. But there was no need for worry. He was greeted by enthusiastic students at both schools.

In his speech at the University of Kansas, he spoke with passion about ending the Vietnam War, reminding the students about the unnamed commander of U.S. forces in Vietnam who had been quoted just the month before as saying that the destruction of a Vietnamese village was necessary in order to save it.

He went on to tell them that all Americans—not just the U.S. government—were part of the decisions being made in the war and that we all bore responsibility for what was happening there. He said, "I don't want to be part of a government, I don't want to be part of the United States, I don't want to be part of the American people, and have them write of us as they wrote of Rome: They made a desert and they called it peace."

He also spoke about the scourge of poverty and said, "Even if we act to erase material poverty, there is another greater task; it is to confront the poverty of satisfaction—purpose and dignity—that afflicts us all. Too much and for too long, we seemed to have surrendered personal excellence and community values in the mere accumulation of material things."

He then launched into a discourse about the Gross National Product (GNP) being used as a measure of American success. His remarks about the GNP were little noticed at the time, but he would repeat them again and again throughout the campaign:

"Our Gross National Product now is over $800 billion a year... [it] counts air pollution and cigarette advertising, and ambulances to clear our highways of carnage.

It counts special locks for our doors and the jails for the people who break them.

It counts the destruction of the redwood and the loss of our natural wonder in chaotic sprawl.

It counts napalm and counts nuclear warheads and armored cars for the police to fight the riots in our cities.

It counts Whitman's rifle and Speck's knife, and the television programs which glorify violence in order to sell toys to our children.

Yet the gross national product does not allow for the health of our children, the quality of their education, or the joy of their play.

It does not include the beauty of our poetry or the

strength of our marriages, the intelligence of our public debate, or the integrity of our public officials.

It measures neither our wit nor our courage, neither our wisdom nor our learning, neither our compassion nor our devotion to our country; it measures everything, in short, except that which makes life worthwhile.

And it can tell us everything about America except why we are proud that we are Americans."

Near the end of his speech, he also paraphrased those lines from George Bernard Shaw that would become a regular part of his campaign appearances: "Some men see things as they are and say, 'why?' I dream of things that never were and say, 'why not?'" That was always a signal to the campaign staff and the press that they should get ready to head out. Occasionally, the Senator would have fun with it, as he did at one stop in Nebraska on a rainy day, when he concluded his speech with, "As George Bernard Shaw said—run for the bus!"

On March 27, the Senator declared his intention to enter the Indiana primary, which was scheduled for May 7, even though his aides advised against it. His rationale: "If we can win in Indiana, we can win in every other state, and win when we go to the convention in August."

Then, on March 31, the unimaginable happened. Lyndon Johnson announced:

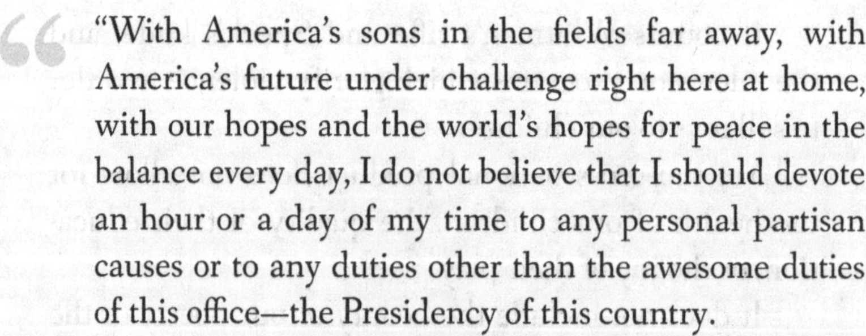

"With America's sons in the fields far away, with America's future under challenge right here at home, with our hopes and the world's hopes for peace in the balance every day, I do not believe that I should devote an hour or a day of my time to any personal partisan causes or to any duties other than the awesome duties of this office—the Presidency of this country.

Accordingly, I shall not seek, and I will not accept, the nomination of my party for another term as your President."

I will never forget that night. I was watching the President's speech live and, when he spoke that last sentence, I could hear loud cheers all over Berkeley. It was like a scene from the film *Network*, when people opened up their windows and started shouting, "I'm as mad as hell, and I'm not going to take this anymore." But instead, the students and others were cheering, as if with one voice, LBJ's decision to step aside.

When RFK learned about the President's withdrawal from the race, he wondered aloud whether his running had influenced Johnson's decision. My guess was that it did. One of the few things I imagine that LBJ couldn't bear was losing to another Kennedy, particularly his nemesis, "Bobby." At least by withdrawing, he wouldn't have to face that humiliation. In fact, he later told Doris Kearns Goodwin that RFK's decision to run for president was "the final straw."

Still, LBJ's withdrawal changed the dynamics of the presidential race in a significant but unknowable way. By removing himself, Johnson (and his unwinnable war) would no longer be a convenient target for either McCarthy or the Senator. Both men were uncertain what that would mean for them.

*Campaigning on March 24, 1968; Credit: Sven Walnum
Collection, JFK Library*

APRIL

On April 4, RFK launched his campaign in Indiana. In the afternoon, the senator spoke to a crowd in Muncie. Then, as he boarded a plane to fly to Indianapolis, he received word that the Reverend Martin Luther King, Jr., had been shot in Memphis. According to some on the plane with him, the Senator broke down in tears.

RFK was scheduled to speak that evening in an Indianapolis ghetto. Even before the shooting of MLK, the Mayor of Indianapolis had warned that it was too dangerous for him to go there. Now his aides suggested that he cancel the appearance. But the Senator refused. There was never any question in his mind that he would speak to the people there.

Adam had prepared some last-minute remarks for him to make, but the Senator brushed them aside; he knew what he was going to say. According to Adam, he did not write a word of the Senator's speech that night; RFK spoke completely extemporaneously—from the heart.

When he arrived, it was clear that most of the crowd had not yet heard the news about Dr. King, who it was now reported had died from his injuries. Historian John R. Bohrer would recount, "As Kennedy approached the back of the flatbed truck where he would speak, reporters noticed he was mouthing some words to himself. According to the *Boston Globe*, it appeared 'almost as if he were saying a silent prayer.' Others, like friend Kenneth O'Donnell, believed that in moments like this one, Kennedy would talk to his late brother, President John F. Kennedy. It is also possible that he was merely imagining what he would say."

Climbing onto the back of that flatbed truck, he opened with this: "I have bad news for you, for all of our fellow citizens, and people who love peace all over the world, and that is that Martin Luther King was shot and killed tonight." There were loud gasps and cries of "No, no" from those gathered there.

He went on to speak about violence and his own sense of loss when President Kennedy was killed. It was the first time that he had ever talked publicly about his brother's death, and he would never do so again.

"For those of you who are black and are tempted to be filled with hatred and mistrust at the injustice of such an act, against all white people, I would only say that I can also feel in my own heart the same kind of feeling. I had a member of my family killed, but he was killed by a white man.

But we have to make an effort in the United States; we have to make an effort to understand, to go beyond these rather difficult times."

He then quoted from Aeschylus:

"My favorite poet was Aeschylus. And he once wrote:
'Even in our sleep, pain which cannot forget
falls drop by drop upon the heart,

until, in our own despair,
against our will, comes wisdom
through the awful grace of God.'"

Adam Walinsky would later remark, "Now there isn't an American politician—I don't know if there's a human being—who at that moment with that crowd could have reached back into his own memory and heart and come up with those words. And that's why he was irreplaceable."

Then, in closing, the Senator said:

"What we need in the United States is not division; what we need in the United States is not hatred; what we need in the United States is not violence and lawlessness, but love, and wisdom, and compassion toward one another; and a feeling of justice toward those who still suffer within our country, whether they be white or whether they be black.

So I ask you tonight to return home, to say a prayer for the family of Martin Luther King—yes, it's true—but more importantly to say a prayer for our own country, which all of us love—a prayer for understanding and that compassion of which I spoke.

Let us dedicate ourselves to what the Greeks wrote so many years ago: to tame the savageness of man and make gentle the life of this world.

Let us dedicate ourselves to that, and say a prayer for our country and for our people."

News of King's death sparked outrage throughout the country, and there was rioting in several cities. But there was no violence that night in Indianapolis.

In respect for Dr. King, the Senator initially canceled all of his scheduled campaign appearances, but after being encouraged by several Black leaders, he decided to go ahead and speak the following day about "the mindless menace of violence." His words on April 5 to the City Club of Cleveland received far less attention than the remarks he had made in Indianapolis the night before, but this speech—in its radical simplicity—was perhaps one of the most moving of his entire career.

He spoke of violence this way:

> Whenever any American's life is taken by another American unnecessarily–whether it is done in the name of the law or in defiance of the law, by one man or by a gang, in cold blood or in passion, in an attack of violence or in response to violence – whenever we tear at the fabric of our lives which another man has painfully and clumsily woven for himself and his children – whenever we do this, then the whole nation is degraded.

He went on to talk passionately about another kind of violence, one that primarily afflicted the poor and the dispossessed—those about whom he cared so much:

> For there is another kind of violence, slower but just as deadly, destructive as the shot or the bomb in the night. This is the violence of institutions – indifference, inaction, and decay.
>
> This is the violence that afflicts the poor, that poisons relations between men because their skin has different colors.
>
> This is a slow destruction of a child by hunger, and schools without books, and homes without heat in the winter.
>
> This is the breaking of a man's spirit by denying

him the chance to stand as a father and as a man amongst other men.

Then finally, he closed with this, followed by a quote from Tennyson:

> Our lives on this planet are too short, the work to be done is too great, to let this spirit flourish any longer in this land of ours.
>
> Of course we cannot banish it with a program, nor with a resolution.
>
> But we can perhaps remember, if only for a time, that those who live with us are our brothers, that they share with us the same short moment of life, that they seek, as we do, nothing but the chance to live out their lives in purpose and happiness, winning what satisfaction and fulfillment they can.
>
> Surely this bond of common fate, this bond of common goals, can begin to teach us something.
>
> Surely we can learn, at the least, to look at those around us as our fellow men, and surely we can begin to work a little harder to bind up the wounds among us, and to become in our hearts brothers and countrymen once again.
>
> Tennyson wrote in Ulysses: that which we are, we are; one equal temper of heroic hearts, made weak by time and fate, but strong in will; to strive, to seek, to find, and not to yield.

The assassination of Dr. King was a terrible shock to all of us and, for me personally, it resurfaced feelings from November 22, 1963, that I thought I had thoroughly dealt with some five years earlier. I couldn't believe that it was happening all over again. The senselessness of such violence was beyond comprehension. It was also a stark reminder of the danger that the Senator himself faced with his high-profile run for the Presidency. Having read some of the threats on his life that were sent to our office on a regular basis, I felt particularly uneasy about his continued campaign for the White House. I knew there must be some deranged individual out there just waiting for the right moment to put a bullet in his head. But I tried as best I could to put those fears aside, to screw my courage, and get on with helping him to win the Democratic nomination. With King's death, there was even more urgency to elect someone who could heal the divisions in our country.

On April 16, the Senator would take time away from his Presidential campaign to travel to the Pine Ridge Indian Reservation in South Dakota. Campaign aides had urged the Senator not to go, telling him that it made no political sense. Getting there was also extremely difficult—the nearest airport was about an hour away and the roads were bad. In fact, RFK advisor Fred Dutton would later recall, "I told him, we're in a campaign, and he should knock off the Injuns." But the Senator was adamant about going ahead with the trip, and Fred's remarks infuriated him. He wrote a note back to Dutton making his feelings perfectly clear: "Those of you who think you're running my campaign don't love Indians the way I do. You're a bunch of bastards."

While he was at the reservation, RFK met with a ten-year-old Lakota Sioux boy named Christopher Pretty Boy, who had lost his parents in a car crash just the week before. RFK invited him and his sister to come spend the upcoming summer with his family at Hyannisport. Tragically, RFK was unable to keep that commitment, and Pretty Boy would also be dead within a year, reportedly from an automobile accident just like his parents.

Three days after his trip to Pine Ridge, on April 19, the Senator was scheduled to deliver a campaign speech at the University of San Francisco (USF) gymnasium. Norbie and I decided to go. I figured it might be the only time I would get to see the Senator before the California primary in June, since he was in and out of the state a lot campaigning for the Oregon and Indiana primaries as well. I made sure that we got there early so that we could nab some good seats.

When we arrived, I immediately spotted Jerry Bruno, who was working as one of RFK's advance men. He was in the gym making sure that everything was set up properly. I hadn't seen Jerry in many months, but thankfully he recognized me and we chatted for a while.

I asked him what route the Senator would be taking to get to the podium, since I wanted to find seats for us where he would be sure to pass by. Jerry indicated that he would be entering from the back and coming down the center aisle to the front of the gym. Fortunately, we were able to grab a couple of seats right on the aisle about ten rows back from the podium.

When the Senator finally arrived, most everyone in the place jumped to their feet, and as he came down the aisle, he was shaking hands with many of the people along the way. As he got to where I was standing, he suddenly stopped in his tracks. Smiling, he reached out his hand to me, and then, to my surprise (and delight), he leaned in and kissed me on the cheek. It was one of the first times that I didn't have to ask him for a kiss.

"What are you doing here, Donna?"

Laughing, I answered, "I came to see you, of course! I wouldn't miss it for anything!"

He squeezed my hand and looked me straight in the eyes. He seemed sad somehow, but that didn't make sense to me. He said, "Thanks for being here," squeezed my hand again, and then moved on.

I later learned that one of the most unpleasant confrontations of the entire Presidential campaign had happened just moments before. As he walked down the aisle shaking hands, a student apparently spat in the Senator's face and screamed, "Fascist pig!" At the time, I had no idea what had just happened. So when he kissed me, I was surprised—it wasn't something he would normally do in public (at least, not without my encouragement). But when I found out about the incident just moments before, it made more sense. I figured that at that point, he was probably just relieved to see a familiar face in the audience. According to Arthur Schlesinger, the Senator later recounted the spitting incident to a friend with "hurt disbelief." So, I was glad that I could provide some brief comfort to him after that dreadful encounter.

Unfortunately, however, when the Senator got up to the podium to speak, there was heckling from an organized group in the audience, with more shouts of "fascist pig." They refused to let him speak, so he finally discarded his prepared text and opened it up to questions, which didn't go much better for him. Sadly, it turned out that a good number of the ill-mannered troublemakers in the crowd were actually from Berkeley. Many of them were members of the left-wing Peace and Freedom Party, which at the time was aligned with the Black Panther Party and was supporting Senator McCarthy.

At one point, a notorious activist in the Bay Area, Jefferson Poland, who was founder of the "Sexual Freedom League" and a contributor to the underground newspaper *Berkeley Barb*, rushed the podium, shouting, "Stop killing black people, you murderers, you murderers... you're always killing black people in Oakland and San Francisco!" It wasn't clear at whom his outrage was aimed, since there were also several local San Francisco politicians on the dais with RFK, but Poland was dragged away by security.

It didn't seem to stop the disruptions, however. The hecklers refused to give the Senator a chance to speak—shouting out epithets and chanting "Free Huey Newton" (Black Panthers co-founder Huey Newton was on trial at that time for murdering an Oakland police officer). Another one of the protestors managed to make it down to the front, just below the podium, and had to be taken away by security as well.

The Senator tried to respond to questions as best he could, but it was extremely difficult. At one point, he was asked whether, as President, he would grant amnesty to deserters from the Vietnam War. He said no—he had no plans to give amnesty to either deserters or to those who went to Canada to avoid the draft, pointing out that young black men were carrying more than their fair share of the burden of military service in Vietnam. His answer drew boos from a good number of people in the audience. He tried to explain further but was shouted down.

While it was part of the campaign strategy to put the Senator in front of unfriendly but polite crowds, this was different. Many in the USF audience were not just unfriendly, but rude as well and determined not to let him speak.*

It was all extremely chaotic that evening, and I felt really badly for the Senator. Frankly, he seemed a bit shell-shocked, and I was as well. But it was quite obvious that the protests had been carefully planned and orchestrated by a group bent on totally disrupting the event.

I would have liked to speak with him afterwards, but under the circumstances, that was also impossible. When it was all over, he was whisked away from the gymnasium for his own safety. Some of the protestors outside actually threw pebbles and rotten apple cores at his motorcade as he was leaving.

Just a week later, the Senator encountered another openly hostile audience when he spoke to medical and nursing students at Indiana University. In his speech to them, he talked about the need for neighborhood clinics and for reforms in the country's medical system to make care accessible to all.

When he opened the floor up to questions, he was asked where the money would come from for his programs and, in his usual blunt manner, he answered: "From you." He returned to the theme of how minorities and poor people were carrying the burden of military service in Vietnam, saying this:

> I look around this room and I don't see many black faces who will become doctors...You don't see many

___

* *As Joe Dolan said, "He was at his best before a polite but hostile audience on a Q and A. That was where he was best as a campaigner..."*

people coming out of the ghettos or off the Indian reservations to medical school.

You are the privileged ones here. It's easy to sit back and say it's the fault of the federal government, but it's our responsibility too.

It's our society, not just our government, that spends twice as much on pets as on the poverty program.

It's the poor who carry the major burden of the struggle in Vietnam. You sit here as white medical students, while black people carry the burden of fighting in Vietnam.

Unlike his event at the University of San Francisco, by the end of his appearance in front of the Indiana medical students, he seemed to have won over the support of a good number of them. It proved prophetic.

RFK flyer—Indiana

MAY

Despite predictions at the outset of the campaign that he would be defeated in Indiana, the Senator actually won the state's primary on May 7, garnering 42 percent of the vote and capturing 56 of its 63 delegates to the Democratic National Convention. Looking at the results, RFK began to believe that he really had a chance to build a coalition of Blacks and working-class whites. He had not only won the majority of Indiana's largest cities (by an overwhelming 85 percent in Black precincts), but he had also carried an impressive number of the largest counties that had gone for George Wallace in the 1964 presidential election.

He took the Nebraska primary on May 14 as well, with 52 percent of the vote. But Oregon would be a different story entirely.

Unfortunately for the Senator, what had proved to be his base of supporters in Indiana ("the have-not coalition") simply did not exist in Oregon. African Americans made up less than one percent of the population, and as RFK would say, the state was "like one giant suburb." In fact, Oregon was far better suited to the likes of Eugene McCarthy. And even though the polls showed RFK slightly ahead, in the waning days of the campaign there, the Senator made the fateful decision not to accept McCarthy's challenge to debate. It would prove to be a deathblow to any hopes of victory there.

On May 28, RFK lost the Oregon primary. It was a real blow and marked the first time that a Kennedy had ever lost an election. He tried not to show the depth of his disappointment, quipping that he would reorganize his campaign: "I have decided to send Freckles home."

So, it was on to California, which became a must-win for him.

Since Berkeley was pretty much a lost cause from the get-go (McCarthy was the clear favorite among students), I had been traveling into San Francisco to volunteer for the Senator's campaign since early spring. Getting there had been difficult, since those were pre–BART (Bay Area Rapid Transit) days. Norbie had a car, and we would sometimes drive into the Market Street headquarters together. Further complicating matters, I was finishing up my studies at Berkeley and was scheduled to graduate in June, so I didn't have a whole lot of free time. I figured that as soon as I graduated, I could join the campaign full time. Although Norbie and I had talked about getting married in September, I was still on the fence about it and reluctant to commit to a specific date.

The truth was that, given the politics of the region, all of Northern California was a hard sell for RFK's campaign. It would ultimately be his showing in Los Angeles County that would put him over the top in California on Election Day. He beat McCarthy in L.A. by some 120,000 votes, with Blacks, Latinos, and working-class whites providing him with large margins.

My RFK campaign staff badge

JUNE

RFK was determined not to make the same mistake in California that he had made in Oregon. He agreed to debate McCarthy, and the match was scheduled for June 1 in the Bay Area. All the political pundits predicted that it would be the decisive factor in determining the winner of the primary. Since the Senator would be staying at the

Fairmont Hotel the night of the debate, I got together with some of the staff for a watch party at the hotel that evening. Of course, we all thought the Senator had won the debate outright, but the press characterized it as a draw. Even so, RFK had done what he needed to do in order to beat expectations that McCarthy would come out on top.

While I was at the hotel that night, I talked to Angie about the possibility of spending a few moments with the Senator the next morning before he left for a rally in Orange County. I told her that my fiancé was eager to meet RFK. Although the Senator was planning to return to the Bay Area the following day, it would be an extremely brief stop during a last whirlwind swing through California, so it was unlikely that I could see him then. As always, his schedule was jam-packed, but Angie assured me that she would try to arrange something. Fortunately—as I knew she would—Angie came through.

So, on the morning of June 2, I returned to the Fairmont Hotel. I was about to begin final exams at Berkeley and had decided against going to the election night victory party on June 4 at the Ambassador Hotel in Los Angeles (although I did arrange for my parents to join Provi there), so I knew this was probably the last time that I would see the Senator before he headed East again after the California primary.

Norbie and I went up to his hotel suite on the top floor of the Fairmont that morning, and we were ushered into a room where the Senator was talking to a few campaign aides. I think Fred Dutton was there, but I can't recall who else. The moment we entered, they all retreated to the other side of the room.

I remember that the Senator was seated in a chair next to a window that overlooked San Francisco Bay, but he got up when I came through the door. He looked more tired than I had ever seen him. There were deep lines around his eyes, and his fingers and palms were swollen and scratched from shaking so many hands. A friend of mine who worked in the campaign, and whose job was to help the Senator navigate through the crowds, said when he pulled on his hand, it felt like the skin was actually going to come off. It was obvious that the campaign had really taken a toll on him, but he nevertheless seemed energized.

Recognizing how extremely busy he was, we declined his offer to sit down. I explained that I just wanted him to meet my fiancé and to wish him good luck in the primary.

I introduced Norbie, and they shook hands. I kissed him on the cheek "for good luck," and he looked directly at me with those piercing blue eyes. In that moment, they seemed an even deeper blue than usual, perhaps in contrast to his tanned and weather-beaten face. Seeing how exhausted he was, I wanted to take him by the hand and lead him to some safe place where he could rest and regain his strength. He seemed so fragile and vulnerable.

He asked if we had set a date for the wedding yet, and I said no—that I was hoping to work on the campaign once he won the nomination, so the marriage would have to wait. What I did not say in that moment—what I hadn't even told Norbie—was that, more and more, I was thinking of *not* getting married; that I had begun to have other ideas about what to do with the rest of my life. I would join the campaign. I would travel the country, and then later, I would set off on my own to see the world. I would go to work in the White House or join the Peace Corps. I would live on a beach in Bali and write a novel about unrequited love. I would march with Cesar. I would go to law school and become a high-paid criminal lawyer. The one thing I would not do was get married...at least not now, anyway. But I kept up the subterfuge.

Digging myself in deeper, I asked the Senator if he would come to the wedding whenever it was. He laughed and said enthusiastically, "Of course, I will!" as if I had just inquired, "Will you have another cup of coffee?"

We chatted with him for a short time longer, and I asked him to inscribe his book, *To Seek a Newer World*, to my parents. I'd brought it with me and intended to give it to my dad as a Father's Day present.

Then, knowing how much he had going on, we started to leave.

Before I went out the door, though, I turned to look at him one more time, and the last thing I said was, "Be careful in L.A. There are a lot of nuts down there, you know." He just brushed it off and waved goodbye, smiling a weary smile. I blew him a final kiss.

Then we left, and I never saw him again.

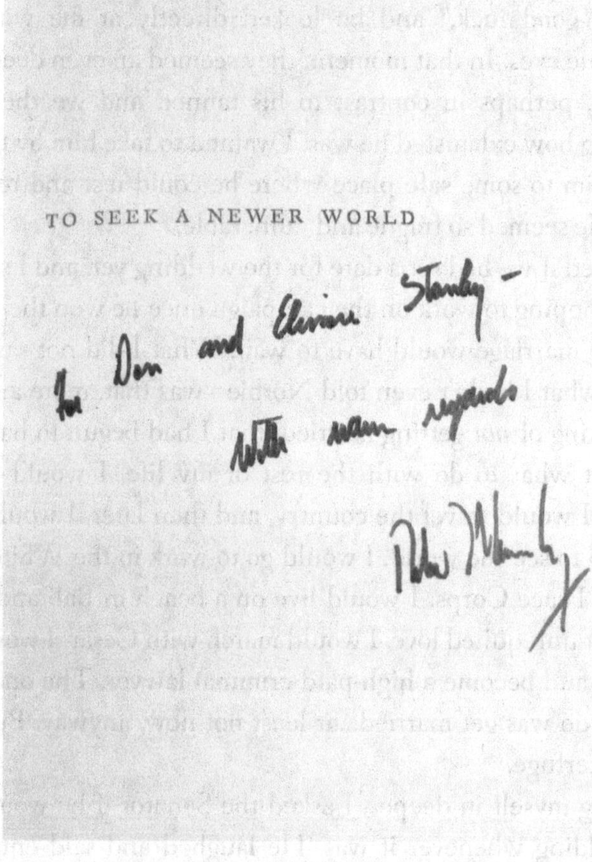

Inscription to my parents — June 2, 1968

RFK pushed himself to his limits during his 1968 presidential campaign; credit: Sven Walnum Collection — JFK Library

Following our meeting, the Senator flew south to attend a rally at Bolsa Grande High School in Garden Grove, before making a spur-of-the-moment decision to take his kids to Disneyland. I was glad to see that he was finally getting in some R&R.

The California primary was just two days away.

On the day before the election, RFK flew more than 1,200 miles —from Los Angeles to San Francisco, then back to Southern California again—appearing in rallies in Long Beach, Watts, and San Diego. The schedule was extremely punishing.

While in San Francisco's Chinatown, a firecracker exploded near him. It sounded like gunshots. The noise was loud enough that Ethel reacted—crouching down in the car—and people in the crowd actually ducked. But the Senator didn't flinch at all, continuing to wave and shake hands.

In San Diego, he got sick to his stomach in the middle of a speech and had to sit down on some stairs next to the stage, burying his head in his hands. He was close to complete collapse.

Chapter 21

The Assassination

Things fall apart; the centre cannot hold;
Mere anarchy is loosed upon the world,
The blood-dimmed tide is loosed, and everywhere
The ceremony of innocence is drowned...
~ W.B. Yeats

At last, it was June 4—primary election day in California. I would cast my first vote ever for the man that I adored.

The Senator spent the morning and afternoon at director John Frankenheimer's house in Malibu. Frankenheimer later drove RFK to the Ambassador Hotel. During the day, the Senator's son—12-year-old David Kennedy—nearly drowned while he was swimming in the Pacific Ocean just outside of Frankenheimer's beach house. Apparently, David had been knocked over by a wave and was trapped on the bottom by the undertow. RFK managed to dive under the water and rescue him, scraping and bruising his own forehead in the process. Frankenheimer gave the Senator some theatrical makeup to hide the bruise, as he would be appearing on television hours later. In fact, the Senator sat down with NBC's Sander Vanocur and CBS's Roger Mudd for interviews in the evening, when the results of the primary were still unclear.

I kept thinking all day long how I should have flown down to L.A. for the victory party, but now it was too late. Instead, Norbie and I planned to camp out in my apartment, studying for finals and watching the election returns.

Late that night, the Senator was leading the California primary with 46.3% of the vote to McCarthy's 41.8%. It was good enough for him to claim victory, so shortly after midnight, in the early morning hours of June 5, he headed down to the ballroom of the Ambassador Hotel to do just that. I was jubilant seeing the Senator give his victory speech. "We are a great country," he said. "An unselfish country and a compassionate country. I intend to make that my basis for running."

Then there was that final upbeat exhortation: "Now it's on to Chicago, and let's win there." The words would haunt me for the rest of my life.

A few minutes later, it became clear that something was terribly wrong. At 12:15 a.m., shots rang out. There was pandemonium in the ballroom, and we heard the words coming from the TV: "The Senator has been shot!"

At that instant, I knew it was all over. I started jumping up and down on the bed, screaming uncontrollably—"They've killed him! They've killed him!" Norbie tried to calm me down, but I was inconsolable.

I sensed his spirit leave, and I knew his life was over. I felt like mine had ended that night, too. It was the beginning of my long descent into hell.

In the days that followed, I began to engage in magical thinking about how I might have prevented the Senator from getting shot if I had been there. It was insane, of course. What could I have done that all the others with the Senator that night were unable to do? But it bothered me that I had been so far away that night—that I hadn't somehow managed to get down to L.A. to be with him on the last night of his life.

The next day was a complete blur. Jerry Bruno would later say that he was able to go in to see the Senator at Good Samaritan Hospital not long before he died. Ethel was holding his hand, and the breathing bag was barely moving. He said that "with all the medical stuff, it wasn't really him," so he left and didn't want to go back.

RFK was still alive, but everyone knew it was hopeless. Although dazed, I began to make plans. There was no time for grief. I knew that somehow I had to attend his funeral—even though it meant that I would miss two final exams at Berkeley and wouldn't graduate on time.

I spoke to my parents, who had been at the Ambassador that night. In fact, they were watching the Senator's victory speech in Provi's hotel room on the fifth floor when it happened. She was in room 507, just down the hall from the Senator's private suite—room 511. Earlier that evening, they had spent time in RFK's campaign suite (room 516), and my mother told me that she had talked for a long time with Annie Glenn, John Glenn's wife.

Provi's room key envelope with my mother's handwriting

Following the shooting, they weren't allowed to leave the hotel, so my mother had volunteered to answer phone calls in the campaign suite. At one point, a *New York Times* reporter called, wanting to know if anyone there had also witnessed President Kennedy being shot in Dallas. She called out the reporter's question, and a voice came from somewhere inside the room: "Tell them yes...and tell them to go to hell!" Later, she helped serve breakfast to the police. "How terrible," she murmured as she passed a plate of scrambled eggs to one of the uniformed young men. "Just a man killed," he replied to her disbelief. "We see it all the time."

Finally, they were free to go. They were recruited to help drive some of the campaign staff to the VIP airport, where chartered planes waited to fly them back to Washington. Provi had left the hotel to help tend to some of the Senator's children. Still wearing their campaign buttons, my parents stopped for coffee at one of the stands at the airport. "How much?" they inquired. There was a pause. The man behind the counter eyed the campaign buttons and streamers and their tear-stained faces. "No charge," he told them. And so they returned to their home—a small eternity since the day before, when they had left.

I spent a good part of June 5 and June 6 meeting with my professors, explaining to them how I had been a staffer for the Senator and —considering how distraught I was—I would be unable to take the final exams as scheduled. Both of my professors agreed to give me an "Incomplete" in their courses and permit me to take the examinations later that summer. My parents generously offered to buy me a round-trip ticket to Washington, D.C., for the funeral.

Nearly 26 hours after he was shot, the Senator died. His death was formally announced fifteen minutes later by Frank Mankiewicz —still wearing a Kennedy campaign pin on his lapel. His statement was short: "Senator Robert Francis Kennedy died at 1:44 am today, June 6, 1968. With Senator Kennedy at the time of his death were his wife, Ethel, his sisters Mrs. Stephen Smith, Mrs. Patricia Lawford, his brother-in-law, Mr. Stephen Smith, and his sister-in-law, Mrs. John F. Kennedy. He was 42 years old."

Jacqueline Kennedy, who spoke to Frank afterward, would talk to him about death—how the Catholic Church and Black churches understood death. She told him how, at Dr. King's funeral, she had looked around at the faces there and had realized that Black people knew death, that they saw it all the time and were ready for it. Then she said something to Frank that he found absolutely chilling: "Well, now we know death, don't we, you and I? As a matter of fact, if it weren't for the children, we'd welcome it."

That afternoon, the Senator's body would be loaded onto an Air Force jet for the flight to New York's La Guardia Airport. A requiem Mass was being planned for June 8 at St. Patrick's Cathedral in New York City, with burial to follow at Arlington. The plane—with *United States of America* emblazoned on the side—was provided by President Johnson. Jackie, who was one of the family members who accompanied the body, only agreed to board the plane after being assured that it was not the same Air Force One that had transported her and her husband's body from Dallas back to Washington on November 22, 1963.

Despite providing transport for the Senator's body, earlier in the day President Johnson—in a final act of spite toward the Senator—had telephoned Secretary of Defense Clark Clifford, demanding to know if RFK had "the right" to be buried at Arlington. Clifford would later recall that the President seemed to be searching for some way to deny the family's request. Even though LBJ could have blocked the Senator's burial there, he finally gave in to Clifford's advice not to do such a "cruel" thing.

Throughout the entire flight from Los Angeles to New York, Senator Edward Kennedy remained by his brother's casket at the front of the airplane. The widow of Martin Luther King, Jr., Coretta Scott King, was also aboard the flight, and at one point the three widows—Jackie, Ethel, and Mrs. King—huddled together in conversation for five or ten minutes.

As the airplane carrying RFK's body crossed the country, I learned from my friends in the Senator's office that the Kennedy family was chartering another plane the next day in the late afternoon to carry staff from D.C.'s National Airport to New York. They were in desperate need of people to work on the funeral arrangements there. I wanted to help—to do this one last thing for him.

Unfortunately, there were no flights from the Bay Area to National Airport that would get me there on time. So instead, I got on a plane to Washington's Dulles Airport that was scheduled to arrive about two hours before the chartered flight was set to depart. It was at least a 45-minute drive from Dulles to National, so it would be a close call whether I could get there in time.

When I arrived at Dulles, I jumped on a shuttle to National Airport. I explained the situation to my fellow passengers, and they were kind enough to let the driver drop me off at the charter terminal first. Incredibly, I made the Kennedy plane with about five or ten minutes to spare.

Upon arriving at La Guardia in New York City, we were taken by bus to the Joseph P. Kennedy offices in the Pan Am Building on Park Avenue, where preparations were being made for the funeral the next day. It was going to require an all-night effort to get everything done. Our work involved mostly sending out telegrams to invitees and fielding telephone inquiries about the funeral and the burial. As I recall, the Senator's brother-in-law, Stephen Smith, was in charge of all the activities that evening. Coffee and sandwiches were brought in at some point to keep us going.

During the night, several aides and friends of the Senator's came by the offices. I specifically remember that John Tunney—Ted Kennedy's former roommate at the University of Virginia Law School—stopped by very late that night or in the early morning hours, and I spoke with him briefly. At the time, he was a Congressman but would successfully run for Senator from California two years later at the age of 36. Ted Kennedy came by the operation at one point too, but I don't remember seeing him. Separate rooms to take care of the different aspects of the funeral had been set up—the phones, invitations, the church, the train, and the Arlington burial. I was in the invitation room and manned the phones for a while as well. Understandably, it was all pretty chaotic.

The first big snag had to do with the invitations. Originally, telegrams were sent out as invitations, but apparently a lot of people didn't receive them because they weren't at home. Then it was decided that we would switch to admission tickets that people could pick up at various campaign offices. I understand that it got pretty bad at some of the ticket distribution sites, with people demanding more tickets than they were entitled to.

We worked through the night, and sometime around 5 a.m., after St. Patrick's was finally closed to the public, some of us made our way over there to pay our respects to the Senator, who was lying in state. It was eerily quiet and mostly dark in the cathedral, with lights along the aisle leading to the casket. It felt quite surreal. I still hadn't accepted the fact that he was really gone. As I sat in a pew a few rows back, staring at the casket, I wanted to scream. I was angry with a God who would permit him to die.

We stayed for about 20 minutes at St. Patrick's and then headed over to the hotel, where the Kennedy family had booked rooms for the staff to sleep. There were three of us women in one room with a double bed. We alternated between sleeping on the floor and in the bed...but the truth was—despite our physical and emotional exhaustion—we didn't really sleep at all.

The funeral service was scheduled to begin at 10:00 that morning, and we would be manning the buses to Penn Station afterward, so we would have to get back over to St. Patrick's in just a couple of hours. Even though we weren't able to sleep at all, lying down and resting for a while was better than nothing.

We arrived at St. Patrick's Cathedral at about 8:00 a.m. Each of us was assigned a specific bus and given instructions on what to do, as well as a list of people who had been invited to travel on the buses to Penn Station, where everyone would board the funeral train. It wasn't clear who initially came up with the idea of a train—apparently someone in the Kennedy family—but it made a lot of sense, given the number of people that had to be transported from New York City to Washington for the burial. Plus, the Senator had loved whistle-stop campaigning, feeling it brought him closer to the people. Now he would be close to them again during the journey to his final resting place.

Once the services in St. Patrick's began, I was able to go inside and watch most of it. I remember in particular listening to Ted Kennedy's eulogy as I stood leaning against one of the pillars in the Cathedral. I was still in a state of shock, and it all seemed unreal—like an Ingmar Bergman film.

"My brother need not be idealized, or enlarged in death beyond what he was in life, but be remembered simply as a good and decent man, who saw wrong and tried to right it, saw suffering and tried to heal it, saw war and tried to stop it.

"Those of us who loved him and who take him to his rest today pray that what he was to us and what he wished for others will someday come to pass for all the world."

"As he said many times, in many parts of this nation, to those he touched and who sought to touch him: Some men see things as they are and say why. I dream things that never were and say why not."

Just before the conclusion of the service, I returned outside to get ready to man the bus to which I'd been assigned. I would be checking the credentials of people boarding. It wasn't difficult work, except for the fact that there were a few folks who didn't have the proper credentials but insisted that they were entitled to get on the bus anyway. The supervisor of the operation had a master guest list that we could check in case a person wasn't on our list for the bus. Some people would be showing the telegrams, and others would have received the admission tickets that were supposed to indicate whether they were invited not only to the Mass but to the funeral train as well.

"Do you have any idea who I am?" was a common refrain. Rather than argue with them, I would refer these cases to the staffer who was supervising to check the master guest list. It wasn't that we were being officious; it was just that space on the buses (and on the train) was extremely limited, so letting someone board who wasn't supposed to be there meant someone else might be denied a spot. Plus, a lot of VIPs would be on the train, so security was another consideration.

> **Requiem Mass**
>
> **for**
>
> # Robert Francis Kennedy
>
> **ST. PATRICK'S CATHEDRAL**
>
> **Saturday, June Eighth**
>
> **Nineteen Hundred and Sixty-Eight**
>
> **at 10:00 A.M.**
>
> **ADMIT ONE**

Admission ticket to the Requiem Mass

ROBERT FRANCIS KENNEDY
November 20, 1925 — June 6, 1968

✝

Dear God,
Please take care of him who tried to take care of yours.

"Come, my friends,
'Tis not too late to seek a newer world"
—Tennyson, Ulysses

"Aeschylus wrote: 'In our sleep, pain that cannot forget falls drop by drop upon the heart and in our own despair, against our will, comes wisdom through the awful grace of God.'

"What we need in the United States . . . is love and wisdom and compassion toward one another, and a feeling of justice toward those who still suffer within our own country, whether they be white or they be black.

"Let us dedicate ourselves to what the Greeks wrote so many years ago: to tame the savageness of man and make gentle the life of the world. Let us dedicate ourselves to that, and say a prayer for our country and for our people."

—Robert F. Kennedy
*Extemporaneous remarks on the death of
Martin Luther King, Indianapolis, Indiana
April 4, 1968*

RFK Mass card

WESTERN UNION
TELEGRAM

512P EDT JUN 7 68
 CT AHD515 AHZ20 AHZ20 PDB AH NEW YORK NY 7 NFT
RUSH DLVRY BY MSGR CHGS GNTEED

 YOU ARE INVITED TO ATTEND A REQUIEM MASS IN MEMORY OF ROBERT
FRANCIS KENNEDY AT ST PATRICKS CATEDRAL IN NEW YORK CITY ON
SATURDAY, JUNE 8, 1968 AT 10:00 AM PLEASE ENTER THROUGH THE
FIFTH AVENUE ENTRANCE BY 9:30 AM
INTERMENT WILL BE AT ARLINGTON CEMETERY, ARLINGTON, VIRGINIA,
AT 5:30 PM
YOU ARE WELCOME TO TRAVEL ON THE FUNERAL TRAIN FROM NEW YORK
TO WASHINGTON. BUSES TO PENNSYLVANIA STATION WILL LEAVE THE
FIFTH AVENUE SIDE OF THE CATHEDRAL IMMEDIATELY FOLLOWING THE
MASS.
 THIS TELEGRAM WILL ADMIT ONLY THE PERSON OR PERSONS TO WHOM

WESTERN UNION
TELEGRAM

IT IS ADDRESSED AND MUST BE RETAINED AND PRESENTED FOR IDENTIFICATION
WHENEVER IT IS REQUESTED
 THE KENNEDY FAMILY.

Telegram to funeral invitees

After loading up the buses, we took off for Penn Station. We finally arrived there and proceeded to climb aboard the funeral train for the long trip back to Washington.

Once on the train, I remember that Coretta Scott King came through our car early on. I was able to talk to her briefly and express my condolences on the loss of her husband just a couple of months before. What a lovely and gracious woman—so composed—and I was honored to meet her.

Later on, Ethel Kennedy also came down the aisle with her son Joe to greet everyone. I couldn't believe her strength in doing so after all she'd been through. She just spoke to me briefly—thanking me for being there. And Joe was quite the grown-up young man that day...no longer the pesky 12-year-old who used to come by the office and break the Senator's autopen signature machine on a regular basis.

Daniel Patrick Moynihan (later to become Senator from New York) was holding an Irish wake in the club car, with many of the Kennedy old-timers getting drunk and telling funny stories about the Senator. I stopped in for just a few moments. While I understood the value of a wake in dealing with grief, I just wasn't ready yet to laugh about the Senator, and I didn't want to drink. With no sleep and with my emotions running high, I was afraid of what would happen if I added alcohol to the mix.

A couple of other memories stand out in my mind from the train. I remember that Jack Paar was weeping uncontrollably. (I had become acquainted with his daughter, Randy, when she worked in the Senator's office one summer, but I don't think she was with her father on the train that day.) I didn't doubt the sincerity of his feelings, but somehow it seemed inappropriate when members of the Senator's own family were managing to keep their emotions in check. But then I remembered how Jack Paar always seemed to be completely self-absorbed, even on *The Tonight Show*, so I wasn't really surprised. Secondly, there was some grumbling about Peter Lawford, who was already inebriated when he boarded the train.

But seeing the thousands lined up along the tracks was incredibly moving—people in tears holding their homemade, handwritten signs ("Goodbye Bobby"), waving American flags, throwing flowers at the train, and singing "The Battle Hymn of the Republic." There were young boys in their Little League baseball uniforms, Black mothers holding their babies in their arms, groups of nuns clutching their rosaries, uniformed firemen and policemen. The people alongside the tracks were Robert Kennedy's kind of people.

The ones sitting inside the train, I wasn't so sure about. I don't know who made the final decisions on the guest list, but in my opinion, a lot of these people were not the sort that RFK would have wanted to be there for his final send-off. Most had probably never even met the Senator, or if they had, they were not people he would remember. As Jeff Greenfield would later remark, they were "the kind of people...who drink all the liquor and eat all the food and really don't know why they are there."

To be honest, I didn't recognize most of those onboard the train. I imagine some were among the thousands involved in his brief Presidential campaign. But there were also those do-you-know-who-I-am types who wanted to be there because they thought they were important and that "anybody who was anybody" was invited. And then there were the Manhattan socialites with their little black Dior dresses who simply had to attend because it was the social event of the year. Onboard, they would gossip about who they'd seen lunching at the Russian Tea Room the week before or gleefully talk about who hadn't made the cut to be on the train. I couldn't help but think that these were the same people the Senator had disparaged when he was campaigning in Indiana—the New York liberals who "spend their time worrying about not being invited to the important parties, or seeing psychiatrists, or... [who] are bored with all their affluence."

As for me, I was mostly in a daze as I sat there—nearly catatonic —still unable to fully process what had happened. Since the day before, I hadn't shed a single tear. I suspected that I would never be able to feel anything again. Most of the time, I spent just gazing out the window at the throngs of people. It seemed that the journey would never end, and in some ways I think we all kind of wished that it wouldn't. Nobody was ready to accept the finality of it all—the ultimate fracturing of our reality. As Dave Powers said, the train should "just keep going...on and on, right off into the Pacific Ocean."

But then finally, after all those endless hours, we were nearing our dreaded destination. Once we passed Baltimore, the mood of those onboard took on a decidedly more somber tone with the realization that the hour of his burial was approaching. It was already dark when we arrived at Union Station in Washington. We got off the train and boarded buses that would take us to Arlington Cemetery.

Passing through the streets of D.C., the memories began to emerge from the shadows and flood my brain. I could visualize the Senator sitting in the front seat of his convertible, heading home from work on a warm summer evening. I could picture him walking across the grass from the Capitol to his office on a bright spring day, his hands shoved deep in his pockets.

Each corner spoke to me in tones of loss.

Then, crossing the bridge to Arlington, there were all the memories of when I first came to Washington. It was the same bridge I had walked over during the many trips that I had made to visit President Kennedy's grave. And now I had come to bury his brother.

We finally arrived just below the gravesite. Someone had phoned ahead to arrange for thousands of candles to be handed out to the mourners once we got to Arlington, so as we exited the buses, we were all given small white candles to hold as we climbed up the hill to where the Senator would be laid to rest—not far from the President. It would be the first nighttime burial in Arlington Cemetery's history.

The service was very short, and then came my turn to say goodbye. I couldn't believe it. I had seen him less than a week before. I had kissed his cheek. And now I kissed the casket that held his body.

Following the gravesite service, several of us were milling around on the street below, waiting for transportation to arrive that would take us back into central Washington. Standing next to me was Joe Dolan and his wife, Marti.

I turned to Joe and said, "It's all over now, isn't it, Joe?" He nodded his head in agreement.

"Yes, it's over."

In that moment, it suddenly hit me—the realization that the Senator was really gone—that I would never see him again. I broke down in tears, and Joe—always ready with a shoulder to cry on—wrapped his arms around me and comforted me.

Other than Joe, I saw none of my friends from the Senator's office. Later, I was told by someone who ran into Adam that night that he was in complete shock. He said to her, "Don't cry. You know we had something; we were part of something very special. Very few people were as lucky. It makes it harder for us now, but in time, it will make it easier." Nearly sixty years on, I am still waiting for it to get easier.

The next day, Jay and I drove up to the gravesite one last time. I would not return for another six years.

In the evening, I caught my flight back to California, not knowing what I would do with the rest of my life.

With Jay—June 9, 1968—still wearing that white dress

Chapter 22

The Aftermath

Tho' much is taken, much abides; and tho'
We are not now that strength which in old days
Moved earth and heaven, that which we are, we are;
One equal temper of heroic hearts,
Made weak by time and fate, but strong in will
To strive, to seek, to find, and not to yield.
~ Alfred, Lord Tennyson

I spent the remaining summer months in Berkeley finishing up my studies and taking those final exams that I'd missed. I would graduate in September, but it seemed an afterthought. There was no graduation ceremony—the school would simply send my diploma to me in the mail. Norbie and I planned to get married on September 14. Yes, I had decided to go ahead with the wedding. The truth was that I needed someone to take care of me. I was a mess. In the period of two months, I'd lost more than 20 pounds. I was depressed all of the time. God knows what I might have done if left to my own devices.

Provi and my friend Jay flew out to Los Angeles for my wedding. It was good to be with them again. I had missed seeing Provi during the funeral. She had been on board the train but had spent the entire time in the front cars helping out Ethel and Jackie and the children.

She told me how distraught Jackie was following the funeral. Provi had been with her in August up at Hyannisport. The former First Lady was drinking too much and would play the Engelbert Humperdinck song "A Man Without Love" over and over again at night as she sat alone in her house, chain-smoking cigarettes. A couple of months later, she would marry Aristotle Onassis. I guess, like me, she needed someone to take care of her, particularly now that "Bobby" was gone too. She was extremely concerned about her safety and that of her children. After RFK's assassination, Jackie became convinced that all the Kennedys were now targets and that only Onassis had the kind of money that could secure her safety and that of her children. When the Senator was alive, he reportedly opposed the marriage and wanted Jackie to wait, but now there was no reason not to go ahead with it.

My mood at the time of my own wedding can best be understood by what I said to my father as he prepared to walk me down the aisle. I turned to him and quipped, "Well, this marriage won't last." Alarmed, he said, "It's not too late, you know—you can still call it off." He stopped in his tracks and looked me directly in the eyes.

"You don't have to do this, you know," he said.

"Yes, I do," I replied.

I don't know why I chose that moment to finally let my father know what I had been feeling for months. Maybe I was reluctant to share with my family the extent of my depression. I had always presented such a brave front to them. And since Norbie and I had been living up in Berkeley that entire summer, they didn't get to see how bad things were with me. Plus, they had gone to so much trouble with the wedding preparations.

Perhaps I should have called it off. But I didn't.

To this day, I think I made the right decision. For all his faults, Norbie did manage to keep me alive following the Senator's death.

For two years, I had trouble functioning. I couldn't work. I could barely get through the day. I don't remember what I did with myself. I do remember that I cried most of the time. Each morning, I would wake up and, on a yellow legal pad, write down a list of things that I could do that day, and each night I would climb back into bed without having checked off a single item on that list. Every now and then, I would seize upon a way forward, only to have it slip from my grasp a short time later. Most days, the sadness would overtake me. I felt like a sleepwalker. I cut myself off from other people. I would just sit around on the couch watching soap operas on TV or lie in bed all day feeling miserable. The grief was clearly visible on my face in photos taken during that period. I could sometimes hide my pain from my family and friends, but rarely from the camera.

Struggling to stay alive—1969

Struggling to stay alive—1969

I had little reason to go on living. But, fortunately, somehow I found a way.

Following the funeral, my parents and I received a thank-you note from Ethel Kennedy acknowledging our letter of condolence, and in the fall of 1968, I received a gift from her—one that she had made for staff and friends of the Senator. It was a Lucite paperweight with the Senator's famous quote engraved in gold:

RFK
Some men see things as they are and say, 'Why?'
I dream of things that never were and say, 'Why not?'

1968

Paperweight—gift from Ethel

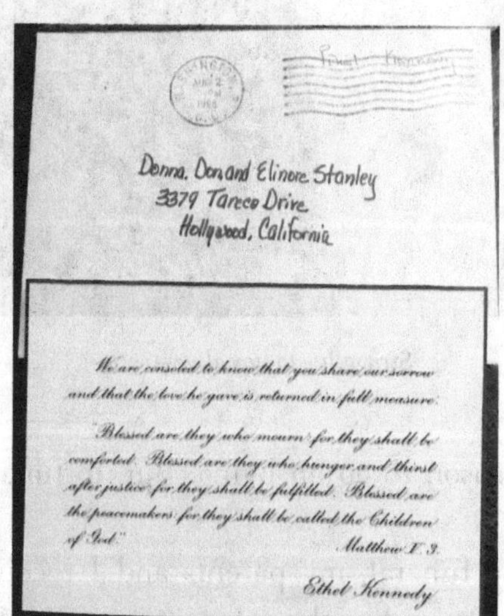

Note from Ethel

Ted Kennedy also kept in touch with RFK's former staff. I'm not sure what year it was—in either 1968 or 1969—he and his wife, Joan, sent me a card at Christmas.

That fall, I also tried doing some drawing and painting to help me in my battle against depression. In addition to a couple of charcoal drawings of RFK, I also painted him in black-and-white acrylic. The painting looks half-finished, but that was my purpose—it was intended to be a statement about how his life and his work were unfinished. I presented the painting to my parents, and it would hang in their bedroom for more than 40 years, until their deaths, when it was returned to me.

My "unfinished" painting of RFK

Norbie and I moved to Los Angeles in 1969, where we lived with my parents for several months. I still wasn't working, and he was having trouble finding work, since he didn't have a green card. Actually, Senator Ted Kennedy was able to help us out with that.

At that time, if a foreign national wanted a green card, he would have to first return to his native country and apply for it there—even if he was married to an American citizen. But through Ted's office, we were able to secure an appointment with the U.S. Consulate in

Tijuana, Mexico, where Norbie could apply for and be issued the green card. It was the only time I ever used my Kennedy connections to obtain a favor, but I was glad I did. It seemed unfair to me that the U.S. government could draft a non-citizen to fight in Vietnam but was unwilling to approve a green card for him to work.

We both finally found employment in 1970. After briefly holding down a couple of jobs in the private sector, I was hired in October of that year by the County of Los Angeles as a budget analyst in the Welfare Department. I would continue to work for the county for nearly 20 years, moving steadily up the career ladder to a financial management position.

Sadly, my predictions on my wedding day about my marriage were borne out. It survived only a few years. One night, Norbie dragged me by the hair and kicked me down the front stairs of our Hollywood Hills home. The next morning, he was remorseful, but we had reached a point of no return.

"I didn't mean to hurt you," he pleaded.

Without hesitation, I said, "Our marriage is over."

And so it was. I felt nothing. I divorced him in 1974 after being separated for more than two years. During the time that he was eligible for the draft, he and I had tried to get me pregnant, but fortunately it never happened.

That blessed event would occur in 1978 after I met the man who would become my second husband. Being a mother would prove to be the greatest joy of my life. That was quite a surprise to me, really. Even as a little girl, I hadn't particularly cared for dolls. I was more of a tomboy than a girlie-girl, and I never imagined that I would ever become a mother. But I can safely say now that if it weren't for my son, my life would have been incomplete. After experiencing so much excitement at such an early age, there was little that could match it. But becoming a mother did.

In 1974, I returned to Washington for a political fundraising event. It was the first time I'd been back to the nation's capital since the Senator's funeral. My old mentor from RFK's office, Joe Dolan, was running in the Democratic primary for U.S. Senator from Colorado. As mentioned before, he was up against a better-known guy named Gary Hart, who would eventually win the nomination.

I was excited to be back in D.C., however, and to get together with some of the staff from the office again, particularly Joe. I hadn't seen him since that awful night that we buried the Senator.

Provi and I planned to make a real trip of it. Following the fundraiser, we went on to New York City. Provi had a cousin there who managed an apartment building on Park Avenue, and she had arranged for us to stay with them.

I will never forget the raucous five-hour bus trip that she and I took from Washington to New York. Provi had prepared buckets of fried chicken and a couple of thermoses filled with daiquiris for just the two of us, and, needless to say, by the time we climbed off the bus in Manhattan, we could barely walk...but what fun we had along the way.

We continued drinking all night long at her cousin's kitchen table, reminiscing about our days together in the Senator's office and her time in the White House. In fact, at one point, her cousin ran out of booze and had to go out in the middle of the night to get some more. He was low on gas in his car, and those were the days of long gas lines, so he first had to wait in line to fill up and then finally found a place in Spanish Harlem where he could buy some whiskey.

I don't know when we actually slept that weekend. I think we tried to just keep drinking—afraid of the hangover if we quit.

The next day, Provi took me over to see Jackie's apartment on Fifth Avenue. Jackie was out of town, so we were able to wander around inside, and I actually took some photos of the place. One of the things that struck me was how there were a couple of racks of her clothing in the middle of the kitchen of all places. Apparently, she had run out of closet space.

Jackie was married to Onassis at this time, so there weren't any photos of President Kennedy sitting around in the main rooms—they were only in the kids' rooms. I remember that Caroline had stuck several photos of her father in the frame of a large mirror atop her dresser. The apartment had a beautiful view of Central Park, but I wasn't really impressed with the decor—it seemed a little old-fashioned to me. My reaction may have been colored, though, since the place was quite dark with all the curtains drawn. I remember there was some sort of animal hide draped over the back of the sofa in the living room. I had never seen that done before.

Nice digs, though, with a private elevator and all, if I'm not mistaken.

Photos of Caroline and John in Jackie's 5th Avenue apartment

On the mirror in Jackie's bedroom

On June 6, 1988, I attended the 20-year memorial service for the Senator at Arlington Cemetery, followed by a reception at Hickory Hill. There would also be a reunion party for the staff that week. Many of the people I hadn't seen at all since the days of the campaign. My nine-year-old son accompanied me to Washington for the events. My husband was unable to make it because of work demands.

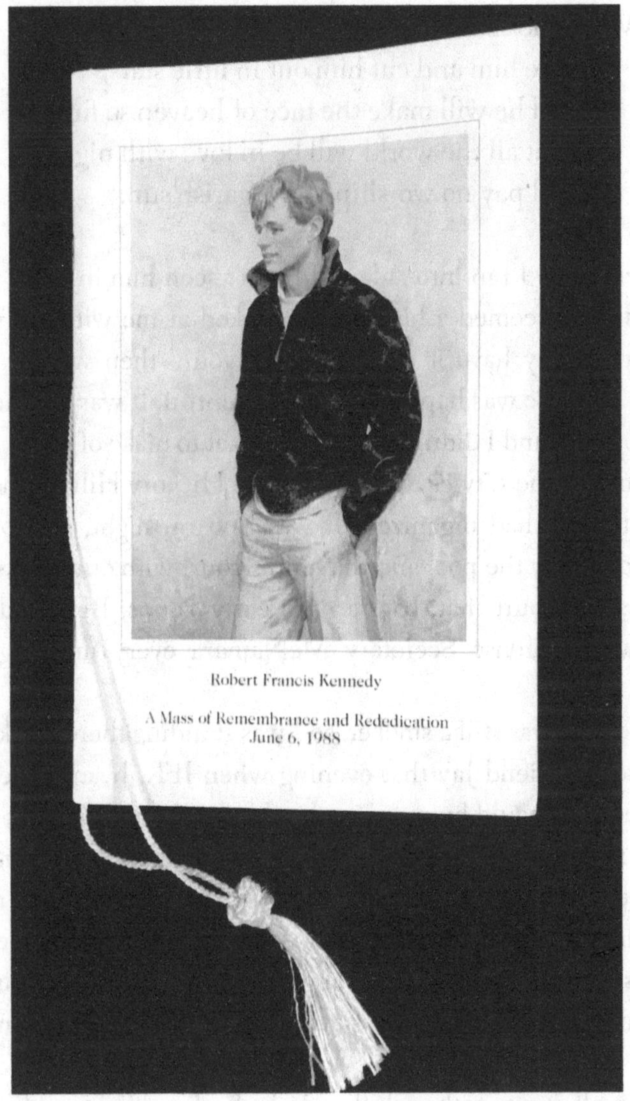

Robert Francis Kennedy

A Mass of Remembrance and Rededication
June 6, 1988

1988 Memorial Service program

RFK's grown children and some of his grandchildren participated in the memorial service, reading parts of his speeches and passages from scripture. John F. Kennedy, Jr. was there and recited the same words from Shakespeare's *Romeo and Juliet* that RFK had quoted at the 1964 Democratic National Convention:

> When he shall die,
>   Take him and cut him out in little stars,
>   And he will make the face of heaven so fine
>   That all the world will be in love with night,
>   And pay no worship to the garish sun.

Afterwards, I ran into Adam. I hadn't seen him in more than 20 years. He still seemed a bit lost. He looked at me with my son and said, "You really have it all now, don't you?" then walked away. I couldn't tell if he was happy for me or resentful. It was a rather peculiar encounter, and I didn't quite know what to make of it.

Following the service, we drove out to Hickory Hill for the reception that Ethel had organized. It was a warm night, so most of us headed down by the pool and the tennis court with our drinks. It was on that same court that, back in the early 1960s, RFK had played tennis with Defense Secretary McNamara every morning before work.

In 1988, I was still a smoker, so I was standing there smoking and talking to my friend Jay that evening when JFK, Jr. approached me and asked if he could bum a cigarette. I knew from Provi that both he and his mother were secret smokers. JFK, Jr. was just 27 years old then, but he was so handsome it took your breath away. That night he mostly hung out with Provi's son, Gustavo. They had been good friends since childhood. My young son and some of the other children spent a good part of the evening on the swings up near the house.

All in all, it was rather chilling to be back at Hickory Hill, where we had whiled away so many lazy summer afternoons. Even though it was crawling with the Senator's family and friends that night, the place seemed so empty without him there.

Getting together for the reunion with former members of RFK's staff was fun, I suppose. While we exchanged promises to keep in touch, most of us knew we probably wouldn't. It was like those high school reunions that you attend every ten years. It's interesting to see people from another period in your life, but you really no longer have anything in common with them other than the past.

In September 1993, my husband and I flew back to Washington for the wedding of Provi's son, Gustavo, who was getting married to Elizabeth Alexander, daughter of Clifford Alexander, former Secretary of the Army under President Carter. The bride was also a poet—she would become best known for reciting one of her poems at the inauguration of President Barack Obama.

Actually, JFK, Jr. was supposed to be the best man at the wedding, and I looked forward to seeing him again. But he was off gallivanting with Daryl Hannah and didn't make it back in time. Just two months earlier, he had quit his job with the Manhattan District Attorney, then spent most of that August with Daryl in Asia. Two years later, he would found *George* Magazine, and six years later, he would be dead.

Jacqueline Kennedy did attend the wedding, however, and she was furious with her son for not showing up. From what Provi told me, Jackie wasn't particularly fond of Daryl Hannah anyway.

The ceremony and reception were held at the vacation home of the bride's parents on Chesapeake Bay. It would be the last time I saw Jacqueline Kennedy Onassis. Even though she hadn't yet talked publicly about her illness, it was obvious observing her at the wedding that she was not well. I suspected then that she'd already been undergoing chemotherapy (although news reports maintained that she didn't start treatments until December) because her hair seemed quite sparse and she looked rather pale. Sadly, she would die just eight months later of non-Hodgkin's lymphoma.

Then, in July 1999, John F. Kennedy, Jr., his wife Carolyn Bessette, and her sister Lauren perished in a tragic plane crash with JFK, Jr. at the controls. Provi may have been the last person to speak with him before he boarded his plane for Hyannis Port. Rory Kennedy was getting married that weekend, and Provi was at the Kennedy compound for the wedding along with other family members. That night, she had prepared John's favorite fish chowder—

a dish that had also been a favorite of his father's—and she told him over the phone that she had it waiting for his arrival. But the plane never arrived.

At his memorial service, his uncle Ted paraphrased the Irish poet Yeats, saying, "We dared to think that this John Kennedy would live to comb gray hair. But, like his father, he had every gift but length of years." It was yet another tragedy for the Kennedy family and for Provi, who had already weathered so much alongside them.

As the years passed, I attended many public and private events in honor of Robert Kennedy. The family made a point of inviting the Senator's former staff to all memorial services and kept us up to date on the development of the human rights organization founded in his name.

EDWARD M. KENNEDY
MASSACHUSETTS

United States Senate

WASHINGTON, D.C. 20510

June 30, 1983

Ms. Donna Stanley
818 Elyria Drive
Los Angeles, California 90065

Dear Donna:

I wanted you to have the enclosed copy of the eloquent homily by Carmine Bellino at the Anniversary Mass for Robert Kennedy last month.

As Carmine said, if Bob could have been there, what a reunion it would have been.

I wish that I could have joined you on June 4, but I was up in Providence for my nephew John's commencement at Brown. I know how close Bob felt to you and all the others who gathered here, and I am grateful for what you have done to honor his memory and to hold his standard high.

Sincerely,

Edward M. Kennedy

Letter from Ted Kennedy

Invitations from the Kennedy family

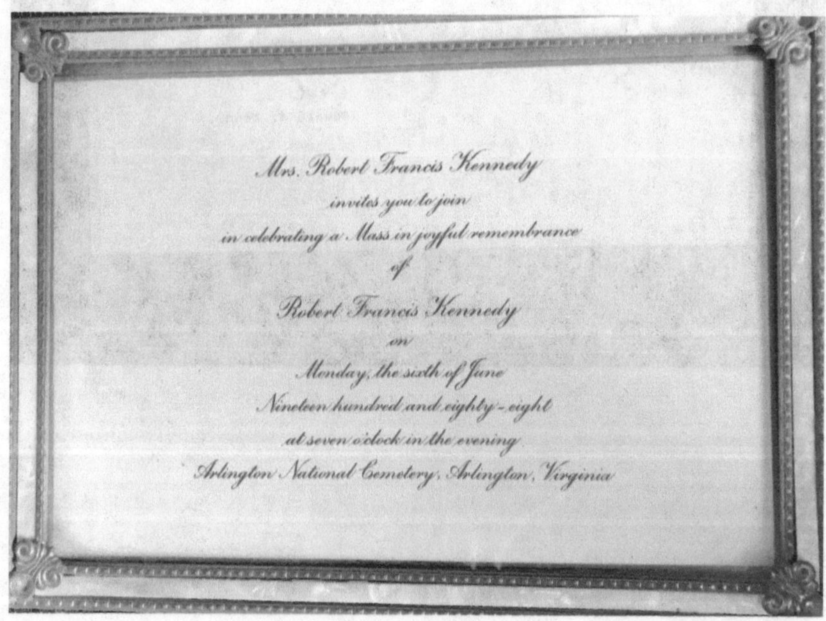

I also established a close relationship with Angie Novello, the Senator's personal secretary. She and Provi lived near one another, and whenever I went to Washington to visit Provi, Angie and I would get together—usually at Provi's apartment. Walking into her home was like taking a trip back in time. The walls were covered with framed prints of paintings of various rooms in the JFK White House, inscribed by Jackie as Christmas gifts to the staff. Provi had preserved so many mementos from her days in the White House that an entire bedroom was filled with memorabilia.

Close-up of White House print inscribed by Jackie for Christmas

*Provi and Angie at Provi's apartment, c. 1970s (Note: White
House print on wall)*

Whenever Angie and I got together, I was tempted to ask her about that October night at the Fairmont Hotel back in 1966, but I never did—and she never breathed a word of it, either. Despite what remained unsaid, we shared many wonderful times over the years.

I'll never forget the summer of 1996, when I traveled to Washington to drop off my teenage son, Ian, for a Junior Statesmen program at Georgetown University. I was only there for a few days and wanted to visit the Senator's grave before I left. Angie offered to drive us to Arlington National Cemetery, but she chose to stay in the car. Ian and I visited the gravesite alone.

I never asked her why.

After I left D.C. for Europe, both Angie and Provi acted as surrogate mothers to Ian—frequently inviting him over for dinner and keeping a watchful eye on him for me.

I am not certain of the exact timing, but in the years preceding her death in 2011, Angie developed Alzheimer's disease and was moved to a nursing home. Unfortunately, I never saw her again. I was heartbroken to later read this account of her funeral, written by Charles Peters for the *Washington Monthly*:

> "During the seven years when Robert Kennedy was one of the most powerful men in the country, you would have thought that the number of Angie's close friends was in the hundreds. Lobbyists, politicians, and reporters would all describe her as one of their pals: 'Angie always takes my calls, and she usually puts me through to Bobby right away.'
>
> "But none of these 'close pals' showed up at the funeral. Aside from her retirement home friends and her wonderful Italian family—originally from Calabria —I seemed to be the only male there. Women were a bit better represented; there were seven, including Ethel Kennedy and her daughters Kerry and Courtney.

Still, when you remember the legions of pals she had in the '60s, you realize just how cruel Washington can be.

"The Washington Post didn't even deem her worthy of an obituary. Angie had a warmer heart and more common sense than most of us will ever possess. She deserved better at the end."

Unfortunately, I was out of the country when she died, or I would most certainly have attended her funeral; and I, for one, have not forgotten Angie and never will. She was an amazing woman: honest, loyal, and kind. She also led an extraordinary life and was a witness to history—a history both tragic and noble. She gave everything she had to one very special man, and in doing so, she made a difference in all of our lives.

Angie rarely talked publicly about the Senator, but she did say this: "I loved Bob Kennedy as a boss and as a friend. He was a great inspiration to all of us who worked for him because he had the uncanny ability of bringing out the best in us."

During that same trip to Washington in 1996, Provi arranged a picnic out at Hickory Hill for me, my son, and other friends. Although Ian had been there before in 1988, this time he was able to play touch football on the lawn in the Kennedy tradition.

Angie, Provi, and my son, Ian — 1996

My son Ian playing touch football at Hickory Hill — 1996

At Hickory Hill with Provi — 1996

Hickory Hill Pool House — 1996

Sadly, Joe Dolan died in 2008. I believe it was in the late 1990s that I last heard from him. It was then that I received a letter from Joe telling me that he was writing a memoir (unfortunately, the letter is undated). His book was to be a collection of remembrances by the people who had worked for John Cand/or Robert Kennedy, and Joe asked me for my input on RFK. In response, I sent him some of my thoughts about the Senator, but to my knowledge, the book was never finished... and sadly, I seem to have lost the piece of it that I wrote. I have no idea what happened to Joe's planned memoir. However, I read in his obituary that his wife, Marti, and their two sons preceded him in death, so perhaps personal tragedy intervened again.

Joe once remarked, "Bobby was the finest man I ever knew . . . he taught me everything I know about politics and about children."

Joseph F. Dolan
4101 So. Colorado Blvd.
Cherry Hills Village, CO 80110
jdolan@mho.net
303-781-8048

Ms. Donna Stanley
818
Los Angeles, CA 90065

Dear Donna:

I am currently writing a memoir about John and Robert Kennedy, and how they related to the people they worked with and for. You can make a valuable contribution. This is not a money making venture for me. All proceeds will go to the Robert Kennedy Foundation. Think back to your relationship to RFK and how you would answer.

Sincerely,

Joe Dolan

P.S. After RFK died, I returned to Colorado whence I had come in 1956. What has your post Kennedy career been?

Letter from Joe Dolan

Provi and I would get together many times throughout the years, both in Washington and California. We also talked on the telephone frequently. She continued to help out Ethel and other members of the family whenever they needed her, and up until John's death, she would spend a part of each summer up in Hyannis Port. Once he died, however, Caroline decided to end that practice, and Provi no longer went up to the Cape. I'm not really sure why, but I know that Provi was terribly hurt by Caroline's decision.

As time passed, Provi began to have mobility problems, but it rarely slowed her down much. Then, in March of 2015, Provi passed away. It really marked the end of an era. I was devastated to lose her—she had been a friend to me at that point for more than 50 years. Gustavo asked me to deliver one of the eulogies at her memorial service, and I did. Clint Hill, Jackie's Secret Service agent on that fateful trip to Dallas, was also supposed to give one of the eulogies, but was unfortunately too ill at the time to make the trip back to Washington.

My remembrance of her read, in part:

> I met Provi for the first time more than 50 years ago when I was just 18 years old. I was an idealistic kid from L.A. who had come to Washington to go to college and to work for Senator Robert Kennedy. Provi was a 40-year-old woman of the world, one who had experienced more life—both its joys and its sorrows—than I could possibly imagine at my young age. But as unlikely as it might seem, the two of us became instant buddies. We were inseparable in those days... and even after I returned to California, Provi and I remained lifelong friends. In fact, she was the only person outside of my immediate family who actually attended both of my weddings.
>
> I like to think that we were kindred spirits because Provi was the kind of woman I always wanted to become—she was smart, savvy, and fearless with a will of solid steel, and as Gustavo put it, "an infallible moral compass." She was loyal to a fault and, like a lioness, she would fiercely defend and protect her friends and her family. Despite the unimaginable tragedies that she

had to deal with in her life, she never faltered. She remained doggedly optimistic, always looking to tomorrow. Provi's glass was never half-empty.

There was nothing that Provi enjoyed more than having fun with her friends and family, and she was always the one to take charge and make it happen—whether it was a pool party out at Hickory Hill or a five-course dinner party at her apartment. She could organize absolutely anything to perfection, even on short notice, and she was one of the best cooks I've ever known.

Most of you already know about Provi's close and enduring relationship with the Kennedy family. I would like to share with you today what she meant to my family. Very simply put, we loved her. We all loved her. My parents fell madly in love with Provi the moment that I introduced them to her back in the summer of 1965 and, for the rest of their lives, they would stop by to see her in Washington whenever their travels took them to the East Coast, or they would fly her out to California for a visit with us.

Provi was someone who, no matter what was going on in her life, would put others first. Despite her incomparable gift for organization and her take-charge attitude, she always led with her heart. Even with the health issues and mobility problems that she had to face in recent years, she always worried more about her friends and loved ones than herself, reaching out to provide comfort or encouragement or a laugh... or even a home-cooked dinner. Although I am more than 20 years her junior, I was constantly in awe of the endless depths of energy and strength of spirit that she possessed.

Others have called Provi "a force of nature," and

indeed, she was. I think that's why I imagined that somehow she would always be with us... like the sun rising in the morning or the flowers blooming in spring. It is difficult for me to picture life without her, but I know that her valiant, unshakable spirit will live on in all of us who loved her and were loved by her. She would want us to move forward, just as she always did in the face of grief. But, oh, how we will miss "the radiance that was once so bright."

I still think of Provi every day, and when I recall those years that we shared back in the Senator's office, I can't help smiling. But I miss her so much.

June 6, 2018, marked the 50th anniversary of RFK's death. The Los Angeles Times was preparing a special feature article about the anniversary and asked its readers to submit their memories of the assassination. In response, I wrote up a short piece and was immediately contacted by the Times for an interview. They came out to my house and spent a good two hours talking to me, not only about the assassination and the days that followed but also about the years I spent working on the Senator's staff. However, very little of my interview was used for their special feature. They did include a very brief video clip and snippets from it in their article, as well as a shot of me holding my inscribed photo of RFK and me together.

Photo of me; credit: Myung J. Chun/L.A. Times

In June 2018, I also attended the 50th anniversary memorial service for RFK at Arlington National Cemetery. It was followed by a luncheon for family and friends at the Irish Ambassador's residence in D.C.

Somehow, the service didn't feel quite as personal as previous ones had. I imagine that it was partly because most of the people speaking there hadn't known the Senator or even met him. And many of those who were close to him had already passed away, so I was saddened to conclude that he now belonged to history.

I did get to reconnect with some of the younger staff who also worked in his office, but now there were very few of us left.

Please Join
Mrs. Robert Kennedy and Family
at a Memorial Service in joyful
celebration of the life of

Robert Francis Kennedy

with Special Remarks by

The Honorable Bill Clinton

Wednesday, June 6, 2018
at 10:00 a.m.

Arlington National Cemetery

Musical prelude at 9:30 a.m.
Memorial begins at 10:00 a.m.

Kindly RSVP at www.RFK50thMemorial.com

Invitation to 50th Anniversary Memorial Service

With Jay at RFK Memorial — Arlington Cemetery, June 6, 2018

In 2018, I also became more involved with the RFK Human Rights organization and attended the Ripple of Hope Awards dinner in New York both that year and the following year. Barack Obama was being honored in 2018, and I was seated just one table away from him, so that was exciting. It was also nice being able to spend some time talking with Peter Edelman that night. While I attended the dinner in 2019 as well, I haven't been back since. The COVID pandemic put a damper on that.

I must say that of all his children and grandchildren, I was most impressed with Joe Kennedy III, and I do hope that he continues to be involved in politics. I was disappointed when he lost the Massachusetts Senate race in 2020 and had to forfeit his Congressional seat, which he'd held since 2012. God knows we need good people now more than ever.

President Obama — next table over at Ripple of Hope Awards

Ripple of Hope Awards Dinner — 2018

With Peter Edelman — 2018

With Rep. Joe Kennedy III — 2019

With Kerry Kennedy — 2019

With Ted Kennedy, Jr. — 2019

Chapter 23

Epilogue

Though nothing can bring back the hour
Of splendour in the grass, of glory in the flower
We will grieve not, rather find
Strength in what remains behind
~ *William Wordsworth*

So here I sit, at nearly 80 years old, facing the final years of my life. I first met Robert Kennedy more than 60 years ago, but it doesn't seem possible that it's been that long since I last saw his face, since I last spoke to him, since he last smiled my way. He has been with me during every step of my journey, has continued to guide the decisions in my life, and will remain here in my heart until I take my last breath.

In 1988, after eighteen years working as a financial manager for Los Angeles County, I became what is popularly known as a "whistleblower." Ironically, it involved the County's mismanagement of federal grant funds for a job training partnership program with the private sector—basically an expansion on some of RFK's original ideas surrounding the Bedford-Stuyvesant experiment. At the time, the intent by department executives was to save county money, but it was to be accomplished by unjustly cutting benefits to the most needy inhabitants of Los Angeles and denying them the opportunity to lift themselves out of poverty or to find permanent work.

It was one of the most difficult decisions of my life to go up against those in power at the county. By doing so, I risked not only my career but my health as well. However, like the Senator, I felt that power without principle was equivalent to corruption, so I wasn't about to back down because of my fears about the personal consequences.

Throughout the three years that followed, I was subjected to all kinds of harassment from my bosses, and I was ultimately forced out of my job. Throughout it all, the only thing that gave me the courage to keep on going was thinking about the Senator and knowing that he would be proud that I was doing the right thing. I eventually won my battle with the county, but it took a tremendous toll on me and on my marriage as well.

Nevertheless, I had no choice. Robert Kennedy had taught me well. In his speech to South African students in June 1966, he said that "each of us can work to change a small portion of events" and that "it is from numberless diverse acts of courage and belief that human history is shaped. Each time a man [or a woman] stands up for an ideal, or acts to improve the lot of others, or strikes out against injustice, he sends a tiny ripple of hope, and crossing each other from a million different centers of energy and daring, those ripples build a current which can sweep down the mightiest walls of oppression and resistance."

But it's not just Robert Kennedy's words that have inspired me over these many years. It is also the memory of his sacrifice. He was willing to give his life for what he believed in. I will forever mourn his loss, but it is some comfort to me remembering those remarkable years that I spent with him. I tell my son that I don't regret being this old, because it allowed me the opportunity to breathe the same air as the Senator.

As Charles Dickens put it, "It was the best of times, it was the worst of times, it was the age of wisdom, it was the age of foolishness, it was the epoch of belief, it was the epoch of incredulity, it was the season of Light, it was the season of Darkness, it was the spring of hope, it was the winter of despair, we had everything before us, we had nothing before us..."

The 1960s were also the best of times and the worst of times. But I wouldn't choose to live in any other era. After all, as Adam once said, we were part of something very special...

The End